HEADED INTO
THE ABYSS

HEADED INTO THE ABYSS

THE STORY OF OUR TIME, AND THE FUTURE WE'LL FACE

BRIAN T. WATSON

Anvilside Press
Swampscott, Massachusetts
2019

ISBN: 978-0-578-59411-8

Designed and typeset by Publishers' Design and Production Services, Inc.

Cover photograph by Brian Watson.

This book is for everyone, but especially for all the very human people in my life who, over the years—with their patience, impatience, generosity, reasoning, understanding, encouragement, and love—have helped me to see humanity fully, and thus be able to write this story.

Man's lusts are fed by his imagination, and he will not be satisfied until the universal objectives which the imagination envisages are attained. His protest against finiteness makes the universal character of his imperial dreams inevitable. In his sanest moments he sees his life fulfilled as an organic part of a harmonious whole. But he has few sane moments; for he is governed more by imagination than by reason, and imagination is compounded of mind and impulse.

Reinhold Niebuhr, 1932

CONTENTS

PREFACE

THIS IS A STARTLING AND UNUSUAL BOOK, so I hope you'll bear with me. In it, I state that civilization is not going to see the light of 2100—perhaps not even 2070—not at least in any form that you'd want to experience. That means that most of us alive today, throughout the world, are going to be part of that collapse and dissolution.

Obviously, I can't be certain of that, but I think it is way more likely than any happier outcome. In this book, I describe where we are now, where we are headed, and how we might change course away from disaster. There are, after all, plenty of constructive measures that we could implement to address most of our difficulties.

But we will not do so. I will explain why that is the case.

On the positive side, you will find that this book connects dots. There are many superb contemporary books that explain one facet or another of our society. Often, they illuminate well the problems and possible solutions in a given area or field of human endeavor or industry. I draw on all that expertise. But today there are few books that step back and survey what it all adds up to. There are few books that examine the dynamics that are created and put in play by the very existence and simultaneous layering and weaving of one problem into another. Like nature, with its infinite number of interwoven ecological relationships and dependencies—so many that we can't know them all—our societies today are complex ecologies that are the products of many simultaneously operating forces. We cannot assess our societies and understand them unless we step back and appreciate the roles and cause-and-effect dynamics of the ingredients and circumstances that we have created in those societies.

This book does that. Uniquely, it conducts an analysis across the full spectrum of forces that are making contemporary society, identifies what is critical among them, and then draws an unusual conclusion. Although the sentences in the book necessarily follow like train cars one after the other, and you can therefore only read one after another, bear in mind that I'd be happiest if there were some way for you to read all the sentences at once. For that would best reflect the complexion and dynamics of society. For everything that I am describing—using unavoidable sequential sentences—is happening all at once, all the time. That simultaneity is an essential feature of our problems and our trajectory and is one of the reasons why we won't unravel the mess we're in.

Like the newspaper columns I wrote for twenty years, this book is for everyone. The citizen, the general reader, the young and the old. Mostly, it is for my fellow human being who is curious about and unsettled by the world around us today. For me, this book is simply a long newspaper column, with the same structure, tone, and purpose that guided that work. It'll take you on a journey, illuminate important realities, and toward the end will gather up its ideas and conclusions to offer you a whole perspective, a clear picture.

While there is plenty of scholarship behind this book—I did my homework—you will find its contents and message accessible and plain-spoken. The straight story I tell in this book is one that most power brokers in society are happy to have you not know. Without much effort, they and the culture and many of the other forces in society act to mask or conceal this story. Nonetheless, as you read, you will recognize a lot in it.

Why would you or anyone want to read a book that describes the coming end of civilization? A book that has no hope? That presents the reasons why we'll fail to adequately address the problems that threaten us? And if my arguments are persuasive, what is left for a reader to do?

I'll say more about this in the Introduction, but I've always believed in studying, learning, and knowledge. Many of my heroes are the men and women who wrote the books that opened the eyes of people everywhere and enlarged the potential of what man can be. Throughout history, these authors often didn't hold back what they knew to be right, even if sometimes it cut against certain cultures or perspectives. Not writing important truths was and is almost unthinkable. The conclusions of this book are grim and nearly unthinkable. There is no question that I wrote it with hopelessness; I believe we will not prevail. But simultaneously I wrote it with gratitude for having the knowledge—drawn partly from others—to see clearly.

I don't believe that most people don't want to know truths, even if they're terrible truths. The arc of human history and the development of societies, and the march of events and their aftermaths, prove that. Even today, in a web-fueled environment of half-truths and intemperate thinking, most people are just trying their best to navigate a difficult time. I think that those who read this book will be grateful to learn the story it tells.

* * * *

This is a story about you. It is about you and your life and your relationship to society. It is a story about the condition of your life.

It is also a story about your society and its relationship to you. It is a story about the forces and influences within that society, and it is a story about the condition of society. All sorts of madnesses abound today throughout societies—here and globally—and they afflict us. They threaten our humanity, our brotherhood, and our very survival.

At the moment, it is October, 2019, and where we are—as individuals and as a society—is a product or consequence of present realities, and of developments that have been unfolding for the past 45 years or so.

Really, of course, picking 45 years is only partially correct. History, time, and the unfolding of events occur along a continuum. To truly explain and understand the nature and shapes of our world and lives, we'd really have to start at the beginning, some time long ago. But for the main discussions and explanations in this book, and the purposes of it, having a sense of what has occurred over the past 45 years is sufficient.

Part of the message of this book, in fact, is to convey to a partly dispirited or uneasy citizenry that we must look harder and deeper to decipher what is going on—and what has gone on—in our societies and the world. We are not used to looking deeply at things. Nor are we good at connecting dots and understanding how forces, actions, and circumstances both exist in and contribute to an entire ecology. This ecology, this context, is a mesh of realities that, taken together, we call society. Today, our unwillingness or inability to see the reasons behind the shape and dynamics of society have left us vulnerable to manipulation or distraction, and ultimately left society in danger of breakdown and collapse.

Today, in our tech-driven, device-addled, tweeting, texting, snapchatting, linking, liking, beeping, 24/7 newsfeed world, it is easy to get caught up in the hyper-present. It is easier than ever to react, to react quickly, to have opinions, to have opinions about nearly everything, and to jump to conclusions. Indeed, much in our connected Webworld encourages us to have those characteristics, to be that way, and to behave in those ways.

In the United States and around the world today, we citizens are still dividing and polarizing, and we face a slew of serious and unprecedented problems. In significant ways, this time is unlike any before. As we examine looming difficulties, history will offer us no hope. Any parallels to earlier epochs only illuminate how different or how much more severe our circumstances are today. This book will attempt to explain those circumstances, and our relationships to them. As people look at and experience our world today, large majorities of us—both rich and poor—have a disquiet in us, and for good reason.

In these pages, I will look at our society and ourselves, and the condition and nature of each. My descriptions and analyses may be illuminating, and that alone is encouraging and useful, and it could indicate that I still have a small hope that we humans could be our smartest selves, and pull ourselves back from any number of abysses we are facing.

But ultimately, my conclusions are bleak because I believe that we will not execute the measures that are necessary to reform, improve, rebalance, and make healthy and sustainable our societies and lives.

I believe that within the United States, and within the world, we are headed for catastrophe. Slowly and steadily and sometimes rapidly we have been and are generating and enlarging circumstances and realities that will ultimately result in the breakdown of societies.

The threats to society now are many. Some are interrelated and some not. Some come from unexpected directions. I do not know which one will bring us down. What is scary and deeply unsettling about this moment is another fact: some of these threats could destabilize and unravel society literally tomorrow morning, or in a week, or a year. Others could be 10, 20, or 30 years away. In any case, regardless of what disasters may transpire in the next two or three decades, by 40 or 50 years from now, for a number of reasons, I believe human society within the United States and across the globe will be deteriorating severely, and be chaotic, frightening, and brutal.

INTRODUCTION

AMERICAN SOCIETY AND THE WORLD TODAY face a number of enormous problems. We are beset by a range of unprecedented developments that are continually worsening and that are—for many reasons—beyond our capacities to respond to.

This book is about those long-building developments and the state of current affairs. It is the story of where we—as individuals, tribes, societies, nations, and civilization—are today, how we got here, and where we're headed. It is about the troubling conditions and compromised health of our society—with the largest focus on American society—and it describes the major, most important and most threatening forces today acting upon or within society.

I describe the current state of ten forces: capitalism, technology, the internet, politics, media, education, human nature, the environment, human population, and transportation, and how the dynamics and circumstances of each are driving our societies in predominantly negative ways. I explain how interconnected and powerful the forces are, and where they are likely to take society—here and globally—in the next few decades and by 2100.

Our prospects for the future—say, 2030 to 2080—are very grim and the book analyzes how we could respond to the biggest forces and realities facing us if we were inclined to or able to. But because we will not be able to respond either fully or optimally, or in a sufficiently timely manner, I explain why our responses will be inadequate.

The book operates at two levels; it analyzes and distills what is significant about each force shaping society, and it tells a big-picture story of what the myriad of parts, factors, and circumstances adds up to. The point of the book is to paint the big picture of our present and future. Wherever on the globe you live, it really is, and will be, the story of our time.

I have written this book primarily for every ordinary American, for the layman reader, for every citizen who wishes to understand our speeding and uncertain present. Because of our polarized and widely distrusting populace, and because of the contents of this book, I feel it necessary to say explicitly that I wrote it with a readership in mind of both Democrats and Republicans, liberals and conservatives, blacks and whites, young and old, and every other person in the country.

While certain groups do bear more responsibility than others in creating our problems—and I discuss the issue frankly—many of the problems I describe have grown almost organically or inevitably from our cultural conceptions of progress itself, and thus are the fault of either everybody or nobody. And many of our problems stem from human nature, advancing technology, globalization, growing populations, and a shrinking world, and thus are difficult to "blame" on someone. In the developed countries especially, we all exist and participate to some degree in the flawed modern world surrounding us and most of us have benefitted from the advances and standards of living in it. Whatever our politics or identity, it is difficult to hold ourselves significantly aloof from either the creation or influences of culture, current events, and our epistemologies; thus we are all to some extent simultaneously responsible and blameless for the shape of society.

In any case, my focus is not on blame but on giving an explanation of where we are and describing the full crises that await us. They are globe-straddling, woven into our present modernity, and permanent. I doubt we'll head them off. I strongly doubt that we'll meet the challenges of changing nearly everything about our many human ways and societies.

Ironically, for all the discord and divisions in the United States and countries across the world, for all the politics, identities, ideologies, and cultures that exist, we are about to experience something entirely unique. Whether we like it or not, every human being on the planet is now connected in a brotherhood of fate.

* * *

I said that this is a story about you and your society, so it is also in some ways a reckoning for me. This story is not abstract or academic; it's personal for you, and it's personal for me. We share a stake in this story. Like you, I do not remain unaffected by our culture and our society. In assessing the present and thinking about our near future, I had to accept what I had learned even though this story will leave most of us in a strange place. What we each do from that place—how we react to this story—will no doubt differ.

For me, relating to you what is written below, especially in this introduction, is somewhat of a departure from my usual writing approach. In 20 years of journalism and reporting, I rarely felt a need or considered it wise to bring my personal experiences openly and explicitly into my writing. In fact, following a widely embraced writing convention, I deliberately and studiously avoided using "I" in my writing, and I did not freely use my personal experiences to buttress or illuminate—or provide evidence for—my writing, arguments, descriptions, explanations, or opinions.

I think I tried to weight my thinking and experience of things as one of many perspectives—rather than give it authorial privilege—alongside the many perspectives of all the others I may have been considering at the moment. I always felt that any one person (including any one author) could experience anything—and it would have some degree of legitimacy—and therefore I always guarded against extrapolating too readily from my (or any individual's) personal experiences. My professional journalistic posture was to be extremely cautious about finding something universal in any individual experience. When I did generalize in my writing I always endeavored to create generalizations and conclusions—or discover something universal—from the largest and widest possible collection of data, observations, reading, and circumstances.

I still do that, and I still believe in that approach, and most of the discussions and conclusions in this book are a product of that method. But far more than anything I have written previously, this book required me to grapple with the truths, horrors, and implications of its contents. And not as some intellectual exercise, but as a story that I too am living in.

Consciously observing, taking note, interviewing, and questioning, I have learned a tremendous amount about people and their thinking, especially during the past 20 years. This book is not remotely a personal memoir, and the 20-year evolution of my personal beliefs—from optimism that we would eventually adequately sort out our biggest problems, to my current belief that we won't—stems mostly from an investigation into actors and forces external to me, but also includes certain personal experiences that illuminated and corroborated my developing conclusions.

I never expected to develop the beliefs and conclusions that I outline in this book. They came slowly, gradually, unwelcome, and unbidden over the course of incessant reading, observation, discussion, and writing during the past two decades.

And in 20 years of writing, this book represents the first time that I have concluded that the weaknesses and limitations of human emotion, human nature, and human capabilities—in combination with the dynamics of the forces that I'll describe—are determining the outcome of the big picture—the ultimate fate of civilization.

I'm 67, and I've had two successful careers. The second one, begun gradually in 1999, is journalism. Moved by what I saw as tremendous contradictions and poor choices within nearly every aspect of society—but most especially in our relationship to the ecosystem—I started to write periodic opinion pieces for a small number of local newspapers. Initially, my goal was to comment on and protest these contradictions; I wanted to bring them to people's attention. I'm sure that I hoped—even dared to imagine—that my columns would help to both raise citizen knowledge and concern and contribute to solutions.

I wrote about current events and a large number of serious subjects—war, religion, terrorism, ISIS, the Mideast, politics, Congress, education, economics, technology, the internet, the environment, global warming, health care, genetic engineering, psychology, psychiatry, philosophy, and epistemology. I wrote about gambling, drug addiction, gun control, race issues, architecture, transportation, movies, and journalism itself.

I read widely and voraciously in books, magazines, and newspapers, and studied hard about all I wrote about. I interviewed politicians, scientists, and business people, and attended public hearings, legislative sessions, conferences, and trade shows. I spoke with citizens everywhere and all the time—at any opportunity or encounter—to pick their brains, learn their viewpoints, and to understand their thinking, perspectives, and epistemology.

I was on a mission, and I was fortunate enough to be able to devote fulltime to it for the past 15 or 16 years. My mission was to understand what was, and is, going on, and to write honestly and clearly about it.

Over time, after the first five years or so, I was able to work myself into a regular columnist position with the *Salem News*, in Salem, Massachusetts. In the early 2000s, the editor there welcomed my columns and encouraged my work. By 2007 or so, I was committed to writing a weekly column of 800 to 850 words (a bit longer than your average op-ed piece). Between 1999 and January of 2017, when I resigned on good terms, I wrote approximately 750 columns. In the last few years of that span, my columns also ran simultaneously in the *Gloucester Times*, in Gloucester, Massachusetts.

I resigned because I had become appalled by the state of so much, and I could no longer write optimistically. There were, and are, of course, plenty of constructive endeavors extant within society, but, examining the developing big picture, I came to believe our prospects are bleak.

I had always been an optimistic person, and I wasn't looking for darkness. My columns had always been characterized by a no-holds-barred description of often grim, difficult, or controversial issues, but they also almost always contained descriptions or recommendations that pointed out possible solutions or ways forward that offered hope. And hope to as many parties as possible. When I reached the point where I no longer believed that possible solutions would be either forthcoming or embraced, I could no longer write the columns about the myriad issues that matter most in the world. I wasn't going to write a column that—to me—lied, but at the same time I wasn't comfortable turning my privileged, weekly, relatively-widely-read opinion pieces into regular messages of gloom and doom. On every issue, there are too many good people working hard to improve things, and they don't need somebody telling them all is lost. And what if I'm wrong?

All of these thoughts led me to resign, feeling that the op-ed genre was no longer adequate or appropriate for what I wanted to say. And blunt truth be told, I was loath to tarnish my reputation with a new and continuing series of columns that would weekly tell readers that things are destined to get worse and worse. Very few people want to hear that, and I'll admit that I cared about retaining my hard-earned identity as a critical-but-always-constructive journalist.

My thinking—my hesitation to be seen as "extreme" in delivering grim pronouncements—has to do with the nature of a column, my professional ambition as a columnist, and the nature of readers. A hopeful, good-news, or constructive column can be easily and safely written. It advances the stature of the writer in the eyes of the editor, the newspaper, and the readers, and within the profession. On any subject, when writing in a positive and optimistic tone, demonstrating familiarity with good sources and background material and then presenting reasoned arguments is usually sufficient to being received well; not every reader will agree with the columnist's position, but almost all will react well to the respect, form, and effort in the piece. Nobody will be offended, and many will like the column.

But write hopelessness into a column—week after week—and you better have bulletproof arguments and strong defensive documentation for those opinions. For undoubtedly you will arouse strong disagreement, hostility, or—worst for a professional op-ed writer, a wannabe influencer—dismissal in the court of public opinion. For lots of reasons, there is a strong, unspoken pressure to conclude columns (and books)—even those bearing seriously bad news or a stinging critique—with some constructive thoughts regarding possible responses to the terrible message the writer has just delivered.

So, because I didn't want to lie, I didn't want to write relentlessly negative columns every week, and I didn't want to lose my influence or my good reputation, I came to view the column as a format that was too small to satisfactorily communicate to the reader the nature of our problems as I had come to see them. A column can certainly usefully start to describe the contours of one discrete issue or problem. But try to describe more than one problem, and also describe how they are interconnected with other problems, and you will rapidly bump up against the limits of 850 words.

On top of those constraints, include a profoundly negative message, and you have a difficult writing task. As I say, I hadn't planned to reach the story and conclusions that I outline in this book. But I experienced my own growth, development, education, and evolution during 18 years of study and column writing. The more I observed, the more I studied our careering society, the more I wrote, the more I came to see the reality that most of the problems and forces and circumstances within society are the products of many factors, relationships, and dynamics. And I was seeing none of it resolving into a good place.

Today's world—the infinite pieces that make up today's world—are hyper-connected and hyper-interdependent, and explaining and critiquing that huge, sweeping mosaic became more than I could do in even serial columns. To say that many circumstances and realities are complicated or have nuances or have many causes, to deliver abysmally grim descriptions and conclusions—and to persuade, be credible, and remain a respected journalist—I needed a longer piece.

In this loud, boisterous internet age, many voices want to tell us that things are simple, that this—or that—is to blame for this—or that—but things are not simple. Instead, they are complicated, overlapping, interrelated, historical, dynamic, simultaneous, logical, illogical, emotional, resolvable, and unresolvable.

Ah, yes, the internet. It too surely played a role in my decision to look for longer-format writing. When I began penning columns in 1999, the internet was still relatively new, relatively small, and mostly constructive. The idea and reality of a whole pulsating, mongrel online world—what I call "Webworld"—was just gearing up.

But in 20 years, its troubling evolution—with a big aspect of it largely a vehicle for hysteria, reaction, division, distraction, oversimplification, falsehoods, and mindlessness—became central to why I view our current situation and problems as unlikely to be satisfactorily resolved. More than any other factor, the place of the internet and Webworld in our world has been the thing that has alarmed me, and has fueled this endeavor to write this book.

As I say, I came to believe our prospects are bleak. I don't see us fixing the critical things that need to be fixed. So, after resigning in 2017, I spent 18 months reading or skimming roughly 120 or so deliberately chosen books and following the news closely and questioning my conclusions. I talked with every scholar, teacher, professional, and ordinary citizen I knew, and many I didn't. Had I missed something?

I came to conclude that I hadn't. In all my reading, I could find no adequate rebuttal to my conclusions regarding the big picture. As I mentioned, plenty of good, recent books identify the difficult issues in various sectors of society, but they all end with a calm advisory to employ the now-well-known reforms that have been proposed in every area. There is almost zero speculation about whether we'll actually do that.

I came to find that shocking. As the forces described in this book become progressively larger, more pervasive, and more destructive, our inattention to them—or outright maintenance of them in their worst forms—becomes shocking.

I came to see that focusing on a future that is 10, 20, 30, or more years out is just not being done, at least not in a public, sustained, or significant way. And almost nobody—except in the environmental sphere—is talking about what the world will look like in, say, 20 or 30 years if the worst consequences of today's problems remain unaddressed.

That is partly because this exercise requires not a specialist in one field but an investigator willing to survey and understand the entire societal landscape—the economy, politics, technologies, education, and media of the nation—and assess our responses to it. The point of this book—to examine the likelihood of our changing the trajectory we are on—is really an investigation into human behavior and the ways that we are interacting with the dominant forces in society. Very few writers are taking on that task.

Perhaps it's too horrible to see or imagine that we won't cope and prevail as a civilization. Citizens and experts alike will give you many reasons why we'll eventually meet our challenges; for most people, it's practically an article of faith. They can barely entertain the idea of civilizational collapse.

It is instructive to notice that it is novelists—not nonfiction writers—who are beginning to write more and more about the near future and our societies in it. They are picturing dystopias, and they are grounding the bases for their stories in the very dysfunctions of the forces I describe in this book. More than the professional practitioners in each field—economics, technology, politics, etc.—novelists exist to depict communities and societies and a time, and to place characters in them. Novelists are interested in humans—how they love, hate, succeed, fail, struggle, behave, and respond to each other and events (tellingly, biographers also do this, although mostly after the fact). Novelists explore human nature and everything that stems from that—weakness, strength, fear, courage, anger, honor, responsibility, immaturity, and generosity. Novelists are interested in emotion, and they understand its outsized and inseparable role in all human behavior.

To write this book, I had to become well informed about the forces and influences shaping society today, but more importantly, I had to discern our responses to them. What have been and are our emotional reactions to them? What have been and are our behavioral responses to them? How self-aware are we about our postures toward these forces?

You will see that our imagination and our emotional selves—and the contest for their control—will be a major factor in how the future unfolds. Some of the smartest, most powerful, and most destructive forces in society—the internet platforms—already understand this, and their dominance and indispensability everywhere are part of the reason why the message of this book has not often been seen (as yet anyway) in many nonfiction books.

* * *

The first half of my working life—from 1978 to about 2002—I was (still am) a registered architect and worked on large and small buildings for a variety of firms in Philadelphia and Boston. In 1988 I went out on my own with another fellow—starting our own firm—and we prospered on small residential projects until closing up shop in 2002.

Although I had been a part-time book reviewer for the *Philadelphia Inquirer* in the early 1980s, I had never intended to leave architecture for journalism. But an architect's training—if good—teaches him to be interested in all aspects of society, to be a student of people, and to be extremely logical, analytical, and far-looking.

I received my Master of Architecture from the University of Pennsylvania in 1978, and my class graduated from Penn at a time when the architecture curriculum there emphasized understanding context, cities, environmental issues, and human nature and behavior, and participating constructively in the long arc of history and civilization. That may sound a bit grand, but that's the way it was. The idealistic notion of seeking what can be, and pursuing it with hope and responsibility, was the message Penn instilled in us.

So, when I left architectural practice for journalism, it was not for me a radical shift. For me, journalism was architecture by a different name.

Both are crafts best served by a loyalty to honest investigation and the pursuit of solutions or conclusions that are free to follow from the circumstances and realities of the problems at hand. And both crafts emphasize seeing the details and the big picture of a thing, and constantly shifting one's focus back and forth, never losing sight of either, and how each—detail and whole—interplays with the other.

Here, at the beginning of the book, I would also like to highlight two points that I want you to bear in mind throughout your reading of the book. One, every person takes (or mistakes) his own limited vision for the horizons of the world. And two, trauma's role in the world is huge and tenacious. These two truths have significance because they relate to the human capacities for growth and change. They identify the existence of two major limitations within society that do not receive enough attention.

As you read through our problems and their possible correctives, please keep in mind that it is only humans who can implement the solutions; and we cannot move faster or further than allowed by either our collective vision of what is desirable or possible, or the overall mental health of our population.

What we imagine as the "horizons" of the world—our conceptions of societies' possible shapes, institutions, relationships, health, prosperity, ecological fitness, and levels of fraternity and justice—depend very much on our personal knowledge and perspectives. The more uninformed or parochial in any way we are, the less potential our vision is apt to hold.

Trauma too plays a part in society's potential. In assessing the likelihood of our responding to the crises I describe in this book, it is critical to be aware that we may be held back by the emotional damage in a large part of the populace. This is an extremely difficult reality to weight appropriately if you personally are whole and healthy and, in addition, do not have to relate in any close or regular way to the personal dysfunction of individuals. Those of us who are empowered, employed in a creative job, and generally doing well are apt consistently to discount this factor.

Perhaps half of the readers of this book will identify with and already understand this point, but the other half may find it startling and new. I will return to this subject material in the chapter on human nature. It will be an eye-opener for some readers, a dose of reality and caution for others, and a reminder, again, that there aren't neat firewalls between our emotional sicknesses and our wonky, creative, if-only-we'd-do-this, think-tank policy prescriptions. There is no magic in our best technologies, wisest policy options, and most generous political compromises that will cause humans to adopt them. Only a society comprised of some large, critical mass of reasonably emotionally healthy and responsible individuals would possess the attributes necessary to sustain civilization indefinitely.

Across the world, there are many types of trauma, and they are of differing character, scope, duration, and severity.

Personally, I can attest to the devastation that one type of trauma can cause. I have been through two brief periods of it myself—long enough to get a look at darkness. But more powerfully, I have observed another individual be laid low more or less permanently by severe and extended traumatic experiences.

While growing up, a close friend of mine was beaten regularly by his father, and deliberately ignored by his mother. Years later, as an adult, he went to therapy to understand his parents' abuse of him and to cope with the consequences it wrought in him. Today, he can speak knowledgeably and coherently about all of it. Nonetheless, he suffers debilitating dysfunctions. He can't recover from any personal conflict. Under any stress at all, his psychological resilience and skills quickly vanish. Then, he just can't help himself from saying—or acting out—the worst possible responses to almost any challenging (for him) stimuli. Repeatedly, he has withdrawn—emotionally and physically and spatially—from many personal relationships.

I am, and his relatives are, mostly helpless to arrest his downward spiral in his worst moments. At those times, he is not happy with his words or his behavior, and never wishes for them to happen.

The power, persistence, grip, and destructiveness of his early-life trauma on him made an indelible impression on me. Despite the therapy that he seems to have taken seriously, his traumatic experiences had many terrible effects on him. His experiences left him with certain degrees of anxiety, distrust, paranoia, and bitterness, and worst of all, created a defensive rigidity to the narratives by which he interprets and understands people, events, and life.

His experiences have boxed him in, putting severe limits on his intellectual and emotional capacities, limiting what he can consider or imagine, restricting what he can see, and arresting his personal growth and development. Whether he is considering human behavior, politics, our own lives and histories, or anything else significant, his feelings and thinking often shrink into small, stunted places.

Most of the time, most of those qualities of his person remain hidden. Only under distress—usually in interactions with other people—does he struggle. He has deliberately developed strategies to avoid being triggered. At times, he actually avoids people. But if his anxieties or fears are triggered, his emotional equilibrium is upset and he becomes in some significant way dysfunctional.

It is sad to watch, it isn't his fault, and he is essentially helpless in the face of his trauma's legacy. At his worst, most overwhelmed moments, he is a prisoner of his damaged psyche.

Now, he is only one person—one American example—and his experiences and trauma were exceedingly severe, but perhaps fifty percent of the American and world population is limited in some significant way by some form and degree of personal trauma. That is an underappreciated fact, but a key one. If we are to realistically evaluate the prospects for human and society survival, we had better start considering the solutions we imagine with the actual populations we have. Trauma today is widespread and it must be considered in any reckoning of the capacities of societies for change and improvement. Also, accordingly, we should view with alarm the events and circumstances today that are continually increasing the numbers of children and adults experiencing trauma. In the chapter on human nature, I will talk more about trauma and the inherent capacities and limitations of the human mind and spirit.

* * * *

At the beginning here, I'll also say a few words about my politics, allegiances, Donald Trump, and related matters. I have always been a registered Democrat, but have not hesitated to vote for Republicans or Independents when their candidates were the better choice. Whether considering a local, state, or national election, I have always focused on the various issues under discussion and weighed the candidates' views and thoughtfulness on them. I've never been a single-issue voter, and I believe that blind allegiance to or dogmatism about any one position or politician or party is a big mistake.

My biggest political sympathies lie with ordinary, working, modest-income citizens—of either party—who aspire to happiness, freedom, peace, success, and a fair shake for all. Although I do not think that the Democratic or Republican parties are equivalent—in many areas they differ greatly—too often politicians from each party display cravenness, dishonesty, hypocrisy, posturing, overweening ambition, and an insufferable determination to be reelected, or well-employed once out of office. That said, in my core I deeply respect politicians, politics, government, public service, and the real skills and experience involved in being a good political leader. Not to excuse the bad behavior or irresponsibility of any politician, elected office can be an extremely difficult job.

Later in this book, when I discuss some of the specific forces buffeting our society and our democracy, I will have some specific criticisms for each party—and not equally. But the main point of this book—to describe the conditions, status, and prospects for this society—does not rely on a partisan loyalty to any political party or a partisan analysis of the current state of things. The realities buffeting and defining our lives are so beyond party considerations; instead, they have to do with power, money, scale, resources, technology, capitalism, economics, and the environment.

As I say, I am writing this book for all ordinary citizens—Republican, Democratic, Independent, Libertarian, Green, or other. Not because we are all the same; we have real and meaningful differences. But this moment in time demands one thing above all from all citizens, and that thing is solidarity. Solidarity with our fellow citizens.

If you prefer to think in terms of enemies, the enemy is not your fellow citizen—whether Democratic or Republican, whether liberal or conservative, whether gay or straight, whether Catholic or atheist, whether ironworker or software engineer, whether rural hunter or urban bike messenger, whether from Texas or Vermont, whether new immigrant or old WASP. The vast majority of us want to be happy, healthy, successful, have a decent job, be reasonably secure (in a variety of ways), and enjoy our leisure time and activities. The vast majority of us also want to enjoy the country emotionally and physically, see it do well, and live up to its (and our) ideals and best promise.

Mostly, our fellow citizen is a good person, a fellow American. But, for reasons—and by techniques—I will describe, ordinary citizens are dividing against each other. Using politics—and being used by politics—we are splintering, fragmenting, deteriorating, and becoming impotent. In direct relationship to the degree of polarization among ordinary citizens within American society, we are helpless to improve our lot in any large, widespread, and sustainable way. I emphasize "ordinary" citizens (of both parties) because obviously there is a very wealthy segment of society that is doing very well.

Regarding Donald Trump, as is widely recognized he was and is a symptom of America's division, not its cause. He certainly adds to the division, but it was partly the division already afflicting America that enabled his ascendance. As such, I am willing to say unequivocally that Trump was and is unfit to be the President but I do not condemn or disparage or misunderstand the citizens who voted for him. I know that among his supporters there are some racists and truly destructive people; but the majority of his voters are good people who have a variety of legitimate, genuine, serious, and not unusual or uncommon concerns.

I emphasize this point: I distinguish mightily between Donald Trump and those who voted for him. I believe that he is a man without principle, character, experience, and the traits and habits that are necessary to lead a great country. But whatever I say about Trump, I am not saying that about his supporters.

To improve, to prosper, to unite, this country does not need Trump; it does need his supporters. By the time he won the vote in November, 2016, I had already decided to soon (in January, 2017) stop writing columns, had already reached the conclusions in this book, and had already seen that the need for ordinary-citizen solidarity was the only ingredient that might offer an effective counter against the forces dominating, wracking, and altering society.

As I write this in October 2019, there are many Democratic presidential candidates vying for the nomination. It's too early to predict the nominee. But whether Trump or the Democrat wins in November 2020, the descriptions and analyses contained in this book will still be pertinent and accurate and its conclusions will still reflect where we are headed. The forces and relationships presently dominating society and us will not change or disappear with the election, no matter who is elected. Our leaders matter—it is important who is President—but this book will describe why we will remain helpless.

* * * *

A few last comments. Again, because of the existence and dynamics of human nature, any observer and writer attempting to judge the path of society has to be pretty conscious of his own place in that firmament. Can he sufficiently prevent his own hopes, disappointments, and energies from coloring his judgements? For there is a growing recognition among people that our personal emotional and physical conditions can have a lot of influence on our perspectives, opinions, and attitudes—especially optimism versus pessimism. Or, in this case, the reference pole I prefer is realism versus either optimism or pessimism. As I've said, there isn't a nifty firewall between the totality of our being and the circumstances of the world. No firewall between the circumstances of the world and our expressions of identity either. I have kept that in mind for two years as I have put together this book. To stay aware of the need for a certain equanimity of judgement, I take the measure of myself with the same lens with which I evaluate others in building the conclusions in this book. For the grimness of my analysis is not lost on me.

Part of the analysis of this book—and part of my judgements about the path of society and our past, present, and future responses to it—hinge on judgements about human nature and human limitations. Often our limitations stem from experiences and factors and an epistemology—that sum total of all the events, education, family, jobs, religion, trauma, age, gender, and lived life and more that makes us who we are—peculiar to us as individuals. Where is each of us in our personal growth and development? Do we each have blind spots, insecurities, or scars which amount to obstacles to agency or cooperation or seeing or understanding?

I will return to these thoughts again. As I discuss the important forces affecting our lives, and analyze their causes, development, and current expression, and our possible responses to them, I hope it becomes evident how huge and critical is the role of human nature, human behavior, human capacities, and human emotion in the trajectory of events. It may seem obvious when you see it written, but it is humans—not the forces around us—who hold the fate of humans in our hands. Life is indeed a play—a story—and we are the actors writing it and acting it.

This is a nonfiction book, but it is a story, and I hope you can see it as that. This is the biggest story of our time. I don't know how you view the world; I don't know what story you hold onto. But an author—or anyone—cannot take away someone's story without giving them a new one. My hope, fellow citizen, is that this book can contribute understandings that cause you to modify and improve the story that you live by.

THE FORCES

I N MANY WAYS, developments in the world are either overtaking us, or
overwhelming us. In the Preface I said that organized society today faces
many threats. These threats can also be characterized as challenges, problems, forces, influences, developments, circumstances, or realities.

In the following chapters I will examine the major forces—the most
significant forces—operating in society today. They are: capitalism; technology; Webworld; politics; media; education; human nature; the environment; human population; and transportation.

Then I will describe a number of miscellaneous forces that are important, but do not rise to the level of universally critical. They are: immigration and refugee migrations; terrorism; black-white relations; health care;
student loan debt; gene editing; war and nuclear war; and religion.

The major forces comprise a large variety of dangers and they are all
quite serious. Some of the forces are relatively discrete realities—meaning
they stand mostly alone—but the majority are related to or connected to
other problems in our list. As such, they don't really have neat edges, nor
are they contained fully within any labels we may give them, or within
any categories we may place them in. I have divided the forces into what
look like tidy subjects, with a seemingly clear name for each, but that
organization is somewhat misleading. Today, more than ever before, these
forces overlap each other, interact with each other, and in many areas
blend seamlessly into each other. And, when compared to their expression
and influence in any previous time, today they have a power and a hold on

society—accompanied by a never-before-seen set of circumstances—that is unprecedented. That is what makes today different.

Some of the forces and threats seem to be more pressing than others, but among them all, I don't know if we can tell which ones are the most dangerous. Part of the difficulty in trying to rank the threats is that their effects may be on different timetables. Many involve uncertainty; we cannot predict the behavior of humans nor—in many cases—the consequences of our actions. We certainly cannot predict with any assurance the dynamics of the natural world and the ecosphere, where those are involved.

These threats and problems and forces are all developing and unfolding simultaneously. We all see or feel them. Although you will read these chapters sequentially, please pretend that you are reading all of them simultaneously. The forces and realities described are laced with each other, and create effects and build strength in association with each other. That cannot be emphasized enough; it is key to appreciating their power and the difficulties we'll face should we try to bring them under control. Let's examine them one by one, to understand them. Then let's consider what would be needed to effectively counter them, and finally let's make a judgement regarding the likelihood of those counters being implemented or undertaken.

CHAPTER 1

CAPITALISM

O F ALL THE MANY FORCES affecting society today, one of the largest and most influential is capitalism. Along with other forces, capitalism has become part of the atmosphere and conditioning milieu by which we live, work, play, see things, interpret things, make choices, and often define our successes and failures.

Two things—sort of reassurances to the readers because of my extensive criticisms below—about this reality are critical to note. First, to a large extent in America, as the march of evolving industrialization steadily transformed the country from a mixture of rural frontier and agrarian communities to a mechanized, commercial economy, capitalism has always been our economic system. It has always been a force in our society. We have modified it, adjusted it, mixed in a bit of socialism, and regulated it more or less, but overall the nation has unequivocally been a capitalist one. So, in my discussion here, I am mostly focused on the degree (relative to the past) to which capitalism is influencing (or dominating) society, and the particular aspects of it that I see as either new or stronger (again, relative to the past) or unprecedented or destructive.

Second, although I will have much to say about the negative effects of capitalism's shape and operation today, I want to make it clear that I believe that capitalism is the best of all the possible ways to organize a nation's economy—especially in a geographically and demographically large and diverse country like the United States. Socialism as an economic system has much to offer, but my preference is for a capitalist economy tempered by smart regulations and socialist aspects where appropriate, and restructured into a sustainable system.

Too much debate today about the economy ignores the reality that we have for about a century had a "blended" economy, that is, one that mixes aspects of both capitalism and socialism. Many areas of both the public and private sectors utilize degrees of socialism, and that has mostly served the nation well. It is silly and dishonest for people to speak as though the choice in front of us is either capitalism or socialism, one or the other. The task we face is much more nuanced and complicated than that. It requires us to examine where and why capitalism is performing poorly or destructively, and then readjust it. In addition, if adopting some "socialistic" approaches in specific areas can help us, then we should consider them. Neither capitalism nor socialism nor a blended economy is a system of government, and regardless of what forms our markets and private sector take, we will still need to resuscitate and maintain our crippled democracy.

Capitalism has given us many good things, including an amazing material-standard of living. The capitalist system has been uniquely well-suited to tap the creativity, individuality, proclivities, energies, and temperament of the American people, and our population has been very productive within its dynamics. But in this book I am not reviewing capitalism's successes. My point here is to focus on the ways that it is failing us—or even encouraging us—to go astray. The chapter that follows contains many generalizations, and it focuses primarily on the negative aspects of our economic system.

* * * *

Today, many important segments or properties of capitalism have become runaway capitalism, out of control, frequently irresponsible, significantly disconnected from ecological sustainability principles, and fueled and measured overwhelmingly by only one parameter—profits. Today's capitalism, in steadily increasing degrees since 1975 or so, has become a cruder, more rapacious system. In contrast to its identity and performance during the postwar years of 1945 to 1975, today's capitalism shortchanges and cares not for workers, has little national loyalty, and with the aid of computerization and highly mobile capital, is able to roam and straddle the globe in search of the most favorable conditions for its operation and purposes. It sharply creates winners and losers, inordinately serves a plutocratic or oligarchic class, and has many citizens thinking that business can replace government. Because large corporations and their lobbyists and ideological allies have captured so many politicians and so many legislative and agency initiatives, capitalism is now outcompeting democracy in many ways. Citizens can be forgiven for thinking that capitalism is our system of government.

Let's look at the characteristics and effects of our version of capitalism as it is designed today.

Probably the most fundamental problem with capitalism today is its need for constant growth. As an operational system, its principles, theories, assumptions, formulas, and success all depend upon the dynamic of constant growth being met. Yet we know today—we did not know in the past—that our finite-sized earth will not forever allow capitalism and its enterprises and products to grow, expand, and proliferate infinitely.

Much of the operation and spread of capitalism involves the design and production of objects and products. Housing, buildings, cars, infrastructure, clothing, food, appliances, computers, toys, and an infinite array of objects are created. Wood, fiberglass, plastic, metal, glass, paper, chemicals, and innumerable materials are produced. Energy, fuel, waste, pollution, heat, and other complex products are processed, consumed, or discharged. As civilization moves, operates, expands, and advances, the capitalist system that organizes our economy steadily uses the earth's raw materials, resources, water, air, soil, and oceans. Those resources and mediums are indisputably finite, as is the ecosystem's capacity to remain healthy, balanced, and life-supporting.

That a finite planet cannot forever support a capitalism-without-limits is a simple and obvious fact. This flaw within capitalism's design is major; it is as though this system was designed for some other planet, one that was ever-expanding, or one with inexhaustible raw materials and resources. This design defect—this disconnect—has always existed, but in centuries past the effects of the flaw were mostly manageable.

In the past, many circumstances were different—in degree—from today that permitted economies to grow unimpeded (in most cases). Both undeveloped land and untapped raw materials were more readily available; exhausting either in one place often simply meant moving on to develop another locale. But today, whether we examine the earth's reserves of temperate woodlands, tropical forests, farmable soil, fresh water, minerals and raw materials, or species and habitat diversity, we find less quantity and less health of those reserves (coal, oil, and natural gas are notable but problematic exceptions).

In the past also, used-up or disposable things could be thrown "away" or burned or dumped. We had sufficient space nearby for convenient, inexpensive landfills, we didn't realize the damage of burning things in the air, and we saw no need for recycling. Our various types of pollution (put into the land, water, or air) were either absorbed or diluted or were sufficiently small to coexist (sometimes badly) with nature. For the longest time—and still partly in the present—we didn't assign any negative monetary costs to pollution or removing natural landscapes; there was no explicit financial penalty associated with those activities. That had the effect of disguising or rendering invisible or removing from consideration the damages we were doing to the environment.

In the recent past (50 to 60 years), after we had identified the damages being done by much of our many types of pollution, we took steps to reduce it and clean the parts of the environment that we had despoiled. And in the past, the earth, its landscapes and atmosphere, its resources and oceans, and its absorption capacities could support and remain relatively stable with the total, global human population and its myriad of developed or developing societies.

Today, however, circumstances have changed, and are continuing to change, and are thereby putting the impossibility of infinite economic growth into high relief. Today, a combination of circumstances is operating in new and unprecedented ways and magnitudes. The current (and growing) global population of 7.8 billion people, the resources we are consuming, the water and soil we are exhausting, and the atmosphere we are altering with carbon dioxide comprise a set of factors that are creating a planetary-scale crisis. As each of those factors grows in magnitude and power, the effect of all of them together will be to cause any number of environmental or ecological catastrophes. In any number of ways, our economic growth, and the pressures it puts on the earth and the natural world are bumping up against the limits of the capacity of the planet's ecosphere (the relatively thin shell of land habitats and the atmosphere girdling the earth) to remain stable enough for human habitation as we know it. I will more specifically discuss the threats to the natural world in the chapter on the environment.

Another qualitative and quantitative difference in the character of today's capitalism can be seen in contemporary globalization. The word "globalization" encompasses a vast array of ideas, practices, and developments. In its broadest sense, it refers to the reciprocal exchange of almost everything—technology, products, resources, culture, entertainment, and ideas—across all parts of the world. Globalization is both a cause and a result of the way in which our world is shrinking.

To some degree, globalization has existed for hundreds of years. But the contemporary phase of what we call "globalization" began in the late 1970s and has operated continuously since then, and with accelerating speed. There are many benefits to globalization, but here I am focused on how its worst aspects and effects have contributed to a capitalism that is distorted and predatory.

In a 45-year process, private businesses and corporations in America and around the world have been able to free themselves from physical and financial dependence on and connection to their home countries, and become free—as never before—to shop the globe for raw materials, best physical locations, financial advantage, taxation advantage, cheapest workers, and new markets.

Private companies have always sought these things, but today's globalization—and the advantages and power that corporations accrue—has become out of control and damaging to the interests of workers, economies, the environment, the sovereignty of nations, the range of cultures of nations, and democracy itself.

As corporations freely roam the globe, they look for countries where they can reduce their labor costs to a bare minimum (in many cases to a point that can only be called labor exploitation) and simultaneously avoid strong environmental regulations. Since the late 1970s, corporations that once called themselves "American" have transferred many millions of jobs from the U.S. to foreign countries. And it should be noted that often these corporations closed factories and offices in the U.S. that were making substantial profits. But the lure of even larger—unnecessarily and destructively large—profits, made by paying foreign workers a tiny fraction of what American workers had been paid, caused companies to relocate to China or still-developing or Third World countries. In Bangladesh, for example, prominent global corporations hire no-name subcontractors to operate 5,200 large garment factories employing about 3.5

million workers. The workers are mostly women and they endure typical sweatshop conditions—low pay, long hours, piecework pressure, abusive bosses, and unsafe or unhealthy building conditions.

For 40 or 45 years, millions of once-well-paying manufacturing and other good jobs have disappeared from the U.S., and in a slow, steady process, the makeup of the American economy has skewed toward poorer-paying service jobs. At the same time, steady computerization and automation and robotization have also acted to eliminate millions of jobs in America.

Ironically today, automation and robotization are progressing rapidly even in China and the Third World countries that once were the destinations for American manufacturing jobs. So when some Americans call for returning manufacturing and other jobs back to the U.S., many of those jobs no longer exist—anywhere. They have been automated out of existence. And as long as the ones that remain are filled with disempowered workers who can be paid pennies, they aren't coming back to America.

With globalization as a backdrop, companies have also been able to gain the upper hand—inordinately—within the United States as they shop around within the country for the most favorable locations here. Playing states off against each other, businesses shop for the most favorable tax treatments, outright subsidies, cheapest labor, and other financial benefits. When a large corporation announces a search for the new location of a major factory or headquarters building, states compete with each other to see who can offer the company the sweetest deal.

For the past 45 years or so, as businesses and corporations and the private sector have been doing well, and as the top 5 or 10 percent of the population has been prospering to a degree that can fairly be described as extraordinarily high, unusual, and unprecedented (with the exception of how wealth got distributed in the Gilded Age), the lower and middle classes of America have been struggling.

Most of working America has actually lost ground in the past 40 years, especially relative to the basic costs of living. Wages have been nearly stagnant for that period, and large and unprecedented numbers—well more than half—of working-class Americans live pretty much paycheck to paycheck. Two-thirds of working Americans cannot fully pay their credit card bills each month, and so must carry a balance forward. Those balances are charged with an average interest rate of 16 percent. Household debt today is extraordinarily high and totals approximately $13 trillion. Many home-owners and workers have debt in the tens of thousands of dollars, with no foreseeable way to pay it off.

Income inequality in the country has grown severe over the past 40 years. The Occupy Wall Street movement in 2011 focused on the wealth gap between the top 1 percent of income earners and the 99 percent below them, and that gap is real. But the real story is the gap between the top 10 percent of Americans and the 90 percent below them.

The wealthiest 10 percent of American families now own 77 per-cent of the country's total household wealth. This is new and different. In 1975 they owned only 35 percent. From 1979 to 2008, the year Wall Street imploded, this favored 10 percent received nearly 100 percent of all the income growth in the country, while the 90 percent of the popula-tion stagnated or lost income. And since the Wall Street meltdown, even though the economy has been steadily recovering and employment rates have been improving, the wealthiest 10 percent of Americans have con-tinued to receive an inordinately disproportionate percentage—literally almost all—of the country's wage and wealth growth. (The past two years have seen hourly wages grow modestly; but they have a long way to rise before they become living wages.)

A few other statistics (of many possible) help to describe the new sever-ity of the income gap in the U.S. The entire bottom half of the nation—roughly 62 million households—possess only 1 percent of the country's wealth. The bottom 80 percent of households owns only 5 percent of the nation's household wealth; they have basically become—in a slow, steady process that began 40 or 45 years ago—frozen out of any upward social mobility.

The top 1 percent of the population now makes, annually, roughly 80 times what the entire bottom half of the adult population earns. And the 20 richest Americans—20 individuals—possess more wealth among them than the entire lower half of the U.S. population.

Emblematic of this skewing of wealth is the gap in salary between ordinary workers and upper-level executives. Since about 1980, there has been a steady and dramatic rise in executive salaries and benefits. Whereas in the 1950s and 1960s a typical business executive might earn 20 or 30 times what the majority of workers in his company might earn, today a typical, relatively high-level executive may earn 300 or 400 times what most of his company's employees earn. And plenty of executives earn 600 or 700 times their typical employee's pay.

Especially at larger companies in the banking, finance, insurance, health care, pharmaceutical, manufacturing, energy, and technology fields, executive pay is often shockingly large—and destructively large given the low pay and economic stagnation at the ordinary employee level. Salaries for each member of upper management—not just the CEO—often range from $5 million to $30 million, and are accompanied by stellar health plans, innumerable perks, enormous bonuses (sometimes bigger than the salaries), and stock awards and stock options.

There is perhaps no better example of the erosion of the social contract than the 45-year trajectory of rising executive compensation. The "social contract" in society is comprised of many parts and relationships. But one aspect of it is the unwritten idea that we all have responsibilities and obligations to each other to strive to see that everyone is doing well and benefiting from America's industry, wealth, and prosperity. When it comes to paying ordinary workers and executives, major corporations have rewritten the social contract largely in their favor. Between 1978 and 2015, the pay of corporate CEOs rose about 900 percent while employee pay was virtually stagnant during that period. The CEOs of fast-food companies, for example, made an average of $24 million each in 2013 while their food-serving employees made an average of $17,000 annually.

Here it would be easy for me to give you a long list of executives and financiers and business managers and their absolutely outrageous salaries and supplementary compensation. Probably the most shocking pay goes to the hedge fund managers on Wall Street. Many of them each routinely make hundreds of millions of dollars a year, and sometimes more than $1 billion (with a "b") in a year. But the point is, tens of thousands of upper-level executives receive extraordinary levels of compensation that are unwarranted, unconscionable, and directly destructive to the economy and our society because those salaries and benefits are a straight theft from—and a cost to—all of the ordinary citizens in the country.

To the degree that those pay packages are excessive, they increase prices and fees to customers, and also increase the burden on taxpayers.

Because salaries and stock awards are tax deductions for the corporations, they are in effect subsidies from the ordinary, tax-paying public.

Many corporations pay workers so poorly—even their fulltime, 40-hour-per-week employees—that large percentages of their workforce must supplement their pay with some type of welfare assistance and food stamps. Fulltime workers in many fields—construction, landscape services, housekeeping, restaurant work, clerical work, retail, fast-food, and others—receive financial assistance through government programs. Very large numbers of fast-food workers—more than half—and bank tellers, for example, also receive welfare or other assistance payments. Just in the State of New York, for example, the government doles out about $700 million a year in assistance to fast-food workers alone.

* * * *

Today, more corporations are ever-larger, and private-sector unions have nearly disappeared (roughly 6.7 percent of private-sector workers are in a union today, versus a peak of 35 percent in 1954). Labor's power is constantly being eroded, while corporations have succeeded in greatly diminishing their own role in providing pension plans and healthcare plans. Corporations also increasingly make use of subcontractors and "independent" contractors to perform work that, formerly, traditional employees would do. This further allows corporations to take reduced responsibility for worker pensions, benefits, healthcare, working conditions, and living wages.

This results in a so-called "gig economy," an economy where large numbers of workers are totally on their own to try to piece together a living without the support, reliability, or security of a traditional, fulltime job with a conventional employer.

At the same time that the private sector was downsizing, outsourcing, de-unionizing, and essentially restructuring and redefining the labor force, the rise of computers, technology, automation, and the digitization of everything was simultaneously empowering corporations to further skew the balance of power against not just manufacturing but all classes of employment and all types of labor. The rise of the internet and connectivity permitted corporations to outsource huge amounts of white-collar office work to locations around the globe. And, ironically, computerization and the wide ecology of the web helped to foster the false notion that a "gig" economy was a real and substantial alternative to the once-traditional, employer-employee shape of the economy. As a result, we have all sorts of diverse "workers," of all ages, attempting to create (or recreate) companies, enterprises, products, services, inventions, apps, gimmicks, and start-ups, and of course, a living wage.

Perhaps best emblematic of "jobs" that are "giggish" and filled by "independent contractors," enabled by computerization and a smartphone app, are the Uber drivers. Working more than 40 hours per week, supplying their own cars, taking on all the risks and responsibilities of the job, and giving Uber a cut of every fare, dedicated drivers typically make between $20,000 and $40,000 a year. Certainly not a living wage. There's a reason driver turnover is so high. And there are plenty of even less remunerative, less dependable, gig jobs than that.

Ironically, some of the most damning examples of major corporations that staff themselves with part-timers, temp workers, subcontractors, and "independent contractors" are the tech companies themselves. Google has more temps than fulltime workers. In March 2019 it had 102,000 fulltime employees and 121,000 temps and "contract" workers. Many of Facebook's content reviewers are subcontractors; they are poorly paid, work under various difficult pressures and conditions, and usually quit after one year because of that.

At this moment, in 2019, the gig economy is mostly a scam that the largest forces in America (the ones discussed in this book) are quite happy to have us believe is really an opportunity for each of us. For the moment, "unemployment" in America is about 3.6 percent, a very low number indeed. But if we understand how that number is calculated, and we examine the nature of the jobs that number represents, we will find that it deceives us into thinking that the labor sector is doing better than it really is, both quantitatively and qualitatively.

First, that "official" unemployment figure does not include workers who have given up looking for a job. It does not include part-time workers who want more hours, but cannot get them. It does not include "underemployed" people, that is, workers who have taken—often reluctantly—a job that is beneath their true work skills because they couldn't find work in their actual trade or profession. The unemployment statistic also does not measure the fact that many workers included in the figure are working two jobs, nor does it reflect the fact that today—way more than, say, 40 years ago—both husband and wife may be required to work to earn enough to support a household.

And of course, the statistic doesn't indicate whether the employed are exploited, intimidated, powerless, in debt, or poorly paid. Roughly 42 million workers—nearly one-third of the workforce—are paid less than $12 per hour. The unemployment statistic doesn't tell us how many workers are putting up with chaotic or abusive scheduling. Almost half of all full-time hourly employees are given little idea, day-to-day and week-to-week, what hours they will be given to work. The statistic doesn't tell us whether workers are receiving employer healthcare or any other benefits, or whether they are freelancers or independent contractors or "gig" workers. Lastly, the statistic does not measure the likely permanence of a job, or whether automation or technology or relocation will soon or ultimately eliminate the job.

Capitalism was not always so distorted by its present degree of near-hostility to labor, and not always so single-mindedly skewed in favor of corporations, and maximizing profits. In the 30-year period from the end of World War II to 1975, capitalism was guided by a set of expectations, norms, principles, and regulations that managed to achieve better performance—some would say a balance—in delivering prosperity across a much wider swath of Americans than capitalism does today.

But starting in the late 1970s, in addition to the changes—environmental damage, globalization, automation, computerization, and labor disempowerment—described above, there were simultaneous political, social, regulatory, and attitudinal changes within society and within the business world that were both cause and effect in contributing to the transformation (by degrees) of the nature and design of capitalism.

In the mid-1970s in academia, there began to be some theorizing in the field of economics that promoted the idea of deregulating certain sectors of the economy that had been regulated since the Gilded Age and—for other sectors—since the Depression. This new thinking came about in response to circumstances. First, during the 1970s, the economy was struggling. There was serious inflation, growing competition from foreign companies, diminished American corporate performance, and slowing consumerism. And secondly, the economy had been performing well—for most people—for 30 years, and so the thinking developed that maybe the need for some of the older regulations was no longer there. There was a rough consensus among many economists that loosening or reducing some regulations could further lift business endeavors and still continue to benefit all (or most) ordinary and working Americans.

Consequently, in the late 1970s, the Ford and Carter administrations and Congress began a gradual process of deregulation of many aspects of the market and economy. Many regulations on the railroad, trucking, and airline industries were altered or removed, and these changes were substantial. They lessened barriers to entry in those industries and they increased the possibilities for more competitive pricing. They reduced the opportunities for companies within those sectors to collectively set prices, and they reduced restrictions relating to carriers and the routes they could control.

Initially, there were many positive benefits to these deregulatory measures. But over time—sometimes decades—and varying for the different industries, not all the consequences were beneficial to everyone. Later, in the 1980s, 1990s, and continuing into the present, some of the deregulation led to more instability in those industry markets, bankruptcies, job losses, reductions in employee pay, the gradual jettisoning of industry-led pension plans, and eventually, consolidation of the numbers of large companies—and the percentages of the markets they serve and control—involved in those three industries.

The Reagan administration and Congress continued Carter's push for deregulation with further measures in the finance, agriculture, and transportation sectors. Perhaps the most consequential of the 1980s deregulation was the repeal of certain rules on savings-and-loan banks and commercial banks. Federal limits on the amount of mortgage interest that savings-and-loan banks could charge were removed, and commercial banks were also given more scope into real estate lending.

At the same time, regulatory oversight of the banks diminished generally. The consequences unfolded relatively quickly. By the late 1980s, many S & Ls had behaved recklessly, loaning foolishly and irresponsibly, and overextending themselves well beyond the value of their deposits. Although the causes of the crisis were many—including inflation, increased competition, and new technology—the primary reason for the debacle was a toxic combination of inadequate regulation, rife bank speculation and incompetence, and greed and outright fraud on the part of the directors and managers of the banks. In the end, roughly one-third of the

3,000 S & Ls in the country failed and the entire S & L industry required about $130 billion from the taxpayers to right itself.

Further changes in capitalism's norms occurred during the Reagan administration. There was a gradual but steady erosion of the idea that businesses or corporations equally served both profit and society. To the degree that that idea had been true in the three decades following World War II, now that posture would get adjusted differently. In the 1980s, there developed the idea that the shareholders of a company held primacy among all of the competing claimants on a business. With a surge of corporate raiders making hostile leveraged buyouts and takeovers, and thereby pressuring corporate executives to maximize profits and shareholder returns—with a new, constant emphasis on short-term stock-price performance—the balances in the social contract got newly weighted.

Simultaneously, business was also wining a higher standing—relative to the past—in the now-constant comparison with government. During the Reagan years, and forever after, the very idea of government was often put on the defensive, and the private sector often enjoyed a reputation as more efficient and innovative than the public sector, which was often derided as bureaucratic, wasteful, and self-serving. This change in public perception—a matter of degree—fed the zeitgeist in favor of deregulation and smaller government roles in almost everything.

Throughout the 1990s, capitalism, businesses, and the market enjoyed a framework and a set of rules that continued to favor them. Corporations became larger, with more leverage over their markets and more power over labor. Lots of mergers occurred in many sectors, and near-monopolies grew. Contract law, patent law, bankruptcy law, arbitration rules, non-compete clauses, advertising, lobbying, and trade agreements all leaned in corporate America's direction.

A good example of rule-making to increase the dominance of the largest companies can be seen in the Telecommunications Act of 1996. It repealed restrictions that limited the size and reach of media companies. The legislation allowed corporations to buy and own properties in the newspaper, TV, radio, movie, telephone, and internet sectors of the economy simultaneously. Consequently, a consolidation of smaller companies occurred, and mega-corporations developed that have awesome power to direct, change, influence, or propel many aspects of news presentation, entertainment, politics, and society itself.

Here it is pertinent to note that modern capitalism, in a developed nation, is always a designed system. It can vary in structure and form, and in its details, and in its operation, regulation, and allocation of rewards. What we call the "free market" is in fact not some natural, inevitable, self-shaping, commercial-exchange space, but instead a particular conception brought about by a myriad of conscious intentions, choices, decisions, and designs. The marketplace of commerce is designed ahead of time, in a deliberate fashion, by humans, not by the natural dynamics of people buying and selling in some sort of free commerce. And this marketplace must be constantly tended, maintained, and adjusted to retain its desired shape, whatever that is during a given period of time. Under capitalism, there are many versions of a "free market" that could be created and successfully utilized. What capitalism and the free market look like—what shape they take—depends simply upon who designs them.

So, in the 1980s, 1990s, and up to the present, when corporations and their lobbies and other allies have been able to gain inordinate influence over Congress and the political system, the entire complex and labyrinthine set of laws and regulations and regulatory agencies that establish and maintain and monitor a legal framework for capitalism and the market reflects greatly the interests of those corporations and lobbies.

So the "market," which many conservatives and corporations are happy to have us think is just naturally and rightly competitive and "free," is actually a highly designed structure, and currently it is weighted quite heavily to the advantage of the wealthy strata of American society and to the large corporations. This has resulted in a capitalism today that—by comparison with the capitalism of the three decades after World War II—too severely disadvantages the interests of labor, the environment, community, and the lives of ordinary people.

A whole range of properties and developments characterizing the edifice and operation of today's capitalism demonstrates—again, I emphasize, by degree and in contrast to 30 years of postwar America—the skewed, winner-take-all nature of today's market: the rise of 5 or 6 enormous banks; the near monopolies of so many firms in so many fields (and the lack of significant anti-trust actions); the unilateral visions and agendas of the biggest high-tech firms; the abuses and unaccountability of the internet and social media platforms; the power and influence of the pharmaceutical companies; the hegemony of the biggest hospital and insurance corporations; the territories and reach of the telecommunications firms; the dictates of the biggest agribusiness companies; the swallowing by their larger competitors of any significant start-up company; the limiting of favorable bankruptcy laws to businesses and corporations, and their frequent use to nullify corporate responsibilities toward labor, health care, and pensions; and the coercive language of contracts to one-sidedly benefit large corporations. All of those items are the reflections and consequences of a capitalism and a market that have been—to a degree substantially higher than in the past—tailored to benefit, primarily, certain segments of our economy and population.

All of the characteristics of capitalism listed above, and the evolution of capitalism generally to become a more predatory, more irresponsible system were facilitated by a larger, more powerful army of business lobbyists that learned how to very effectively influence politicians and government to obtain the playing field that big business wanted. In the chapter on politics, I will have more to say about the role of lobbyists and money in government.

Additionally, the 1990s and the 2000s saw new growth in the financial sector of the economy. Critically facilitated by the incredible rise of the computer and digital technology, the financial services piece of the economy—always viewed as necessary but once seen as a sort of secondary, support activity in service to the "real" goods-and-services productivity sectors of the economy—grew into a significant business in its own right. But it was a business designed almost exclusively for the purpose of sucking investment money, fees, profits, and wealth from the many productive sectors of the economy, and giving the vast majority of it to—it must be said—a greedy, parasitic, already-rich Wall Street gang.

Helped along by deregulation and the removal of rules and oversight that once placed prohibitions on a range of bank activities, the Wall Street financial sector became a bazaar of speculative investment activities for the sole purpose of making money. All sorts of unprecedented investment vehicles, financial schemes, junk securities, and other dubious machinations were utilized, and it is no exaggeration to say that the Wall Street financial sector was totally out of control in the decade prior to its meltdown in 2007 and 2008.

The new financial "instruments" (ways to organize, package, and sell various assets of varying value) were complex and opaque in the sense that it was difficult to evaluate the true value and true reliability of investing in them. They were packages of dicey loans, subprime mortgage bonds, credit default swaps, collateralized debt obligations, "synthetic" versions of those, and hybrid collections of mortgages, student loans, insurance policies, and credit card debt all being bought, sold, reorganized, bought and sold again, and insured for and against. These instruments were in a meaningful sense mostly just "constructs" with which to speculate unrestrainedly. It was a dizzying, confusing, and corrupted process.

The private-sector ratings agencies—Moody's, Standard & Poor's, and Fitch—that were supposed to give honest appraisals of the various financial investment packages that the banks were selling, did not do their job. Instead, they went along with the banks' deceptive arrangements and practices, assigning triple-A ratings to a slew of types of loans that were highly likely to be defaulted on. The ratings agencies were hired by and paid by the banks, so there were strong financial incentives for the agencies to inflate the worth and investment-grade quality of the various packages and thus stay in the good graces of the banks, and thus continue to receive the banks' business.

In the absence of oversight and responsibility by either government or the private sector, the financial sector degenerated ultimately into a veritable casino, where bankers, brokers, traders, investment managers, insurers, and hedge fund mathematicians made reckless wagers on anything and everything that wasn't nailed down. When millions of faulty home mortgages started to be in default, the fraud behind mortgage-backed securities was exposed, and the entire house of cards collapsed.

The banks, eager to accumulate sheer numbers of mortgages with which to enlarge a lucrative fee-sales-investment vehicles market, for ten years had been irresponsibly handing out home mortgages to unqualified, credit-poor, insufficient-income, and mostly unsavvy applicants. This was not in response to any new government program or incentive, nor to any new government pressure. And the mortgage applicants—the borrowers—hadn't suddenly become somehow more dishonest than they had ever been. What had changed however, was bank behavior. The banks basically stopped doing due diligence and good practices, and instead awarded mortgages that they knew weren't warranted, and they often crafted mortgage language that compounded the financial impossibility of homeowners from ever meeting the terms of their payment schedule. Millions of homes went into foreclosure. About 6 million owners lost their homes outright. And to this day, especially in struggling, hollowed-out regions of the country, millions of homeowners still owe more money on their mortgages than their houses are worth.

Although many factors caused the banking meltdown, the major one was the enormous extent of reckless, unregulated bank behavior. With so many complex, opaque financial instruments that often did not show up on the banks' conventional balance sheets, or were otherwise nearly impossible to track and understand, there were insufficient controls and restraints on the speculative activities of bankers and traders.

It hadn't always been that way. As I have mentioned, during the Reagan administration, rules on banks were relaxed, and that deregulatory trend continued through the Bush I, Clinton, and Bush II administrations. During that time—about 30 years—there was a steady liberalization of regulations that defined allowable bank activities and practices.

Prior to all of those administrations, an extensive set of laws, regulations, and requirements had provided rules establishing and governing limits on the bank practices of lending, investing, trading, hedging, and market-making. The Glass-Steagall Act, which had been in place since 1933, and the rules of many other regulatory agencies and protocols were like the guardrails and reflectors along a highway's edge, providing a margin of safety and direction and guidance to a bank's business path.

The Glass-Steagall Act had been one of the more significant regulatory controls until it was dismantled. The GSA placed a sort of "firewall" between the activities of traditional, community commercial banks and the activities of the usually larger and more audacious investment banks and firms. Under the GSA, commercial banks that accepted FDIC-insured deposits and lent money to homeowners and small businesses—using longstanding best practices that had traditionally been proven to be prudent—were prohibited from engaging in the riskier businesses of speculative investment, opaque swaps-dealing, hedge fund activities, market-making, and "synthetic" financial products—in short, many of the activities that played a large role in making the Wall Street crisis so serious and far-reaching. The theory (borne out in practice) was that the banks should not be allowed to gamble with depositors' savings accounts. By contrast, the investment and securities firms were governed by a different set of rules.

But throughout the 1980s and 1990s, both commercial and investment banks lobbied continuously to slowly dismantle the firewall. As the two bank types increasingly associated, the regulatory agencies and the courts repeatedly decided in favor of loosening the GSA prohibitions. Finally, in 1999, the Glass-Steagall Act was repealed, although that was just making official what was already substantially the reality.

The final item in the list of factors that gives capitalism the character and consequences that it has today is taxation. Taxation policies play an enormous role in our country and the way that our economy is organized, shaped, expressed, and directed. Taxation policies help to determine how the money generated by our economy is distributed, saved, spent, or invested. They can reward or punish any actor—individuals, groups, unions, businesses, political parties, nations—with varying rates, incentives, disincentives, or subsidies, and they largely determine the amount of revenue that our local, state, and federal governments will have to operate.

There are, of course, taxes on individuals and businesses. The federal income tax was legislated by Congress in 1909 and ratified by the states in 1913, when it became effective. It has always been a progressive or graduated income tax, meaning that individuals paid it at a rate that varied by their income level. But over the years, both the tax rates and the number of different brackets have varied widely.

Between 1945 and 1971, there were a lot more income brackets—anywhere from 24 to 33 different brackets—in the tax code than in recent decades. That was a good thing because it meant that the rate at which any one earner was taxed was able to be more closely attuned to what that worker earned. Rather than lumping together a wide group of workers—earning quite a range of wages or salaries—and taxing them at the same rate, multiple tax brackets (or gradations) permitted taxation levels that more closely reflected citizens' ability to pay them.

We can contrast this graduated income tax with a "flat" income tax, which would have only one tax bracket for everybody. Under such a system, every earner, regardless of his salary or income, would be taxed at the same rate, say, 15 percent. The worker who makes $35,000 a year would be taxed at the same 15 percent as the worker who makes $10 million a year. The significant drawback to the flat tax system is that it ignores the reality that lower-income earners have far less ability to make a tax contribution than upper-income earners. Citizens at the modest end of the income spectrum often spend every dollar of their weekly paycheck on living expenses whereas wealthy earners are able to save much of their income. It is true that in almost any tax scheme, graduated or flat, upper-income citizens pay more taxes in absolute quantity of dollars than do poorer citizens. That reflects two realities: the ability of wealthier citizens to contribute more; and the need to raise sufficient revenue for the government to operate.

After 1971, the number of different tax brackets in the tax code began a steady descent toward fewer brackets. From a postwar high of 33 different brackets in 1971 to a low of only 2 brackets in 1988, and only 7 today, the tax code rates are now applied in divisions that are less responsive to citizens' range of incomes than they used to be. Of course, a complete picture of one's tax burden would also have to factor in deductions, subsidies, exemptions, and other relevant components of one's financial and taxpayer status.

Since World War II, tax rates generally—but especially on the wealthy—have been reduced too. From 1946 to 1964, the top tax rate varied somewhat but was always in the high 80s or 90s as a percentage. In 1952, for example, the top income bracket was pegged at 92 percent (although, after deductions and other allowed provisions, often the actual tax owed was about 50 percent). In 1964, tax rates were substantially reduced, and the top rate was lowered to 77 percent. It remained in the 70s until President Reagan's administration (and Congress) lowered it to 50 percent in 1982, then ultimately to 28 percent in 1988. Generally speaking, the taxation rates on lower tax brackets were reduced too. The top income tax bracket today is taxed at 37 percent. Of course, as I have mentioned, any individual's actual tax payment depends upon a myriad of other additional factors.

It is important to note that few upper-income taxpayers pay taxes at the rates listed on the tax tables. Because wealthy people invariably have a range of assets and benefits—multiple homes, stocks, bonds, dividends, and other investments—they are able to take advantage of quite a number of deductions and other provisions written into the tax code. Many investment gains, for example, are taxed at lower rates than ordinary wages or salaries. Ultimately, it is not at all unusual for wealthy people to have a federal income tax bill in the 15 to 20 percent range, far less than a casual observer might suspect if he were looking at their large incomes.

Large corporations also frequently benefit from a favorable tax code. Over the past 40 years, with deregulation, globalization, computerization, and the increasing role and power of money and lobbies in government, large corporations have been able to influence the myriad provisions of the tax code, and take advantage of them. With tax law, contract law, labor law, financial law, antitrust tolerances, bankruptcy law, and offshoring rules all favoring corporations—many globe-straddling—they have been able to reduce their tax burdens to often minimal levels. Many successful corporations sometimes have paid no federal taxes at all.

Perhaps the best, recent example of how the provisions of the tax code benefit the powerful can be seen in Amazon's 2018 tax payment. Despite taking in $11 billion in revenue, it paid exactly zero in corporate taxes last year. Through legal deductions, it managed to essentially shelter its earnings from taxation. In addition to taking tax deductions for equipment purchases, research and development costs, and investments—all arguably defensible—it also took deductions on all the stock options and stock awards it gave to executives and employees as part of their compensation. Amazon gave out $1 billion in stock-based compensation, all deductible. This is totally legal, but it is essentially welfare subsidized by the public tax dollar. Executives who are already receiving millions in outright salary then receive millions in stock awards, all courtesy of a dysfunctional tax code that has the average struggling American worker contributing his tax dollars to Amazon.

Despite enjoying tax provisions that only a mega-corporation could love, the industry lobbyists never rest. The tax bill passed in December 2017 by the Trump administration and the Republican Congress further reduced the corporate tax rate—if companies paid at all—from 35 percent to 21 percent. Part of the reasoning for this was to encourage businesses to bring back into the United States many billions of dollars that they had parked overseas to avoid taxation. Many corporations indeed brought much of their offshore money back into the country, but what they did with it was disappointing. Although a few companies made a big show of handing out small bonuses to workers or raising some wages by modest amounts, the lion's share of the money went to stock buybacks and corporate coffers. Companies purchased quantities of their own stock, thereby raising the share price, helping the stockholders, and benefitting the executives. There's no question that the corporations themselves viewed the repatriated money as a windfall. And the new tax rate of 21 percent was even lower than they had lobbied for. The tax bill did juice the economy a bit for the short-term. But the economy was already healthy and humming, and it simply didn't need another stimulus. Meanwhile, the lost revenue to the government will have serious and long-term consequences.

The economy today (August 2019) is operating well, but only if we measure it by longstanding conventional standards and assumptions. Unemployment is low and there is little inflation. Wages increased by about 3 percent between May 2018 and May 2019. Consumers are spending their money and many businesses are doing well. Stock market share prices generally are high, and corporate profits are strong. But all of those positive indices come at a price; they mask the dysfunctional and damaging aspects of capitalism that I have described. They don't tell us about the unfairness of the current tax code, continuing income inequality, the quality and pay of jobs, the continuing offshoring and automation, the dependencies and vulnerabilities of web-networked industries and infrastructure, the impact of inadequate regulation and oversight, the loss of revenue to the government, the debt level of students and citizens and governments, the reliance on mass consumerism, the reliance on fossil fuels and natural resources, the damage to the atmosphere and biosphere, and the nearly nonexistent responses to global warming and other building crises around the globe. So yes, the economy is doing well if we essentially ignore the future, both near and distant, and the path we're on.

* * * *

It's important for citizens to understand the specific form that capitalism takes today. The details matter. If your brother called you on the phone and said, "I just bought a new car," but that's all he told you, you would know nothing about that automobile. You wouldn't know if it's a sports car, a sedan, a crossover, a hybrid, or an SUV. You wouldn't know its make, model, color, engine size, seating capacity, or its mileage. You wouldn't know its interior features, upholstery, options, level of practicality, or level of luxury.

Similarly, if you don't know the particular structure and features of our capitalism, you really don't know much about our system. In the same way that automobiles can vary from each other in significant ways and still be automobiles, so capitalism can take any shape and still be capitalism.

For forty years, capitalism has been morphing as I have described in this chapter. It has happened gradually, incrementally, and rarely dramatically. Citizens, understandably, missed a lot of what was going on; they were also deliberately deceived and misled about much of this change (more about that later). Our economic system is now an operation devoted overwhelmingly to serving the wealthy.

Citizens have woken up, at least somewhat. They feel—correctly—that they have been shafted. That is part of the reason Donald Trump was elected President in November 2016.

Whether citizens will be able to learn enough to competently judge the causes behind and the contours and effects of today's capitalism remains to be seen. Currently, capitalism—as presently designed—is one of the major forces exerting a net poisonous pull on the shape and direction of American society, American democracy, and many societies around the world. It poses a threat to all of civilization.

CHAPTER 2

TECHNOLOGY

WE HAVE LOOKED AT THE FORCE IN SOCIETY that we call "capitalism." Like all the other forces discussed in this book, it doesn't really exist contained within a nice neat category, and other large forces simultaneously are partly part of it or intertwined within it or overlap it somehow. What we call "technology" is a major force that is operating in society today. In its relationship to both capitalism and society, it can be thought of—variously and at different times—as a cousin, facilitator, servant, spur, leader, distorter, destructive agent, constructive agent, or completely independent agent. And because technology encompasses such a huge array of inventions, devices, processes, assumptions, and implications, it can be all of those agents simultaneously. Different parts of it will possess different characteristics and imperatives, acting in different ways on various parts of capitalism, society, and the natural world. Technology can be cause or effect, or often both simultaneously. But whatever it is, in its nearly infinite forms and effects, it is never neutral, especially today. It is always a force, and never neutral.

At first blush, this may seem incorrect. Isn't technology just a tool, a machine, an invention, an inanimate object or process? How can it be not neutral? Often, explainers or defenders of some technology will say that technology is just a tool, and that what gives it its direction or value (or non-neutrality) is how we use it. This seems sort of right, but it isn't.

Every man-made invention or machine or tool—whether discovered deliberately or accidently—springs from the imagination, creativity, and inventiveness of man. And that man is a human being at a certain point along an evolutionary path, and in a certain physical space and society, at a point along the long arc of history and progress, and a product of his own lifetime of education, experience, observation, and epistemology. As such, his inventions and tools spring from—and are "limited" or "liberated" by—a powerful and complicated context. And it is from within that particular context and perspective that man designs what he may need, want, or randomly discover. He may even design something simply because he can. Man invents things for a multitude of reasons: for his job, profit, necessity, love, pleasure, respect, pride, competition, control, health, war, progress, modernity, style, and sometimes just for a challenge. He may design things to reinforce the status quo, change it, undermine it, or question it. If we understand all of the many and possible motivations and dynamics behind tools and technology, we can realize that technology is never neutral, and that inventions don't necessarily equate with "progress."

Technology is not a new force in society. Since Paleolithic man first picked up a usefully shaped stone, he has been crafting things, discovering things, and utilizing them—all the while being shaped by them in return.

Throughout history, and especially since the Industrial Revolution that started around 1750, man's inventions, machines, processes, and technology have been incredibly powerful forces. For better and for worse, they have often had major impacts on the natural environment, human health, living conditions and the standard of living, the shape and scale of war, the globalization of commerce, the organization of society and government, our educational levels, and even on the way we think and feel.

And over the past centuries, technology and technological change have been—and can be—a product of individual genius, individual effort, group initiative, private or public endeavors, corporations or laboratories, democratic or unilateral actions, good or bad intentions, secret or open processes, or any number of protagonists, dynamics, or ways.

So, as in previous epochs, technology is an active force today. I am particularly interested in identifying the technologies that today are most buffeting us, or that are creating consequences and dynamics that are most buffeting us.

After thousands of corporations in the 1980s and 1990s relocated their assembly lines and production lines to locations out of the country—to take advantage of cheap foreign labor—the next shock to the American worker came from developments that were purely technological. After the year 2000 especially, automation began to take an increasing toll on workers, eliminating jobs in a wide variety of industries and fields.

The invention of the computer itself—and later the internet—has played a seminal and interwoven role in both job elimination and automation. At the most elementary level, the quick and wide adoption in the late 1980s of the desktop computer eliminated significant numbers of secretarial jobs. Business executives, architects, engineers, lawyers, doctors, administrators, government officials, and all sorts of white-collar, desk-job positions that had once been accompanied by secretarial support staff no longer required that assistance. With the advent of the personal computer, most of the personnel filling white-collar occupations were expected to do their own typing, scheduling, and file management. (Of course, the name of this work was changed to "word processing," partly to mask the demotion, and partly to put a gloss and a certain hip level of sophistication on what was once an entry-level task.) Over a decade and a half, between 1990 and 2005, millions of secretarial and office administration jobs were eliminated. It was the first of many job losses that we can attribute directly to the computer, and to the digital realm. (There has been new job creation too, as a result of the birth of the computer industry.)

Word processing was one thing. But computers and digital technology—after 2000—soon made inroads into a myriad of industries and areas, and really threatened many longstanding occupations. Advanced digital technology made possible robots and robotic-like automation. In almost every manufacturing sector, automation became more widespread, resulting in faster, more accurate, more consistent, higher quality, and less costly goods, products, and services. Not least, for the profit margins of corporations, automation eliminated millions of human workers and their wages. Automated assembly machinery doesn't require pay, sick time, pensions, health care, motivation, negotiation, or rest. It can be operated 24 hours a day and it can be located or relocated, speedily, anywhere in the world. And as a bonus for corporations, the mere existence of lots of laid-off workers, and lots of workers worried about losing their jobs, and lots of overqualified workers competing for lesser jobs, had (and has) the effect of undermining and making anxious all workers, thereby placing downward pressure on all wages generally, as corporations gained a dominating position relative to the power of labor. (In 2019 we have very low unemployment, but as I explained in the last chapter, the official unemployment figure does not convey—at all—a meaningful descriptive picture of the conditions and economic health of the average American worker.)

Automation has eliminated huge numbers of jobs in auto assembly, apparel production, textiles, electronics and appliances assembly, machining, farming, woodworking, plastics, furniture-building, and a wide variety of other materials production and parts and products assembly. This has been an unfolding and accelerating phenomenon in the United States for the past 30 years or so. It continues today and will continue to threaten and take away a widening array of jobs. And it is important to remember that this reality is playing out now in China and other developing nations too. Although during the initial and middle phases of globalization—say, roughly 1975 to 1995—those up-and-coming Third World countries arguably benefitted from the large and rapid infusion of manufacturing factories and their jobs, today those countries are experiencing the same automation of their once-secure (albeit low-paying) factory, manufacturing, and sweatshop jobs. With computerization and robotization advancing literally everywhere, it is now truly a globalized labor market. Increasingly, there is (and will be) no haven anywhere in the world where labor has the power to compete with the companies and forces and developments that determine the shape and rules of the economy.

Large numbers of jobs are being lost in the retail sector as internet shopping and online businesses have—and continue to—cut into the available market of consumer purchasing. Steadily, small brick-and-mortar stores are closing because they cannot compete with the lower prices, instant delivery, and convenience of online browsing and purchasing. Purchases from websites like Amazon and eBay are providing ever-larger shares of the goods consumed in America. Consequently, retail store clerks, cashiers, display stockers, and the tradesmen who maintain the physical buildings are disappearing, and will continue to disappear. (Amazon in particular is a giant. It has 150 warehouses located in dozens of states, and supplies goods or services to more than 2 million small businesses. It is growing rapidly, and has developed a formidable lobbying presence in Washington, D.C. to protect its interests.)

And, irony on top of misfortune, we are rapidly approaching the time when automation and robotic technology will replace stockers and packers in the warehouses and in other jobs that still require human labor. That automation—with robotic systems currently being researched and developed for the jobs—is coming.

In addition to the ongoing demise of retail stores and their jobs, significant labor replacement is planned for the millions of jobs currently existing within the fast-food restaurant chains. Self-serve order-and-pay kiosks have already been introduced in many of the franchises, which will slowly eliminate most cashiers, and robotic automation is being developed to soon replace the humans currently making the hamburgers, chicken, tacos, and other meals served up from the back-kitchen assembly line. Although these fast-food service-sector jobs are very low-wage, and often involve abusive working conditions and unreliable scheduling, they have been—and are—a last-resort lifeline for many economically struggling workers. Young people, middle-age people, immigrants, and even very old, so-called "retirees" have had to resort to those difficult subsistence jobs in order to survive at all. So, automating them out of existence will be a catastrophe for many workers with few other options.

Similarly, automation is currently replacing check-out cashiers and clerks in increasing numbers of grocery stores, lumber and home-goods stores, big-box stories, coffee chain shops, rental car agencies, and other enterprises. Every time we select and use a self-checkout line, we are feeding the data-collection process that is refining the software that is fine-tuning the mechanics of self-checkout. Eventually, there will be no cashiers in these stores.

Automation is making inroads into white-collar jobs as well. Various types of software have been developed—and are being developed—to replace technicians in fields as widely diverse as medicine, architecture, engineering, law, finance, pharmacology, journalism, telecommunications, insurance, accounting, and many others. Almost every American job that involves eight hours a day of sitting at a computer, or otherwise manipulating words, numbers, or data on a connected device, is at high risk for replacement by robots or automation, or some other machine embodying smart software or artificial intelligence. Even jobs that require human judgement and interpreting human emotion—jobs that we might not dream could be done by machines—will soon become vulnerable to artificial intelligence. Some doctors, therapists, interviewers, receptionists, phone operators in call centers, and many others will find smart computers competing for their work.

Many people seeking work have already experienced the tyranny of artificial intelligence. Their resumes are screened by algorithms, their job interviews take place remotely while they answer questions on a computer or talk into a camera, and their entire performance—including voice tone, modulation, and mood—is evaluated by a machine. They may be eliminated from employment consideration without ever having spoken to another human.

The technology companies have invested heavily in programs to build machine intelligence. In addition to developing the sophisticated hardware, software, and algorithms that A.I. relies on, tech employees are—sometimes manually and sometimes using computers—feeding massive amounts of data of all sorts into the software of computers to help build A.I. The tech companies also employ tens of thousands of workers around the world to identify and label a wide array of images, words, drawings, and photos which can then be fed into computers systems to "teach" them to understand what they are "seeing." (Working for subcontractors of the big tech firms, these employees are poorly paid laborers in China, India, Nepal, the Philippines, East Africa, and the U.S.) Thus programmed, the A.I. bots can then search or scan videos or text or other sorts of content to perform many tasks. For example, smart computers are used now in language translation, identifying defective products, and object or facial recognition applications. Alarmingly or happily, depending upon the application, the capabilities of facial recognition systems are already quite impressive, even while the accuracy of the systems is improved every year.

Advances in artificial intelligence have been phenomenal—are still ongoing rapidly—and promise to replace humans in many roles. As an early example, the display of artificial intelligence by IBM's "Watson" (no relation) computer in defeating its human opponent in 2011 on the set of the TV game show "Jeopardy!" was impressive, and yet it was only the beginning. Watson's software had been developed to the point where it was able to quickly identify and process subtle "human" language and thinking expressions, characteristics, ambiguities, and capacities and tics like nuance, humor, irony, puns, idioms, colloquialisms, inference, correlation, confidence, and more. Holding vast quantities of data, and empowered with sophisticated software and algorithms, Watson is capable of analysis, comparison, the ranking of information, and even identifying if it has sufficient information to answer a question or solve a problem. In the next 5 to 20 years, we will be shocked at the range of complex, higher-knowledge jobs that AI will take over from humans.

Further threatening jobs, the power and capabilities of computers like Watson have been multiplied, in a sense, by grouping them together in "the cloud," the name for the storage "location" of infinite amounts of data and the name for the capacities of millions of remote, dispersed servers, many of which are connected to each other in networks and connected to the internet. Many private companies own these physical, networked servers—pieces of the cloud—and they sell both storage capacity and advanced computing services to a wide range of other private companies. This has the effect of making ever more powerful computing services more available to more people and companies. Not every individual nor every business need have its own formidable computer network, nor therefore an IT (information technology) staff.

Robots, automation, and artificial intelligence are poised to replace or eliminate many white-collar jobs. And the time horizon in which this will occur is from now (since automation is underway already) through the next two decades and beyond. This is a process that will not stop. A huge, shocking chunk of job eliminations—maybe 30 to 40 to 50 million jobs—in the U.S. could occur during the next 20 to 30 years or so.

The inventions of drones and autonomous-driving vehicles are also poised to be adopted, and they will both eliminate substantial numbers of jobs. They are also examples of detrimental technologies being foisted upon a powerless public. Drones have already started to perform a myriad of inspection and monitoring tasks; these applications often occur in remote or hard-to-reach areas and are genuinely useful and valuable. However, drones are poised to become ubiquitous and obnoxious vehicles in the delivery process. E-commerce businesses, grocery stores, fast-food restaurants, and all sorts of convenience stores are in the process of testing drone delivery of their products. Google and Amazon especially are pursuing this development. Amazon is dominant in the online shopping sector and will aggressively expand into delivery by drone. It will market and sell the deliveries by emphasizing to customers how quickly they will receive their merchandise. This is truly a case of business creating new and silly "needs" and desires in consumers; for there is no good reason that a buyer needs his purchase immediately (obviously, we can make exceptions, say, for medical situations). This is the desire for instant gratification taken to absurd levels. The costs to society and nature will be terrible. The drones used to deliver packages are not small, recreational models; they are large, noisy, have wings, and 10 to 14 propellers, and are about four to six feet long. In tests in Canberra, Australia, they scared adults, children, animals, and birds. We will see, hear, and experience them in our skies, neighborhoods, and natural landscapes as they become ubiquitous. They will be an extremely damaging presence in our daily experience of the outdoor world. Even if eventually they are made smaller and quieter, they will be a nervous, discordant element constantly interrupting our field of vision. The larger, longer-range, winged drones will be developed to complement the existing, wingless, short-range quadcopters and octocopters that we are already familiar with.

Similarly, commercial trucks—especially long-haul highway trucks—are expected to become driverless in the near future (within 5 to 10 years), and eliminate many professional drivers from the interstate regional-hub-to-regional-hub runs. Human drivers would still take trailers from a given regional hub to a particular final street destination. But there will be substantial job loss. Again, nobody requested the invention of drones or autonomous trucks; the tech sector, with its vision of all-things-automated and web-connected, has its own imperatives, and it doesn't solicit our opinions prior to introducing products. But their impacts on our lives will be significant.

Other types of professional drivers will be replaced too. The people who drive taxis, limos, hail-services, buses, and delivery services that cannot be replaced by drones are all vulnerable. Professional drivers number about 4.5 million people in total (including truck drivers) so their replacement would be no small disruption.

The recent invention of 3-D printing and its ongoing improvement promises to eliminate yet more jobs. As it becomes possible for each of us individually to fabricate many objects that we need—or just want—plenty of producers, stores, and craftsmen will be adversely affected. This is an area where the quantity of job loss is difficult to predict. Manufacturers themselves may find that they can produce some component parts (of larger products) on-site, printing with machines, and thereby eliminate some parts suppliers or subcontractors. Again, a lot of this potential for eliminating jobs and workers may take 5 or 10 years or so, and beyond, to play out, but 3-D printing is present, reliable, practical, and advancing rapidly.

There are other aspects of computers, digital technology, online devices, and the internet that eliminate jobs in subtler ways. As more and more people spend more and more time using web-connected devices (whether laptops, phones, or tablets), other non-digital or pre-computer-age activities and entertainments receive less attention or patronage. Traditional hobby stores—with plastic models and other crafts—have essentially disappeared. Especially in urban areas—and partly as a result of land development erasing natural habitat—fishing, exploring, purely recreational bike riding, pickup sports games, and much informal outdoor youth activity have waned. Billiards and bowling leagues are reduced in number. Of course, many factors are involved in the popularity of any given hobby or pastime. But today, all possible activities must compete with the online offering of engagements. To the extent that any non-digital activity supports industries, products, jobs, or even just the preservation of outdoor spaces, they are eroded when they are losing that contest with online gaming, online recreation, web-surfing, and social media engagement.

Online games themselves are an invention made possible by, and enhanced by, digital technology. Nearly infinite in number and variety, these games—along with millions of apps—offer entertainment, distraction, data, information, feedback, and a host of other increasingly popular ways to spend time on, or utilize, the internet. I will have much more to say about gaming in the chapter on Webworld.

Virtual reality is another development in the digital technological world that is poised to make itself felt in many ways. It is being employed now in many fields, and it will soon become a larger part of the social, recreational, industrial, and business landscapes. Architects, engineers, scientists, manufacturers, technicians, educators, pilots, doctors, and many others already use virtual reality to model, simulate, envision, teach, and train. For an architect or a medical student, for example, virtual reality is an amazing tool: virtually "walking" an architectural client right through the spaces of his prospective building in a realistic, simulated, three-dimensional experience; or, for a medical intern, touring inside the human body and its organs in a miniature, simulated journey, is a new, powerful, and unprecedented technological capacity. And for its potential in the entertainment industry, virtual reality is being developed with great anticipation; it almost surely will prove to provide irresistible virtual—not real—environments and experiences. (Some aspects of the gaming, apps, and virtual reality advancements do, obviously, result in new job gains in providing those technical creations.)

Professional journalism is another area that has suffered tremendous job loss because of the internet. Since 1990, newspapers and magazines have been repeatedly downsized or closed. As readers of the news migrate to online sources, and advertising that used to appear in and support newspapers now patronizes websites, blogs, and social media, the papers have experienced huge revenue losses and have laid off reporters and staff. Most newspapers are a thinner shadow of what they once were, and fully half of the papers that existed in the country in 1990 have completely closed. That means we have lost nearly 2000 papers. I will have more to say about this in the next chapter.

* * * *

The increasing levels of automation of so many devices and processes, combined with an increasing likelihood that they will in some way rely on or offer a connection to the internet, are manifestations of an ongoing effort to create an "Internet of Things." Product designers, manufacturers, software engineers, and technology companies use that phrase—sometimes abbreviated to "I o T"—to describe their goal to eventually have every single physical object and process connected to the internet. Many objects and processes already are.

In private homes, refrigerators, toasters, coffee makers, vacuums, thermostats, baby monitors, lighting, televisions, speakers (there are already voice-activated Amazon Echo speakers in 50 million homes), toys, garage doors, washing machines, security systems, and many other appliances and devices increasingly are connected to the internet. They are turned on or off, timed, adjusted, monitored, and even interconnected by the internet. Slowly, even smaller objects—objects with no moving parts or operational complexity—are and will be connected to the web.

Newer private automobiles are thoroughly connected—constantly—to the web. With incredibly complex on-board computers and software, cars are constantly sending, receiving, and storing information. Newer cars often automatically receive software updates without any knowledge on the part of, or initiative by, the owner.

At the large commercial and business scales, the Internet of Things is also advancing. Obviously, all computerized office systems are connected. But so too is nearly every aspect of every business, save some of the most basic or necessarily hand-crafted manual and physical work.

Machinery and processes are all web-connected. Banks, grocery stores, clothing stores, warehouses, hospitals, factories, power plants, airports, the financial system, stock market trading, communication systems, the electrical grid, water supply and treatment systems, gas stations, anti-pollution controls, military equipment, the nation's offensive and defensive military capabilities, the nation's security and intelligence apparatus, government at every level, and every other imaginable infrastructure—throughout every corner of society—are all tied into the internet in one fashion or another.

Even human beings are now starting to be directly connected to the internet. A few businesses have offered their employees the option of having a computer chip surgically implanted inside their hand. This chip, which contains each employee's unique password, can be scanned and "read" remotely by other web-connected devices. The chip enables the employee to be checked in and out of a given location, or to purchase and pay for items in the employee cafeteria. Obviously, the functions, tasks, and monitoring that the chip technically permits will be expanded as time passes and as both employees and society become accustomed to what is actually quite a disturbing idea—people with internal computer chips. But at the companies where chips have been offered, most employees agree to have them implanted.

A number of companies are working on the creation of an even more invasive computer-to-human connection. They are developing methods to run tiny, filament-like wires through the skull and directly into the brain. These thread-like wires will connect to one or two small computer receivers and transmitters located discreetly on the body (perhaps behind the ear). The entire system will be internet-connected and information will move in both directions—to and from the human and the web. Initially, it will be used to assist people with physical disabilities, but the technology eventually will be available to all people.

In promoting the Internet of Things, technology engineers and corporations are selling the idea that connecting objects to the web allows greater automation, with more precise operation and control, and with more efficiency. And indeed, that is often true. There are some real advantages to connecting some things to the web. For many machines and processes, there are truly impressive gains in manageability, coordination, efficiency, capability, speed, reliability, precision, and safety. Many, many valuable, beneficial, and unprecedented capacities and advances and results have come out of connectivity and the Internet of Things.

The promoters of this across-the-board connectivity also laud the immense levels of data generation and collection that accompanies the Internet of Things. The data itself is about an immense—and growing—amount of activity and things. And it circulates in every direction among people, machines, processes, systems, corporations, nations, and environments.

The data are about how machines are working, how processes and systems are working, what people are doing, and where geographically every thing and every person is. The data constantly—in every conceivable field, profession, and enterprise—monitor, track, collate, catalogue, and tabulate. Data today is nearly infinite, and about a nearly infinite number of things.

The data serve a multitude of purposes. It can serve as feedback that is used to improve machinery, processes, and artificial intelligence. It can assist human workers to perform more accurately and skillfully. It can show us aspects of things, and teach us things, that we could not otherwise know. It is not my intention here to even begin to survey the variety and uses of data.

This is a chapter about technology, but we've got to take a minute and talk about data and its relationship to government, the economy, and us.

The amount of data being amassed by the private sector and by governments—domestically and around the world—is staggering. The data is used for purposes good and bad. Obviously, authoritarian regimes in China and Russia and elsewhere use surveillance and data collection to monitor the activities of their citizens and to elicit compliant, conforming, obedient behavior.

Here in the United States, despite the fears of many, and despite the collection of data by our intelligence agencies, it is my belief that citizens who worry about surveillance and oppression by our own government are looking in the wrong direction. There are a number of serious threats posed by data collection and surveillance, but at the present time—and for any meaningful or relevant future period of time—those threats come almost solely from the private sector. I'll explain that in a minute.

Understanding why our government doesn't need or want to become authoritarian, or oppress us (here I am speaking about oppression in the largest, state-driven, overt, Orwellian sense, because there are plenty of real and societal oppressions imposed upon us), requires understanding that, for the most part, we are an obedient citizenry, behaving in ways that mostly support the dominant power structure. For the most part, we live, work, shop, drive, vote, take vacations, have recreation, watch sports, gamble (casinos and lotteries), spend hours online, go to church, make families, socialize our children, behave reasonably well, and generally support our communities and country and the larger society—and deliberately or by default therefore, support the dominant power structure and arrangements.

Of all the ways we are "obedient," or relatively passive in the face of today's realities, it is our shopping behaviors, combined with our transfixion with all things online, that are the most important to the oligarchic, plutocratic, and capitalistic forces—combined with a government captured by them—in power today. It would be redundant for our government to oppress a citizenry—us—who are already behaving, in every regard, in ways that thoroughly and completely support and reinforce that government, its operators, and its power.

As I describe in the discussion of capitalism today, and politics today, the distortion of those two forces into mechanisms by which the wealthy elite—maybe the top 1 to 5 percent of the American population—control and direct both the economy and the government to do their bidding is their single biggest and most critical victory over the citizenry. Because those plutocratic and oligarchic operators essentially own the economy and the government, and design the details of both—with market and policy frameworks—overt, heavy-handed, repressive state and authoritarian measures are not needed. We shop and shop and shop, and we spend hours and hours and hours on websites, blogs, and social media, and those are the key behaviors that build, strengthen, and sustain the status quo, in its every manifestation.

I would never claim that a government, even an American one, could never become authoritarian, but currently the corporate and political winners in our society see no need whatsoever to mess with a formula that continues to make them rich and powerful. The capitalist-political system is rigged alright, and oppression (of the kind citizens would notice) wasn't and isn't necessary.

Now back to data.

So the massive amount of data being collected by the government is not intended to threaten us. That data is indeed gathered in a genuine effort to identify and head off actual security threats, whether they be domestic or foreign terrorists, or just genuinely bad people intent on a wide range of criminal or destructive activity.

The real threat, as I mentioned earlier, is the constant and increasing collection of data by the private sector. This data, whether collected by the big internet and social media platforms or the smallest businesses, is used primarily for the purposes of advertising to us, selling us products or ideas, engaging us in various ways to spend more time on the internet, and generally building and reinforcing a certain cultural posture. This "cultural posture" can be thought of as the sum total of our behaviors and our attitudes and our perspectives on all things status quo.

I refer to the data as a threat because it is collected and wielded with such unprecedented precision, power, and effectiveness, and because of its purposes. And because the corporations and powers behind the data collection are most satisfied when we are relatively unaware and unalarmed about all of the dynamics involved with data, the economy, our behavior, and the internet.

As we saw in the chapter on capitalism, and as we will see in the chapter on nature, the economy as it is currently designed and operating is not serving the ordinary citizen, nor is it protecting the planet's resources and ecosystems. Ordinary working-class and middle-class citizens are being badly victimized by our predatory economy and are losing ground financially in many ways. Our jobs are at risk, our savings are low, our debts are high, and all the major forces acting on our lives—the forces described in this book—are pushing in ominous directions.

Given that context, any powers that act to get us to spend yet more money, acquire yet more things, take on more debt, spend more time online, know less about today's actual realities, or otherwise waste our time, energy, and resources, are a large threat. Yet I can say without exaggeration, those are the goals to which private, commercial data are being applied.

When we are online, where most data about us is being collected, every click, like, share, or thumbs-up we post is recorded and catalogued. Every article we read, ad we look at, video we watch, link we make, tweet we send, photo we post, and website we visit is observed and noted. Every email we send, blog we read, newsfeed we check, comment we make, and emoji we choose, is digitally seen and stored. All of it—24/7 and without exception—gets amalgamated and assembled into our own unique, personal, descriptive profile. A picture of our life, habits and interests, history, age, race, religion, health, occupation, marital status, education, address, income and financial situation, political and sexual orientation, and much other information gets assembled and becomes stored and available online. The profile may contain some inaccuracies, but mostly it's uncannily accurate. And it is continually added to as we repeatedly go online.

This data gets "weaponized." It is used against us, and against our interests. It is used to make us into impulsive, impressionable, status-seeking, silly, distracted, acquisitive, consuming, web-addicted people. The data is used both to hook us into consuming as much online entertainment and content as possible, and to purchase more goods and services generally. It is used to modify, change, and direct both our moods and our behavior.

Capitalism has always tried to do this—has always had these twin goals of selling entertainment and products. Capitalism has always tried to know us—as customers—and influence us to give up our money to it. But today, capitalism has unprecedented power. The invention of the internet, and the data collection that goes along with it, allows all the many enterprises of the market to track, tally, and target us with ads, videos, articles, newsfeeds, links, and more that flatter and seduce us. Today, prompted by computer code-algorithm technology that didn't exist even 15 years ago, we are more likely than ever to spend, consume, click, surf, and view. Computers and the dynamics of the internet have helped to create a capitalism on steroids, a capitalism with unprecedented power, scale, precision, and irresistibility.

Again, the key factor to remember, if you are protesting that capitalism and market forces have always tried to get us to be free-spending consumers, is that today the citizen-consumer is faced with a computerized capitalism that is unlike anything in the history of economics. Software programs and algorithms know us, know human nature and behavior, and are taking advantage of us to a degree that has never been done before.

* * * *

Another consequence of our constant and increasing use of computers and connected devices is a continually growing dependence on them. Here I am referring strictly to what I'll call a "practical" dependence rather than a psychological dependence. In the next chapter I will describe our growing psychological dependence on computers, the internet, and connectivity.

At a strictly practical and operational level, we have created enormous dependencies on computers and their uninterrupted connections to the internet. At every level of society—from our personal lives to our businesses to our towns to our entire society—we rely on computers and connectivity from the moment we wake up to the moment we fall asleep.

At a personal level, we employ our smart-phones and laptops and tablets and e-readers for seemingly everything: communications; scheduling; navigation; news; music; entertainment; work; shopping; purchasing; and countless other tasks and purposes. We rely on the myriad of capacities built into these devices as well as constantly adding innumerable supplementary apps to expand the features of the devices—and enlarge our reliance on them.

At the business and commercial levels, as I have mentioned, we thoroughly rely on computers and connectivity for nearly everything. Today, most stores, businesses, factories, and commercial enterprises simply could not open for business, or conduct business, without computers and connectivity to the internet. Whether it's communicating, tallying data, restocking, purchasing, banking, manufacturing, litigating, managing, or any other function, very little of this can occur for very long today without connected computers.

On the days when either our computers or connectivity is down, our enterprises come to a near halt. Whether at the personal, business, societal, regional, or national level, when our computers or their connections to the internet, or the internet itself, go down, we basically become paralyzed and are able to actually work at very few tasks. We have become nearly totally dependent upon having functioning computers to run our businesses and to do our jobs.

Most of us are familiar with the inconvenience of a relatively brief interruption in the service to or the usability of our individual computers. If our computer freezes, crashes, malfunctions, is hacked, gets a virus, or otherwise becomes inoperable, we can take the steps to repair it, clean it, or replace it. And if internet service (by the provider) to the computer is interrupted, generally a solution restores the service within hours or days.

We understand computer outages at the individual level because we have experienced them, and therefore we have an idea of our level of dependence on computers individually. But at the commercial and business and infrastructure levels, most of us don't realize the degree of dependence that we have created with connectivity.

It is impossible to overstate the magnitude of this dependence. And so it creates a vulnerability—or really, an infinite number of vulnerabilities—that is shockingly large and shockingly serious.

Over the past few years, we have seen some of these vulnerabilities exploited in various ways, and with varying degrees of severity, and for varying purposes.

At the smallest level of computer hacking, it is not uncommon for personal computers to be commandeered by bad actors who can freeze the screen and operation of the machine. The criminals, who hope to make money, will send a screen message to the computer threatening to destroy its files and data unless the operator (you) makes a payment to the hijackers. This method, holding computers hostage for ransom payments, has been used successfully against individuals, businesses, hospitals, police departments, government agencies, and even entire towns and cities.

At another level of vulnerability, entire networks of computers—linked within a single business, institution, agency, or enterprise—are often broken into and commandeered or hacked for the purpose of stealing data. This goes on all the time, although the public usually hears only about the largest or most dramatic ones. Most businesses and enterprises are not eager to let their customers, clients, or the general public know that their digital systems have been hacked, breached, held for ransom, or otherwise compromised.

One of the worst attacks on a corporate network occurred during the summer of 2017. For about two months, hackers infiltrated the computer systems of Equifax, the national credit reporting agency, and methodically stole data from the company's digital files. The cyber-thieves took the names, addresses, and Social Security numbers of roughly 148 million people, and were also able to take the passport numbers, drivers-license numbers, and credit card information of smaller numbers of people. Incredibly, Equifax had known for months prior to the break-in that its system software had a vulnerability, but its internal memorandum system was out-of-date and thus the appropriate technical personnel were never notified of the need to repair the software.

Similarly, Home Depot and Target have been hit with successful hacking events. In 2013, Target's network was accessed by intruders who stole personal data on 70 million customers and information on 40 million credit and debit card accounts. In 2014, Home Depot's system was hacked and the account numbers of 56 million credit and debit cards were stolen.

In 2014, eBay's computer system was breached and the names, addresses, user names, passwords, email addresses, phone numbers, and birth dates of all 145 million users were stolen.

Municipalities are also frequent targets for hackers. In March of 2018 the computer network of the city of Atlanta government offices was breached by a ransomware intrusion that demanded a payment of $51,000. Many online city services and operations became inaccessible for a week or two and some data was lost. In the end the city did not pay the ransom but instead spent about $10 million or more to patch, replace, and upgrade its computer system.

Cyberattacks against municipalities are increasing too. In the first eight months of 2019, there have already been at least 40 successful hijackings—including Baltimore, Albany, Dallas, and Laredo—of municipal computer systems. In Texas alone, 22 towns and cities had their computers shut down and held for ransom. Small and medium-sized towns make easy, tempting targets because often they haven't spent their relatively limited resources on installing the latest security software.

Alarmingly, not even our military and intelligence agencies are satisfactorily protected from digital attacks. In 2013 the computer networks of the National Security Agency (NSA) were penetrated by unauthorized agents—still not yet identified—and massive amounts of data and top-secret operational protocols were stolen. In 2016, the hackers published some of the protocols, which were (and are) various ways to infiltrate the computer systems and networks of adversaries or anyone whose computers you wish to illegally enter or incapacitate. For years, the NSA had been discovering and stockpiling these hacking tools and techniques for potential and actual use by the U.S. government. We have used these software tools to spy on or sabotage other countries (the Stuxnet attack in 2010, which caused centrifuges in Iran's uranium processing system to spin out of control, is just one example of an American use of malware to attack an adversary).

So when malicious hackers penetrated the NSA's network—or were somehow given the files (nobody knows)—it was a disaster of colossal scale. Since 2016, the hackers—known as the Shadow Brokers—have periodically posted onto the web all kinds of what are effectively software hacking instructions. These instructions describe how to take advantage of weaknesses or flaws or errors in a wide range of popular software systems and programs that are used by billions of people in corporations, institutions, governments, and individually around the world.

And since 2016, there have been many serious hacking events where techniques developed by the NSA—and now in the hands of criminals, pirates, terrorists, nations, and other rogue actors—have been used to disrupt, destroy, modify, or hold ransom a broad range of computer systems and networks.

One of the more serious hacks occurred in May of 2017 and froze the computers in a large variety of enterprises in parts of England, India, Taiwan, Ukraine, China, Russia, and many other countries. Called "WannaCry," the digital assault encrypted the data on hundreds of thousands of computers and requested the payment of a ransom before the thieves would release the computers back into normal operation. One of the hardest hit networks during the assault was the British National Health Service, which was disrupted for a number of days. Many of its services and operations had to be shut down, and its ability to manage, diagnose, and treat patients during that period was negatively affected. A huge number—70,000—of its computers and web-connected equipment, such as blood-storage refrigerators, MRI scanners, and phones were frozen out of service by the hacking software.

Also affected by the WannaCry malware were banks, universities, manufacturers, and many other businesses. In the attacks, as in many other cyber invasions, the ransom amount requested—$300—was relatively modest. That serves to increase the likelihood that victims will pay the ransom. And the criminals make their money by the sheer number of actual and future victims targeted. In the case of WannaCry, the perpetrators collected about $130,000, a relatively small total. However, the real danger and cost to society is less in the ransoms paid than in the vastly larger sums that must be spent, after an attack, to repair the damage. Usually, some data has been lost, some computers and devices must be abandoned, software must be updated or upgraded, and new security measures (of all types) must be implemented. Additionally, valuable business time and revenue have been lost. Because businesses are very image-conscious and want always to project an air of ultra-competence, and because they pass along to their customers their costs of doing business, they are often less than forthcoming about revealing either when they are hacked or how much it has damaged or cost their operations. Thus, it is usually very difficult to fully tally—across the economy—the total costs of any given cyber attack. Estimates of the grand cost of WannaCry range from $1 billion to many billions.

There are a nearly infinite number of ways to hack into or infect computers and their networks. An exhaustive list and description of such actual and potential tools and techniques could be an entire book all by itself. Criminals can "phish" with emails, hide malware in spam, implant contagious worms and viruses on otherwise innocent and upstanding websites, disseminate poisonous "clickbait," link compromised and captured computers into massive "botnets," overwhelm websites with "denial-of-service" attacks, contaminate all sorts of otherwise benign apps, and infiltrate computers and networks in thousands of other ways.

Many times, computer users do not even know their computers have been breached. With botnets, for example, an entire network of compromised computers gets silently and secretly linked by a single malicious "worm" which may initially do nothing at all. The botnet may lie in wait for weeks or months until it receives instructions from the hackers. Then, utilizing the power of many computers, it may be mobilized for hacking in any number of ways. The infamous "Conficker" worm, which at one point in 2009 had infested itself in 9 million computers, was a frightening demonstration of the capability of hackers to create a really large botnet. Ultimately—and puzzlingly—Conficker was never really utilized by its creators in any substantial criminal or destructive activity. Many internet security experts speculate that Conficker may have been created as an experiment or a warning. Had it been unleashed in any coordinated way—in pursuit of malicious ends—it could have been a disaster, overwhelming whole corporations or institutions or possibly even large regions of the internet itself.

Another level of vulnerability—perhaps the most serious of all—is found in the structure and operation of the internet itself. Successful attacks on pieces of the internet have large consequences, halting normal operations for all the individuals, companies, institutions, and government that are served by the affected portion of the internet.

In October of 2016, the public got a look at what an attack on the internet can do. A major company called "Dyn" (since purchased by Oracle) that was one of many involved in receiving and directing online traffic was targeted by a "distributed denial-of-service" attack. Nearly simultaneously, the company was bombarded with hundreds of thousands, or millions (it is unclear), of requests for online connections. This had the effect of overwhelming the capacities of Dyn's computerized routing machinery to handle the volume, and so, on and off for a day, Dyn could not maintain uninterrupted internet service for large portions of the east coast of the United States, and some portions elsewhere.

The malicious requests for connections came from a botnet that had a unique wrinkle, for that time. It was one of the first botnets to infect and employ not just conventional computers but also to use a range of devices that are part of the Internet of Things. Now digital, computerized, and connected to the web, and therefore hackable, are devices such as baby monitors, video recorders, printers, home thermostats, home routers, and closed-circuit TV cameras. The hackers who attacked Dyn had commandeered hundreds of thousands of these ordinary devices and used them to dispatch their bogus messages to Dyn. Eventually, after a disrupted day in which individuals and companies lost time, money, and resources, Dyn was able to fend off the attack and restore normal internet service.

But the attack really demonstrated yet another vulnerability that exists in our new and ever-expanding digital world: the many devices being hooked up to the web in the so-called Internet of Things do not have adequate security measures protecting their digital operations. Unlike our personal computers, which have some degree of security built into their programs and operating systems, and generally also are protected by customized user names and passwords, the proliferation of so-called "smart" devices (thermostats, appliances, cameras, etc.) comprising the growing list of gadgets in the Internet of Things are often cheaply and sloppily made and have poor security software. They come with less internal security, and they use generic, default user names and passwords that many consumers don't bother to change. Some of the devices don't even give the user the option to enter a new, unique, customized password.

So now, in addition to all of the desktop computers, laptops, tablets, phones, and watches that we must defend against cyber intrusions of one sort or another, we can add millions—and the number will continue to grow steadily through the billions—of internet-connected, everyday objects.

If the operation of the internet system itself is interrupted—the most serious hack of all—there is another dangerous vulnerability that is closely associated with that. That danger is the potential for the nation's electrical grid to fail. The electrical grid sprawls across the country in a massive infrastructure of power plants, substations, transformers, equipment, and power lines. Nearly all of that infrastructure is today monitored and controlled by computers. The electrical demand on all parts of the system is monitored by computers, and the electrical power sent to users is regulated and allocated by computers.

Furthermore, because electrical loads and demands—and the power sent to them—vary constantly, the overall grid system and the electricity flowing in every direction within it require a nonstop and sophisticated charting, balancing, and rebalancing to keep the system operating satisfactorily. Electrical power today is generated from many sources—oil, natural gas, coal, wood products, wind, solar, nuclear, hydroelectric—and consequently the costs and quantities of electricity available from different power plants can vary on an hourly and daily basis. Matching—and taking account of—demand, capacities available, pricing, time, and where on the grid the power will both originate and be sent is an integrated task that today is performed almost wholly by computers and computer-controlled instrumentation and equipment.

These computers and the networks that they operate on are continuously connected to the internet. It is no exaggeration to say that human beings alone—without computers—could no longer maintain the balancing and rebalancing that occurs within the electrical grid, if the internet went down over wide areas of the country for a sustained period of time, say, many days or a week or more. So, let's repeat that; if the internet fails, is hacked, is sabotaged, or goes down for any reason—over a wide area of the United States and for a significant period of time—effectively the entire electrical grid would fail, and no electricity (with relatively tiny, decentralized exceptions) would be sent anywhere.

And of course the reverse is true too. In a kind of circular dependency and vulnerability, if the electrical grid were for any reason to be the first element of our infrastructure to fail, then the internet would fail for lack of electrical power. So too would every computer, laptop, phone, network, and Internet-of-Things device that requires either or both electrical power and a connection to the web.

So, the electrical grid depends upon computers and the internet; and computers and the internet depend upon the electrical grid. A significant interruption to either will halt the other, and modern society as we know it would come to a halt.

Now, it is important to say that the interruptions I am referring to are not like any we have had so far. When the internet—or electrical power—gets interrupted for a few hours or a few days, and the outage is local or regional, we have been able to manage those relatively limited events. Most power plants, internet providers, corporations, hospitals, institutions, and government facilities have backup generators, alternative web resources, and emergency protocols. Often, these have been successfully used to manage bad situations. Generators, for example, often have three days of fuel.

When I warn here about our extreme vulnerability—brought on by our complete dependence on computers—I am referring to an internet or electrical failure that is perhaps weeks or months long, and one that is spread across the entire country.

If the internet fails, and consequently then too the electrical grid, would the impact on society really be as dire as I am saying? Unequivocally yes, and to appreciate how grim things would get, and how relatively quickly they would get there, we must understand how incredibly reliant on computers we have made every facet and level of society. We have woven them into everything.

Without an operational internet, grocery stores would not get restocked, gas stations would not get refueled, banks would cease to permit withdrawals or other operations, credit cards would not work, smart-phones would be useless, telecommunications would go dead, trucking and airline flights would halt, wastewater would not get treated, and the water supply itself would halt or become unreliable.

Without the web, factories would cease production, fuel would not get refined, the entire financial system would become inert, police and fire operations would dwindle, and governments would become ineffective.

Without the web, buildings would have neither heat nor air-conditioning, automobile traffic and mass transit would halt, hospitals and medical care would degrade, schools would shut down, and work itself—normal jobs—would cease.

How quickly would these conditions become widespread? In the cities and dense metropolitan areas, one week or longer without the internet could begin the deterioration I am describing. One month without computers and the web would surely be devastating. In rural areas, where some last vestiges of decentralized (not computerized) services still exist, and where food, fuel, and water supplies are still produced and procured locally, it might take longer before an internet and electrical outage would result in devastation.

How would citizens—especially in the cities—respond? If every single system of communication, food and water supply, mobility, medical care, employment, and finance broke down, how would we cope? Without heating or cooling, without any emergency services, without any money or use for it, how would we cope? How quickly would chaos, illness, crime, and deaths become widespread?

We can barely imagine these things. They are unbearably unthinkable. But they all would occur, and occur relatively quickly, in the absence of computers and the internet, and the resulting absence of electrical power.

One of the most important points to note as we think about the forces on society is that this digitally-technologically vulnerable state of affairs did not exist—at all—only 35 or 40 years ago. In, say, 1980, most every important infrastructure system was not connected to the internet, and not run and managed by computers. Factories, banks, hospitals, refineries, stores, warehouses, offices, and most importantly, the electrical grid itself were still independent of the internet. To the degree that they used computers at all, that automation had not yet risen to today's level of dependence where a protracted computer outage would halt entire enterprises and halt the normal operation of the whole economy itself.

In this chapter I have focused on how technology, computerization, automation, and robotization have eliminated millions of jobs in many sectors of the economy, and how those forces will inexorably erase millions more. This job loss—due to the digital technologies—has occurred during the past 35 years, and the next 20 to 25 years will see even more devastating replacement of human workers.

There have of course been some number of new jobs created by the digital technologies. An entire tech sector of the economy has been created in Silicon Valley, Boston, New York, and other high-tech hubs, and today many of America's most profitable and successful companies owe their productivity and very existence to computers. Companies, such as Amazon, Apple, Facebook, Google, Microsoft, Dell, Oracle, Cisco, and Intel employ thousands of workers and generate billions of dollars in revenue. And in smaller companies across the country, there are software engineers, information technology specialists, video game designers, telecom workers, scientists, geneticists, contractors, and others whose work exists as a consequence of computers, robots, and the internet. Uber and Lyft drivers and Airbnb proprietors wouldn't exist without the internet.

But what is also unfortunately true is that, speaking generally, the big and small tech companies and enterprises are able to generate any given amount of revenue and profit with far fewer workers than did more "traditional" companies of the past (pre-computer age). Many companies today that make products or apps or services for uses on or related to the internet do so with shockingly few employees—sometimes numbering in the dozens. These companies are often worth a lot of money. In the past—before computers—they typically would have employed many times more workers to attain the valuations, productivity, and place in the economy that they hold today.

Overall, human labor is losing out. Overall, computers, automation, and robotization have eliminated far more jobs than they have created. And this reality will continue, and get worse. Computers, robots, and drones continue to be improved, and continue to possess greater and greater capabilities. Software engineers are working hard to write ever more sophisticated code and to further develop artificial intelligence. More and more people, in more and more occupations, will be replaced as computers "learn" how to do their jobs. The irony is that as all of us use computers to do our jobs, software engineers are tracking and cataloguing our keystrokes to use to "teach" computers and "intelligent" machines how to do whatever it is that we are doing. In effect, by simply executing our work tasks every day, we are providing the data (immense quantities of it) with which artificial intelligence is "trained." As I mentioned earlier in this chapter, both blue-collar and white-collar jobs are vulnerable to ever-smarter computers. Ultimately, even many computer programmers, software engineers, code writers, and repairmen of all things digital will increasingly be replaced by more formidable computers and ever-faster "machine learning." Increasingly, computers can troubleshoot and "repair" other computers, and artificial intelligence is well on the way to achieving the capacity to "teach" other connected devices.

Another by-product of the advance of digital technology is a slow, sometimes subtle, undermining of the economic health and very existence of physical places. I will have more to say about this in the following chapter on "Webworld." I mentioned already the closing of retail shops and stores and the loss of jobs that results, as more of us increasingly shop online. But the shuttering of businesses has consequences beyond job loss. As stores, offices, and enterprises empty out, and downtowns and suburbs and malls and regional nodes all become quieter and less peopled, the organization and value of the physical environment changes. In many cases, the downtowns and other built places become less dynamic and less attractive. With fewer small-scale mixed uses, and with less foot-traffic, the importance of particular places diminishes, and care for them and about them diminishes as well.

In many cities, certain once-vibrant retail-enterprise streets have been so affected by online shopping—and the consequent demise of stores— that a phenomenon called "pop-up" stores has begun. New store owners— and their prospective landlords—have become so apprehensive about competing with the online-sales world that they've come up with an idea to test the local market prior to committing to a 1-year or multi-year lease. Instead, both shop owner and landlord agree to an initial 1-month lease to see if the proposed retail shop sells enough merchandise to be viable. The pop-up shops are generally small and more often than not they don't last long. Slowly, physical places lose a consistent, memorable, imageful identity.

Another reflection of the difficulties that traditional stores are having can be seen in the proliferation of self-serve kiosks. With no human workers, these small stand-alone structures are located on sidewalks, in malls, or in larger "box" stores. Part of the automation of everything, they can sell a variety of items, they are cheap to build and operate, and they add nothing meaningful or substantive to a physical place. They further contribute to the message that physical places are transient, anonymous, carelessly assembled (and easily disassembled), and perhaps not actually important.

The slow loss of the landscape of physical places also has a bad effect on the quality of new construction and the budgeting of money for municipal and public green places generally. These effects are not always obvious, and they are difficult to prove in any easy cause-and-effect demonstration, but new construction in a time when physical placeness is continually less important than it was before digital technology, is cheaper, less ambitious, less noble, and less public-oriented. Similarly, in the digital era, public open space, green space, landscaping, and urban trees and vegetation generally are subtly and continually diminished in quality, quantity, and importance.

The ultimate digital technology for undermining and diminishing the one-time primacy and importance of the physical environment may well be virtual reality. Currently being developed rapidly, virtual reality helmets and headsets allow us to experience any location or physical surroundings—imaginary or real—in increasingly realistic sensory experiences. The surroundings that we see inside our headsets can be programmed to be exact facsimiles of actual places—say, Venice or Rome—or they can be some imagined fantasy landscape that we (or the programmers) dream up. It is conceivable that within, say, 10 years, we may choose to wear improved headsets frequently to provide us with ambient background visuals and acoustics while we work or relax. Many people already wear music headsets—and for long periods of time. If virtual, background, visual "scenes"—simulating full immersion in a three-dimensional environment—can provide us a setting in a "place" of our own choosing, many people will probably opt for that too. The value of real physical "placeness" will continue to be diminished. Replacing our actual surroundings—whether it be our office or the outdoors—with some simulated contextual backdrop may seem somewhat outlandish, but there are many computer engineers working right now to create that option.

As in all things digital, generational change plays a role in this ongoing transformation. Our expectations generally for the beauty, interest, coherence, and indispensability of physical places are constantly being eroded by the growing capacities of the digital world. Our attention to the online world squeezes out the attention that we bring to the layout of the physical world. As the imageability and planned quality of towns and cities continually deteriorate, and as older citizens naturally die, and younger citizens are born, the overall population slowly takes to measuring the attributes of the built environment—especially in the public sphere—by a new baseline, that is, the only environments it has known. So, again slowly and subtly, lower-quality built environments and smaller expectations for them become the new norms for progressive generations. Essentially, over time, younger generations literally can't know or feel what they—and their cities—are missing.

The reality that—obvious on the face of it—each generation has a difficult time fully knowing and appreciating things and conditions that existed before its lifetime, plays a powerful role in the insinuation of all-things-digital into all facets of life. Quite naturally, through nobody's fault, differences in the capacities of successive generations to see, feel, perceive, comprehend, and judge the changes to society and human behavior and human habits of mind from pre-web to post-web life, is a constant dynamic to bear in mind as we examine the effects and consequences of digital technology, online life, AI, and automation.

Looking at history, this dynamic has parallels. In any age, the younger the person, the fewer references he has, or has experienced, of a totally previous era. But this time is different, and the dynamic contains real dangers. Because of the nature of the threats embodied in the new digital and AI technologies and the internet, and because many of them involve fundamentally changing the way people think, talk, process information, and behave, and because the stakes today involve the very survival of democracy, the ecosphere, and civilization itself, it is probably critical—in a way that has not existed in the past—to be conscious of what changes we are embracing or defaulting into. I will talk further about more of those changes in subsequent chapters.

* * * *

As I wrote at the beginning of this chapter, society has always had to contend with technology as a force—a force for better or for worse, but either way a force often in some regard "disruptive." This has been the case especially with digital technology, as computers and the internet together are a force that cuts across nearly every aspect of society and the economy.

An important component—one not frequently enough remarked on—of this digital force is the powerful faith and optimism and vision that its promoters hold. The Silicon Valley entrepreneurs, inventors, wizards, computer scientists, software engineers, encryption experts, and code magicians who have created our astounding digital machinery and the internet hold an unshakeable, near-religious belief in the rightness and wisdom of their work. They believe unequivocally in their computers and in the data that computers collect and assess. They believe in the efficiency with which computers and robots and artificial intelligence perform tasks. They are motivated to make computers faster, more accurate, more intelligent, more versatile, and more formidable. To them, digital technology is wholly elegant and beguiling, and they fully believe that if something can be done—technically—with computerization or automation or robotization, it should be done.

Complementing their extreme faith—what in any other endeavor would be called a fanaticism—in digital machinery is a corresponding view that humans are flawed, slow, mistake-prone, inefficient, unreliable, and mortal. Don't misunderstand this, they like humans and consider them sometimes useful or necessary. But really capable, high-level computer scientists and software writers and robot designers live in a professional environment where the new machines, algorithms, and software are meant to—in the present and even more so in the future—outshine the humans.

In the Silicon Valley tech firms, new machines that can do extraordinary things are being researched and prototyped constantly. Tech engineers are constantly enlarging the capabilities of computerized machinery, and are constantly developing new digital-technological possibilities and seeing new horizons beckoning now and in the near future.

As these engineers imagine and build the computers and robots of the near-future—utilizing rapid advances in artificial intelligence, machine learning, virtual reality, and 3-D printing—they both consciously and subconsciously constantly compare the performance of their machines to the capabilities of humans. Humans are the natural benchmark, obviously. And what Silicon Valley has learned is that the capacities of humans are relatively static while the capacities of machines are unlimited. Therefore, in the Silicon Valley culture, software and machinery are exciting, and humans are not.

What this Silicon Valley perspective translates into within the industry is a contagious enthusiasm, an innocent and well-meaning boosterism, a near-blind embrace of all computer advancement, and a no-questions-asked agenda in support of advancing digital technology. And this perspective—because there is no powerful competing narrative—has substantially been adopted by the public and by government.

Consequently, for the past 35 years or so, the computer industry—which is basically, totally unregulated in any meaningful way—has researched, designed, invented, and produced an entire economy-transforming and society-shaking industry without so much as a public discussion. For all that time, a technology of unprecedented scope and power—like no technology before it—was able to be woven into the economy and society without anyone's permission. And until only very recently, the American public participated enthusiastically as an unquestioning cheerleader in pushing this force into and across everything.

CHAPTER 3

WEBWORLD

IN THE CHAPTER ON TECHNOLOGY, I described how the relatively recent invention and proliferation of computers, smartphones, and connected devices has been a powerful and growing force across society and the economy. This force—unlike technologies of the past—possesses characteristics of power, range, scope, and persistence (or ubiquity) that are astounding.

Closely associated with the technology of computers—and now and increasingly nearly inseparable from it—is the internet. The internet is itself an invention, a new "technology," but it has come to be so ubiquitous and to seem so organic and second-nature, that it is easy to forget how new, novel, radical, amazing, and transforming it is—and that it is indeed a technology. As older people die off, and the population eventually comes to consist of citizens who never knew a world without the internet, it will become unthinkable and unimaginable to picture life and commerce without it.

Really, technology and the internet are two halves of a digital juggernaut of a force, and although this book separates them into two chapters for purposes of description, they are thoroughly woven together in practice. The internet consists of hardware, software, servers, routers, browsers, modems, cabling, electronic signals and pulses, computers, devices, apps, programs, protocols, and other components variously linked and supporting giant, sprawling communication webs or networks. We call this "the internet" but it is really an enormous collection of many networks. It is, therefore, decentralized in some ways, and centralized in others.

The internet as it is built and used today contains nearly an infinite array of products, services, communications, tools, purposes, and effects. It is used by 4.5 billion people across the world, is constantly growing and spreading, and has enjoyed a nearly universal, mostly uncritical, welcoming embrace by widely diverse users everywhere. Even where authoritarian governments, like those in China and Russia, fear an open, unfettered internet, they have nonetheless embraced and propagated their own national version of a network, one that they use to reinforce and promote the semi-restricted societies that they have created.

The internet is so large, so multifaceted, and so diverse, that about the only common denominator that crosses all aspects and expressions of it is connectivity itself. If something—a computer, an app, an alarm system, a toaster, a game—is connected and therefore "online," it is part of the internet. I use the word "Webworld" to identify and label and summarize the vast online agglomeration of tools, services, websites, games, blogs, videos, podcasts, apps, and other content and their dynamics and effects. If the label "Webworld" conveys a faint sense of otherworldliness, fictitiousness, or fantasy, it is meant to. If the term also seems slightly disparaging, it is meant to be. For a significant portion of the internet and its dynamics promotes lies, fantasies, distractions, delusions, destructive effects, and insanities.

I don't know if other observers have used this word "Webworld." You would think they would have. It seems so natural, fitting, and obvious. Yet in all my reading about the internet, I don't recall ever having come across it. I find that odd. Is it because few commentators want to seem hostile to a huge, new, not-going-away, modern technology? Or, they don't want to appear Luddite? Or, they don't want to sum up the entire internet venture with one semi-pejorative label?

* * * *

When the internet was first being created, in a long process that really began in the early 1960s, it was a product of scientists, engineers, and academicians working in various places—but perhaps most substantially and initially at DARPA, the Defense Advanced Research Projects Agency funded by the government (and housed at the Pentagon) to research computer technology projects generally. The government hoped there might be some future military value to whatever the researchers came up with, but that possibility never became the driving force for the scientists and engineers doing the actual research work.

Instead, they held what could almost be called the opposite of a military-is-relevant view. They envisioned a new tool with which to communicate and collaborate with their intellectual peers across the United States, across institutions, and across the globe. They imagined a digital, decentralized, computer-managed communications network that would be speedy, direct, versatile, and—in actual practice—probably mostly exclusive to serious scientists and academicians in all fields. It would be democratic and open to all, but the internet's designers always assumed that, sort of by default, only earnest scholarly types would utilize it.

In the 1960s and the 1970s, they envisioned the web as a giant and constantly growing information source, akin to a set of encyclopedias—or an online library—that is constantly being updated in every subject area. They saw this network as being welcomed and supported by scientists and academicians in every field—the humanities, sciences, medicine, health, education, engineering, and many others. The network would function as a library, research laboratory, discussion forum, and easy, frictionless communications medium. And because all parties interested or involved in a subject, experiment, or discussion—regardless of their location or the institution they were working for—would or could at any time tap into the network information, this would have the dual effect of more quickly advancing research and the development of knowledge while also drawing from and informing the widest possible relevant audience.

In 1962, DARPA-funded engineers created the first internet-like computer network. Called "ARPANET," it connected four college campuses and allowed scientists at each institution to share information quickly and simultaneously with all the others.

In 1970, a group of computer engineers—a bit uneasy associating with the Pentagon imprimatur—broke off from DARPA and formed an independent, parallel group, called PARC, for Palo Alto Research Center. Simultaneously, DARPA and PARC continued to develop the ARPANET, the personal computer, and other digital and networking innovations. By the mid-1970s, the ARPANET had facilitated the formation of virtual communities of scientists and engineers across the globe.

Those early web designers and users had the best of intentions. They were not motivated by dreams of making money with their new network;

their primary goal was to build the purest and most elegant solution to crafting a revolutionary new digital communications tool. Their enthusiasm for the project was totally positive, optimistic, public spirited, and innocent. And, significantly, because they had such high hopes for what computers, networked communications, infinite information, and humans could accomplish together, their enthusiasm was also utopian.

As opposed to what much of the internet has become—trashy, divisive, political, destructive, and overwhelmingly commercial—the early internet pioneers had in mind a truly constructive, democratic, decentralized, self-managing (meaning, user-managing) mechanism that would be a force for education, enlightenment, and individual empowerment. They felt that a world-wide web would be an irresistible force for enhanced cooperation and understanding among diverse peoples. Although their focus was on individuals—and the increase in knowledge accruing individual by individual—rather than on any articulated collective or society, their assumption was that societies would only benefit and improve as their internet connected citizens.

With a viewpoint that today seems naïve, the early web designers came pretty close to believing that just sharing all the knowledge and information in the world would cause magic to happen. By "magic" I mean a universal, global embrace of the idea that we are here to learn, become smarter, do better, and improve societies everywhere. For a number of reasons, it is worth emphasizing the idealism behind the founding of the internet. First, it contrasts with so much of how and why the internet is used today. Second, some portion of the idealism and utopianism survives today in the perspectives and behavior of current Silicon Valley tech firms, and knowing that will help us understand Webworld as a force. And last, our continuing awareness of the genuine good intentions behind the creation of the web has played a role, and still plays a role, in giving somewhat of a carte blanche to Silicon Valley as it has introduced, developed, and promoted the entire computer and internet and digital revolution. I will have more to say about this persistent idealism as our story progresses.

But now back to our thumbnail sketch of the evolution of the web. During the 1980s, we saw computers and the web mature. In the decade between 1980 and 1990, the internet was transformed from a small, elite academic tool to a broad commercial venture. Microsoft and Apple grew and prospered in that period, and Webworld was well on its way. In 1988, after the technology to send vast volumes of text speedily over the internet had been perfected, the term "World-Wide Web" was coined.

After 1990, computers proliferated in the developed world and the uses of the internet became thoroughly multi-dimensional: academic; scientific; creative; commercial; religious; political; personal; and other. In 1994 Amazon was founded, in 1995 eBay, in 1998 PayPal and Google, and in 2004 Facebook.

So, indeed, at its best the internet has wonderfully fulfilled its inventors' goals that it be an infinitely expanding information source and an effective tool for communications and collaboration. The web performs those two foundational tasks well with text, video, audio, photos, virtual reality, and other formats. And it does those jobs for anyone, anywhere, thus fulfilling its inventors' intentions that it be open, democratic, free (relatively), and unregulated by any central governing body. Whether you are a business, government, church, club, cult, group, or individual, the web is open to you. You can live in the city or the country, in the First World or the Third, and you'll have equal access to Webworld, 24/7.

In many ways, the internet has been a positive invention. I could write many pages describing the benefits of connectivity and Webworld. But this chapter will focus only on the negative and destructive aspects of the internet. The internet and Webworld are an enormous force across the world today, and it is my belief that that force is—on balance—more negative than positive. I think that Webworld, its dynamics, and the consequences it engenders are contributing to—and in some cases causing—a number of current ongoing crises in America and in other nations. In thinking about Webworld, and evaluating its power, it is important to remember that Webworld is a force that blends and straddles and modifies and is part of all the other forces discussed in this book. And again, its characteristics, reach, and power to create consequences are unprecedented in the history of technology. (It is possible that the invention of language itself, the invention of agriculture, and the printing of books are equally huge events in the march of technology.)

One of the most obvious and deleterious impacts of the birth of the internet has been its effects on newspapers. Since 1990 or so, when the web really started to come into its own, it has put roughly 1900 high-quality daily and weekly newspapers out of business; and that occurred while the U.S. population grew by 80 million people. Traditional (pre-web) newspapers relied heavily on advertising—especially the classified ads—to make sufficient revenue. Because huge amounts of advertising switched from the newspapers to the internet, the papers no longer had the budgets to pay reporters, editors, photographers, printers, and op-ed writers. Many newspapers have closed entirely. All the others have had to cut large numbers of staff, and many papers also reduced the number of pages they publish. Still others reduced the physical dimensions of their pages. The financial pressure on newspapers is unrelenting still, and every year brings further reductions in the quantity of papers nationally, their size, and the number of reporters and writers at them.

This loss of papers is an incredibly serious and unprecedented development. In a democracy such as ours, the Fourth Estate, as the press is known, plays a critical role in observing the government and the private sector, reporting on politicians and businessmen and legislation, offering opinion and commentary, giving voice to citizens, and helping to inform and educate voters. In a democracy, the allocation and use of power—public and private—is important, and the press takes seriously its mission to hold power to account. So having fewer newspapers and fewer reporters means—quite directly—that there is less coverage of the government, the private sector, and all else. This loss is critical.

The internet has not been fully able to duplicate the roles played by newspapers. While traditional newspapers have their online versions, the internet hasn't made up for the loss of so many other papers and journalists, nor do its new offerings have the resources, mission, and professionalism of serious journalism.

The growth of the internet has seen the proliferation of all sorts of "news" offerings. Oftentimes, websites are mere aggregators of articles written for traditional newspapers—so they haven't added to the amount of journalism being produced. Other websites offer news that has been selected to present only one side of some issue or ideological argument. Still other websites—the worst of all—deliberately distort, mislead, provoke, and lie with their content.

Although traditional pre-web newspapers usually had some ideological leanings, most reliable dailies confined their cheerleading—their editorial board biases—to clearly identifiable opinion pieces on the op-ed or editorial pages, and even consistently located those essays on the back page of a section. That was a physical design meant to signal to the reader the not-neutral nature of those pieces. Conversely, all the "reporting" articles in the main sections of the papers were supposed to (and by and large did) present a straight description—as fully as possible—of current events and developments. (Of course, which stories a newspaper chooses to feature on its front page could and usually does involve editorial judgement, and sometimes bias.)

Mostly, the internet has not followed the strict editing, formatting, and opinion-versus-reporting, firewall-division models of traditional papers. Instead, a bizarre circus of media and human dynamics are at play on the web, resulting in a chaotic and fragmented and often unedited collection of material.

Pre-web newspapers were relatively orderly things. With the exception of some special papers like the *New York Times* and the *Wall Street Journal*, papers had defined local audiences, tried to appeal to a decent cross-section of that audience, had a stable revenue base, and could go about their business in a consistent, reliable, relatively transparent, and sober way. They were staffed with paid, professional journalists. There were lurid-press exceptions to this Fourth Estate mission, of course, but most everybody knew the difference between a reasonably serious paper and a sensation-selling tabloid.

The development of the internet radically changed the business calculations that once worked for journalism. Online, it is still advertising revenue that funds journalism and other content. But online, any newspaper or website is now competing with literally millions of news sources, blogs, videos, and apps. And the possible audience is huge and unknown, no longer confined to any local geographical area. And worst of all for traditional newspapers, advertisers now may shop around among many online venues for the most suitable places for their advertising. Consequently, newspapers (and everybody else online) cannot charge advertisers anywhere near as much as they used to be able to charge. And there are fewer advertisers to go around, relative to the number of "publications" on the web.

This competition for advertisers has come to define the web. Advertisers want to place their ads in front of the most eyeballs, so they sign up with websites and other online places that receive the most attention. Here's where things start to go awry. It turns out that serious, detailed, lengthy, calm, even-handed news reporting is not particularly popular, at least when competing with other types of content. What the majority of Americans prefer—or are seduced into—is web material that is sensational, emotional, simple or simplified, and brief. If it cannot be those things, then at a minimum it must—if it is "news" content—align with the opinions and narratives that people already hold within their heads.

The natural desire of people to be affirmed, and to live a life surrounded by words and stories that reflect and reinforce their beliefs and perspectives and ways, leads them to be online within an internet "bubble" or "silo." We all look for what we like on the internet, and mostly that is all we see.

For the last 15 or 20 years, with the rise of Google, Apple, Amazon, and Facebook, the human tendency to affirm only our own epistemology has received powerful corporate support and encouragement. Because those four companies are responsible for putting on our computer screens nearly everything most of us see, and because they make their money by selling advertising, they have designed huge protocols and systems to feed us mostly information and visuals that we will like. Even our search results are tailored to each of us; if ten of us were to look up some item, we'd each receive a different list of results, and even a different number of results. The companies' algorithms track our destinations on the web, what articles we read, what videos we watch, what searches we make, what ads we look at, what products we buy, and much, much more. Facebook, for example, tracks our physical locations, political opinions, personal interests and habits, education, income, time online, even our brand of smartphone, and much more. The company does this so it can better convince advertisers to pay it to place their ads in front of the audiences—us—most likely to buy the advertised products or services or political beliefs. The biggest internet companies are actively weaponizing ad technology against us.

So with regard to the news, the money-making incentives that fuel the operation of the internet are working against traditional, broad presentations of the news. Relatively few people want their political opinions challenged regularly, and most citizens will not or cannot take the time to become deeply or sufficiently informed regarding current events and their real meaning for their own lives. So we click the web content that we like, the algorithms increasingly present us with more of the same, and we spiral down deeper and deeper into our own happy version of the world. The "silo" that each of us lives in is the product of a team effort: we indicate our preferences, opinions, and entire epistemology to Google, Facebook, Twitter, other companies, the algorithms, the advertisers, our friends, our followers, and all of Webworld, and they respond by sending us content that mirrors that picture of who we are. We now live in visual and print echo chambers.

Aside from the slow death of good newspapers, what does this mean for our knowledge and attitudes? Well, egged on, pumped up, and reinforced by the internet, we all think we know more than we do, we think we're right most of the time, we think we're in the majority or mainstream of "reasonable" thought, and we're apt to have a very poor understanding of ideas or people that we don't agree with.

It is important to note here that people have always had these tendencies. What is different and unprecedented today is the existence of the internet and its role in enlarging, magnifying, hardening, and weaponizing these tendencies and their consequences.

In the political realm, human nature combines with the dynamics of the operation of Webworld to exacerbate and create division, alienation, impatience, anger, ignorance, misunderstanding, suspicion, and fragmentation among the citizenry. Webworld is constantly enlarging the divisions between people and then being employed by them to assault the thinking and beliefs of their fellow Americans.

Victimized by the entire spectrum of online sites, blogs, videos, apps, programs, and social media platforms that make up Webworld, we are hardening our prejudices, falling into "us versus them" thinking, becoming vulnerable to virulent ideologies, and doubting the goodness, motives, and patriotism of our fellow Americans. We are becoming less tolerant, less discerning, more emotional and reactive, and more easily distracted by matters that should receive less of our attention.

Many of us—egged on by Webworld dynamics—are susceptible to believing false accusations, conspiracy theories, and poisonous ideas. Many citizens have become so buffeted by Webworld that they simply don't know what to think. They do not know who to trust. They have become so paranoid or cynical or distrustful that they question whether facts can exist at all, and whether anyone can be believed. They close down and become unreachable. Many citizens choose not to read any news at all.

Of course, the troublesome dynamics of the internet were not launched onto a pure and rational population to begin with. The ordinary citizenry—when Facebook, Twitter, Reddit, and 15 million or so apps were unleashed to them and on them—were not prospering, thriving, and healthy. They were already underemployed, underpaid, in debt, financially precarious, anxious, resentful, disempowered, and disrespected. In the chapters on capitalism and technology, I have described how both of those fields have evolved over the past 45 years or so in ways that have severely hurt ordinary working Americans. Whether it be by job loss, wage stagnation, tax policies, or globalization, ordinary Americans have been abused and victimized. Furthermore, for 40 years, they have been misled or lied to by their government and the private sector about the economic repercussions that these changes over four decades have brought. So when Webworld came along, with its easy, interactive possibilities for anyone with a keyboard to have a voice, it is no wonder that a simmering, long-disenfranchised citizenry took to it with zeal, anger, carelessness, and hostility.

Today, the online world and the political world have degenerated into places and conditions that are thoroughly polarized and destructive. There are loud, irrational voices online and in politics that—because of Webworld, the circumstances of the world, and what we have become—are dominating and driving what is possible and what is not possible.

* * * *

Today, the traditional, serious press is slowly but steadily eroding away. Many people don't realize this, or are not bothered by it. More and more citizens get their news from the internet, and not by simply reading their newspaper on it. Instead, some two-thirds to three-quarters of Americans tap into a "news-feed" which continually comes to their smartphone or device from some social media platform or site or app. This news-feed generally includes content that has been selected to appeal to them.

In addition to the natural erosion of newspapers under financial duress—and the erosion of the professional journalism that creates them—the sheer ease of putting content onto the web was and is an opportunity for malicious actors to get into the "news" business. There has been an explosion online of websites and social media blogs that pretend to offer legitimate news reports and legitimate commentary, but that in fact are extremely biased and misleading and hold some narrow, often extremist agenda. These sites often hold a vision of a certain society that they are pursuing, and so they write and select stories that will advance that vision. Simultaneously, they will criticize other ideas, cultures, and people that they disagree with. What makes their online offerings so destructive can be either the goals themselves—say, misogynistic, anti-Semitic, white supremacist, autocratic—or the methods they employ to promote their vision—lies, distortions, bigotry, knowingly false accusation, or conspiracy-mongering.

Webworld allows extremists of all types to publicize their craziness or their poison, and to recruit other adherents to their cause. Prior to the existence of the internet, it was far more difficult for people with bizarre or antisocial views to find each other, to sell their propaganda, and to be in the news. Before the web existed, the editors at traditional newspapers and magazines acted as the filters and gatekeepers who reviewed articles, opinion pieces, and letters to the editor before they appeared in a publication. Material that was deemed racist, irresponsible, marginal, or outright bizarre would not get printed. But Webworld has no, or few, or insufficient editors and gatekeepers, and thus all sorts of destructive material—both text and photos—get put online.

There are entire communities of nutcases, whack jobs, extremists, militias, anarchists, terrorists, pedophiles, sociopaths, and other deviants who gather together online to support each other and to put hideous, pornographic, violent, criminal, or fascist content on the internet. Much of the internet is a cesspool of one sort or another. Many ordinary, normal, decent Americans who use the internet only lightly or for benign purposes, are unaware of both the amount and the viciousness of the darkest aspects of the web, and thus they underestimate its quantity, influence, and effects.

There are many clear examples of dangerous online communities that Webworld has facilitated and that wouldn't have reached the "success" and prominence that they did without it. Maybe the worst one has been ISIS, the fundamentalist Islamic State group that has been fighting fanatically and with horrifying gruesomeness in Iraq and Syria (and elsewhere). ISIS could not have thrived without the internet. It employed social media specialists and brainwashed and recruited roughly 40,000 alienated young men to join it. Aided immensely by the global reach of Webworld, ISIS drew converts from Africa, Europe, the Mideast, and Central Asia. Even today, after losing much of the physical territory it once held in Iraq and Syria, it maintains an internet presence (somewhat diminished) and still has tens of thousands of adherents around the world.

Another corrosive group that has benefitted enormously from the internet is the neo-Nazi rabble in the U.S. Connecting by website, list-serves, social media, and other web vehicles, these demented individuals—who would otherwise be far more isolated—reinforce each other's thinking, share and spew propaganda and hate, and come together for rallies and other public displays. The dynamics of the internet encourage them, empower them, sustain them, help them multiply, and make it difficult for them to be definitively marginalized.

One of the most bizarre groups found online is the "incel" community. Demonstrating how Webworld pumps oxygen into the most insane minds on the planet, men—"incels"—who have never had sexual intercourse with a woman and who are frustrated and angry about it have found each other online and have created an affirming culture for themselves. These men, who are socially incompetent or just seriously odd or worse, and who have been consistently rejected by women, have become dangerously hostile to them and society. Online, they rant to each other, unite emotionally, and rev each other up. They have posted videos and comments advocating the rape of women and other hateful actions and attitudes. There have been at least two instances in recent years when enraged "incel" individuals went on mass killing sprees in public places. Although there is no way to know the total number of incels in the U.S. and the world, it no doubt numbers in the hundreds of thousands, probably millions (though they may not all comment online). Just on the internet platform Reddit alone, about 40,000 members were banned from the service.

I can't emphasize enough the role of the internet in connecting extremists, sociopaths, the dangerously angry and alienated, the grossly uneducated, the lost, the traumatized, and other people who—for a large variety of reasons and forces, most of them outlined in this book—are near the edge of sanity or desperate or otherwise vulnerable to their own throbbing emotional condition or to the influence of others who are also—consciously or unconsciously—thrashing about.

Look at the role of the internet in the hands of the killers in mass shootings. Using contemptible websites like 8chan and others—essentially unmoderated and X-rated sites—the sick and murderous minds post vile content, feed each other's anger and self-righteousness, and rev each other up. They talk about hurting people, and sometimes they carry out their threats. In 2019, on at least two occasions, killers posted manifestos online before carrying out mass shootings. The manifestos are meant to spread their poison and encourage other members of their web communities to commit violence. In the Christchurch, New Zealand massacre at a mosque, and during other shootings, the shooters have even live-streamed onto the web their rampages while they were executing people.

Unhinged or violent people—in every era—have always existed. But before the invention of the internet, they were mostly isolated. They could respond physically—with their bodily presence—but they could not easily initiate and maintain contact with compatriots with any sort of communications tool that remotely compared with the internet in speed, immediacy, credibility, and reach.

In the 1920s, '30s, and '40s, for example, the U.S. saw large numbers of citizens in or supporting the Ku Klux Klan. But its adherents had to attend rallies in person, had to rely on leaders and ringleaders, and had no communications vehicle to initiate contact with fellow members or spread reinforcing messages. It must be remembered too that the popularity of the Klan in its time existed in the contextual soil of that era. The wide civil rights movement and the gradual education of the American people through it had yet to come. Today in 2019, our nation's norms regarding the treatment of blacks have come a long way, and it is with that backdrop in mind that we should see the growth of bigotry and hate on the internet for the truly retrograde development that it is.

Today, the web and its social media platforms are instrumental in allowing racist extremism—and any other kind of extremism—to proliferate. Before the internet, people with destructive voices and horribly misguided messages would not have found each other—not with the ease and magnitude that is occurring today. They would have remained relatively isolated, without a megaphone, and the rest of society could probably have marginalized them successfully. The rest of society would be working with the help of the norms and conventions and, yes, even common courtesy and decency, that existed and were widely embraced in, say, the year 1985 or so in America. Today, through constant battering on the web, and under constant assault by conspiracy mongers, trolls, and cynics, the words "common decency" and "courtesy" are widely disparaged or mocked and have lost their power to call up the better angels of our nature or to unite citizens in a general posture of respect.

Here, the 24/7 nature of Webworld, and the enormous size of it, also plays a role. Any call to decency, any pause for widespread general reflection, is immediately overwhelmed by the continued operation of all other parts of Webworld, which will not be pausing, or allowing a moment's grace, or being in any way cooperative with any attempt to reduce confrontation on the web. Today, reason and patience are up against an uncontrolled global force—with attributes unlike any in the past—that never rests.

Another factor that helps to explain the durability of some of the extremism on the web is the rise of cable television. Proliferating after the mid-1980s or so, cable TV and its hundreds of channels sucked ordinary Americans away from the three major network news channels, and reduced the number of citizens watching any serious news at all (for a democracy, this was a bad development). After the explosion of cable, many citizens instead chose to watch entertainment, seduced by a nearly infinite array of subjects, some of which each citizen would find irresistible. Other citizens, still interested in news, selected cable news that reflected their political thinking and leanings. Fox News was the original "news" show that deliberately and strongly adopted a political viewpoint as its own, and that colored (or tainted) nearly everything presented on the show. MSNBC followed in 1996. And there are many other cable stations that similarly exist to reinforce and spread a political ideology. (I do not think that they are all equally egregious and will discuss this further in the chapters on politics and media.)

But the proliferation of many news stations helped to divide ordinary Americans, and helped to seed the ground for the introduction and development of Webworld silos. Some of those silos are extremist, or at the very least politically uncompromising, and there are cable TV stations that consciously complement the messaging found on the internet.

Further complementing and reinforcing the targeted messages disseminated on agenda-driven websites and in social media communities is talk radio. Again, like cable television, the explosion in talk radio stations is a relatively new development, occurring roughly between 1987 and 2004, and continuing right up to the present. Because of the repeal of the Fairness Doctrine in 1987, which had required roughly balanced (but not equal) presentations of partisan political reporting and commenting, broadcasters in both TV and radio became free to lobby ideologically and relentlessly for certain political viewpoints. For a number of reasons, radio talk shows that promoted a conservative, libertarian, or strongly right-wing viewpoint proliferated and thrived. Today, conservative talk-radio outlets vastly outnumber liberal and middle-of-the-road stations (more on talk radio in the chapters on politics and media).

So today, unlike during the pre-internet era, a powerful synergy operates between Webworld, talk radio, and cable television. Especially on the right, they operate together very effectively to be a juggernaut of a force. The synergy repeats and amplifies the messaging of the listeners, and allows them to directly contact each other. Thus, the energy and fanaticism behind the ideology never flag: there are always adherents online conversing, pumping out information and revving and rallying the group.

In the late 1920s and the first half of the 1930s, Father Charles Coughlin and Senator Huey Long were two populists who were demagogic. If they had been complemented by cable television and Webworld, they may have realized their ambitions. As it was, Coughlin's radio-broadcasted speeches were heard by 30 or 40 million people, an astounding number in the country then of 125 million people. Although each man was deeply flawed, and their case histories are instructive, their ultimate fall from influence (Long was assassinated) should not give us any reassurance that either populism or demagoguery could not succeed in the U.S. today. The existence of Webworld and the interplay of its dynamics make no such confidence possible.

* * * *

Obviously, the most extreme examples of online garbage are easy to condemn. But in some ways, the more insidious consequences of the free-for-all that Webworld has become can be seen in the proliferation of shrill, one-sided political sites, blogs, list-serves, and other internet vehicles. They too create their own true-believer community and slowly and steadily influence and brainwash their regular users. Anyone who doesn't agree with them is to be condemned, maybe ridiculed and insulted. The "other side" is alien, and determined to oppress our side; we have nothing in common with them—no common ground—and no compromise is possible with them.

The rise of the most poisonous commentary of the alt-right is an example of this. Crazy conspiracy theories, misguided thoughts on who the "enemies" of the country are (never mind the shut-down thinking that would brand other ordinary citizens "enemies," simply because they disagree with you), and undiscerning dismissal of all mainstream media reporting are examples of the sort of echo-chamber thinking that those in alt-right Webworld embrace and disseminate.

Over time, because of all of the dynamics outlined above, and because of all the participation that citizens can have on the internet, they come to think of themselves as reporters or journalists or commentators. They come to have an inflated sense of themselves. Many web users send emails, links, likes, comments, tweets, and all sorts of other posts—especially about politics and current events—and so in a way they become the center or director of their own web experience. They pick their websites and newsfeeds, they judge and talk back to the content they see, and they interact with some community of other web users. Many users even explicitly strive to become "influencers," and thereby gain attention, followers, stature, and possibly paid (by advertisers) sponsorships.

This aspect of the internet—the idea that anybody can go to any site, look up any question, find any fact, research any issue, rebut any argument, post any comment or write any opinion, and elicit replies and reaction—is largely responsible for the current disparaging view of expertise. Heavy web users have come to think of themselves as the equal of experts. Any person, no matter how ignorant or injudicious, may post a comment or send a tweet, and there for everyone to see—in black and white print and neat and in tidy website or social media graphics just like all the other comments—will be his personal and equal contribution to whatever everyone is looking at.

The disparagement of expertise is also fed by the anonymity permitted in most parts of Webworld, and also by the unaccountability and arrogance that Webworld can easily foster in anybody, but especially in people who may have personal difficulties or little true power in their lives. Webworld allows people to create and curate an online identity and persona, and that dynamic doesn't facilitate humility or modesty. Webworld inhabitants can easily become the stars—in their own eyes—of their own online presence, and beyond that they can become trolls, provocateurs, or cynical know-it-alls. The idea of expertise erodes.

* * *

There are other aspects and features of Webworld which are contributing to its overall negativity as a force in society. Related to the ongoing diminishment of traditional newspapers, and related to increasing attacks on the mainstream media—which are sowing mistrust of longstanding, traditional news sources—is the large use of the internet and social media to plant and spread fake news, false stories, and rumors, and generally cause even more distrust and chaos across society. Especially in the areas of politics, websites and social media are constantly being seeded with content that is meant to mislead, frighten, or confuse people. This is done for a variety of reasons. Sometimes the people responsible are simply trying to make money; sometimes the provocateurs are partisans of a particular cause; and sometimes the false-content campaigns are part of a competition between nations.

One of the clearest examples of fake and provocative news items being injected into the online news landscape occurred in the run-up to the 2016 presidential election. With both government agents and private citizens working on its behalf, Russia placed all kinds of phony and shrill material onto the web and engaged in a campaign to create discord and division across American society. Russia has an actual state agency devoted to this work, and it utilized Facebook, Twitter, Reddit, YouTube, and other platforms to spread divisive political content across the web. Although the Russian efforts aimed nasty and hyper-partisan material at both Republican and Democratic news consumers, it found—through trial-and-error—that anti-Hillary and pro-Trump material generated the most views, likes, clicks, links, tweets, and retweets. In addition, Russian President Vladimir Putin appeared to favor Donald Trump in the election, and this may have added a factor to Russia's more general goal to poison the American online news environment. Putin's larger goal is to weaken the United States and undermine democracy, and exploiting Webworld's dynamics is one way to aid that effort.

On Facebook and Instagram alone, Russia's workers posted some 80,000 inflammatory items that were seen (or could have been seen) by approximately 150 million people. These items ranged from political advertisements (that Russia purchased) to fake news articles to fake photos. Russian agents also set up lots of phony Facebook accounts to impersonate ordinary American citizens and then created Facebook pages to generate interest in controversial political material. Using Facebook's data metrics, they were able to run political advertisements that targeted people who were likely to be impressed by those ads. These gullible victims then shared the fake material tens of thousands of times with their friends. Russia also used YouTube videos to create content that was viewed millions of times, and it employed roughly 50,000 bots (automated accounts) on Twitter to post millions of election-related tweets which were seen (and retweeted) by millions of American citizens. The Russian tweets received nearly 300 million views. The Russians also created podcasts, posted Vine videos, and blogged on Tumblr. They spread propaganda and disinformation across the internet for potential voters to see.

On another cyber front, Russian military intelligence officers (many now indicted) hacked into the computer system of the Democratic National Committee in 2016. They stole tens of thousands of emails and gave them—through an intermediary—to Wikileaks to release publicly. The officers also obtained about 50,000 emails of John Podesta, Hillary Clinton's campaign chairman. These emails, which of course were never intended for public consumption, were given to Wikileaks too, and for the last month of the 2016 presidential campaign that organization published some number of them nearly every day.

In addition to Russia's work to dupe American citizens, many entrepreneurial young men located in various countries around the world also engaged in the same deceits. In Macedonia especially, there were many teenagers who, seeing an opportunity to make easy money, set up deceptive Facebook and Twitter accounts, ran fake-news stories, used provocative political advertising, and collected payments whenever online readers clicked on ads seen on their websites. Their postings fed social conflict and vitriol and magnified existing divisions within the electorate. They too discovered that anti-Hillary material generated the highest numbers of clicks, shares, and retweets.

Between the efforts of the Russian intelligence officers and those of the independent private-sector trolls, there was a significant amount of hacking, posing, disruption, and mistrust injected into Webworld in the year preceding the 2016 presidential election. These dynamics further divided a U.S. citizenry already polarized, and undermined confidence in our electoral system, our sense of mutual fairness, and in one another.

Similar to the subversion and attacks carried out by Russia, other nations have been victimized by online treachery. Prior to Brazil's presidential election in the fall of 2018, the contents on YouTube and the smartphone messaging app, "WhatsApp," were used to sow untruths and rumors in the Brazilian citizenry. Because of its low cost in Brazil, 120 million people there use the app, and it became a tool of trolls and those who wanted to skew the election unfairly. Because messages on WhatsApp are encrypted, it was easy for provocateurs to send lies and divisive content across the service, and it was nearly impossible to counter them.

The same thing has happened in Myanmar, Sri Lanka, Kenya, Sudan, India, Malaysia, and other countries. Social media is relatively new to those countries, and people there—perhaps even more than in the U.S.—are susceptible to its never-seen-before capabilities to feed mayhem. In those countries, Facebook and WhatsApp have been used extensively to spread false news, slander, hoaxes, and rumors. The purpose behind all of that distortion is to sow prejudice and hate and separate the population into warring groups. There has been serious violence—especially in Myanmar—as a direct result of the goading content on social media.

Authoritarian states employ the capabilities of the internet in still other ways. The government of China controls its own version of the internet, and decides what its citizens can and cannot see. Censorship is widespread and internet constraints are complemented throughout society by web-connected surveillance cameras everywhere, indoors and outside. And Venezuela, Iran, Russia, Egypt, and many other countries use the web to both monitor their citizens and to ply them with propaganda.

Another more subtle dynamic of Webworld that operates in authoritarian countries (and that also operates in democracies) is its capability to slowly, steadily—almost imperceptibly—entertain and seduce the citizenry. If Webworld can substantially occupy the time and energy and attention of a nation's people, it makes less necessary an authoritarian government's overt measures at control or repression. If a citizen who lives in China, Russia, Vietnam, India, Hungary, or many other imperfect nations can look at online porn, comedians, games, entertaining YouTube (or similar platform) videos, and other pleasurable content, and spend hours submerged in one way or another in Webworld, then he is distracted from a focus on his real-world life and conditions.

Additionally, especially in China, which is communist, the subtle Webworld embrace and promotion of a capitalistic and consumerist acquisitiveness also helps to distract many citizens from chafing under some restrictions on freedom and conditions that an American would find excessive. China's economy and material standards of living are growing, and those improvements naturally temper the negative impact of some of the "big brother" aspects of Chinese society. The internet, filled with glitter, entertainment, and 24/7 advertisements for products to desire, can turn the heads and minds of citizens in a communist country just as well as they can in a free America.

* * * *

But let's get back to other damaging aspects of Webworld operating in the United States. Among young children, teenagers, and college students, there is often (maybe usually) an unhealthy level of attention and concern paid to and for the internet and social media. Starting at a very early age— anywhere from age 4 to 10—more and more children are getting their own smartphones or tablets and living large pieces of their lives and experiences on or through the connected device. The phone or tablet is a medium through which their lives and experiences are filtered and mediated.

In steady, gradual, and increasing fashion, young people are becoming keen to use their web-connected devices for as much as possible, and for as long as possible. No child or teen is ever unhappy to use his device, or be "on" his device; he is often unhappy to have to put it down, for any reason. With tablet or phone in hand, children and teens are never bored and never have to—or care to—experience a quiet or reflective or truly solitary moment; they are constantly in touch with others online and constantly watching videos. Between the messages, photos, and videos sent by friends, and the endless string of videos recommended by the web platforms, young people are digitally stimulated from the moment they awake until the moment they fall asleep.

Younger children increasingly use their devices for learning, for playing games, and for entertainment or passing time (parents of the youngest children often use the devices essentially as babysitters).

By the time children are in middle school, the smartphone and social media are starting to capture them in insidious and destructive ways. They start to have a presence and an identity and a "profile" on the various social media platforms. They develop a self-consciousness about how they "look" on social media. They actively and deliberately "curate" their posts, photos, selfies, comments, and image online. In Webworld, they want to be quick, clever, cool, ironic, attractive, popular, and hip to everything else online. They also want to be liked, friended, followed, shared, retweeted, smiled at, linked to, and more.

Children, teens, and college kids have always wanted to be popular and cool. Before the existence of the internet, they found ample ways to pursue those goals. They also had plenty of ways to be mean or bullying, if they wanted to be. The differences the internet makes are ones of degree, power, intensity, time-on-task, audience size, and oftentimes a new focus on commercialization and celebrity. And those differences make the tools and consequences of the internet absolutely unprecedented.

First, the near-universal embrace of smartphones and social media make it nearly impossible for a young person (as opposed to an old-age adult) to not participate in the online world. It would be difficult for a young person to not have something—Facebook, Instagram, Snapchat, Twitter, TikTok, WhatsApp, or other—with which to communicate with his peers. And, once in Webworld, it is exceedingly difficult for a young person to remain aloof from its pressures and dynamics.

Second, Webworld is seductive and addictive. The more you use it, the more its algorithms feed you what you like, and the more you feel loved, appreciated, and affirmed. There are millions of apps to select from, and some will seem just tailored to you and your life. If you are a teen, and the dynamics of Webworld are working out well for you (i.e., you are popular and not bullied), you will find that your online silo can be orderly, predictable, familiar and unchallenging, comforting, and safe. You may prefer it to the "real" world.

Some high school and college students, in fact, become so enamored by and integrated into the online world that they seek to become "influencers" within it. Whether it be by creating and building a popular blog, managing a widely read, personal Twitter profile, or becoming a spokesperson and sponsor for commercial products, many young people seek mini-celebrity status or financial gain by using the tools of social media.

Paid influencers, for example, agree to post comments, shoot videos, and take selfies—all of which will mention or promote various consumer goods—a certain number of times per month. The influencers sign a contract with a company (that sells, say, lingerie or hair products) which will specify the amount and type of online promotion required, and will set the terms of payment to the young influencer. The influencer, or "brand ambassador," as corporations like to call them, will then use Instagram, Snapchat, Twitter, Facebook, and other messaging platforms to literally model and showcase the product they are being paid to use, endorse, and promote. On some college campuses, their contract may even require the participating student to set up tables at or near university events so that they may actually hawk their goods directly to fellow students.

The large role of social media in the lives of children, teens, and college-age young people, combined with Webworld's inundation by and deliberate partnership with commercialization, has the effect on young people of stamping the commercial world with an imprimatur of respectability, harmlessness, desirability, and hipness. Again, what's new about this today (post internet) is the degree and emphasis. The interwovenness of social media and commercialization changes the values and perspectives of young people, manipulates them, and makes it much harder for them to develop a healthily skeptical and wise critique of—and balanced posture toward—commercialization, advertising, consumption, materialism, and even the larger design of our market system. Participating so actively in the display and selling of products changes the values of young people. Slowly, undramatically, and over time, those values get degraded. It is a corruption of their minds at an age when they should be allowed and encouraged to think clearly and critically about all parts of their world.

"Corruption of their minds" may seem a strong description of the consequences that they experience as a result of web dynamics, but it really is an apt description. Young people are being encouraged to think of themselves literally as "brands." Not just the products they pose with, but they themselves. Part of the point of all that curating of their images and profiles online is to develop an identity and a persona that is marketable. To whom they should be marketable can vary. It may be to friends, Webworld strangers and followers, colleges, companies and corporations, employers, the gig economy, or some as-yet-unknown entity or opportunity in the future.

Part of curating an image online is often the pursuit of celebrity, or at least getting noticed. Webworld, with its over-the-top emphasis on titillation, stimulation, drama, conflict, hype, and buzz, is tailor-made for Hollywood, celebrities, glamour, excesses of all types, and competition for fame (some people, even those who are already famous or popular, are so desperate for celebrity status that they "purchase" fake fans from online companies that then attach thousands of phony followers to the wannabe-famous or already-famous person's social media account). And lots of Webworld's dynamics emphasize the visual and the superficial. Young people see and admire all this and—again, slowly, undramatically, and sometimes unconsciously—are pursuing celebrity for themselves, and for its own sake. In Webworld, everyone is encouraged to be a star, and in Webworld everyone is rewarded and affirmed for being a star.

It should be noted that, while all young people are affected by internet dynamics, it is girls and young women who are most vulnerable to certain aspects of social media. Girls are more likely than boys to seek an attention and a celebrity that is based on beauty and physical appearance. Because of remaining and longstanding biases and double standards in our culture, girls and young women are far likelier than boys and young men to curate an online profile that showcases their hairstyle, body shape, physical attributes, clothes, jewelry, and sexuality. Girls constantly monitor their appearance, and take nonstop, great care in maintaining only the "hottest" pictures of themselves online.

The content that predominates on the internet helps to shape teen attitudes and anxieties. Webworld is saturated with pornography, advertising, commercial values, and image-consciousness and image-worship. Because young people spend so much time online, all of those features steadily and slowly condition them—boys and girls alike—to absorb the perspectives and values behind those realities. And girls and young women respond too often by seeing their worth as dependent upon their physical beauty. Again, this dynamic is not new in the culture, but it works with unprecedented power, ubiquity, and effectiveness in the Webworld age.

The prevalence of pornography online leads to other consequences today, and ones not limited only to youth. The sheer amount and easy availability of online porn dwarfs what was present in pre-internet times; today there are literally hundreds of millions of images and videos of soft- and hard-core porn cached in Webworld, including videos of sexual abuse and torture of children. Some of it is encrypted, or on the dark web, or behind ultra-long passwords. People—overwhelmingly men—who grew up with the internet are watching far more porn, and spending far more time looking at it, than did people before the advent of Webworld. As such, it is one more of the multitude of significant distracting options available on the web. There are many indications that—for many men—watching porn has the negative effects of changing their expectations about feminine beauty and about what healthy sex is, and reducing their desire for intimacy. Among significant numbers of couples, online porn is responsible for destroying trust, intimacy, sex, and the relationships and marriages themselves. Furthermore, many regular porn viewers who are young, and who also use social media heavily, are becoming less competent at the once-conventional skills of talking, socializing, dating, and developing healthy romantic friendships which could become romantic relationships.

* * * *

Another offering on the web—one that engages and afflicts males more than females—is all of the gaming available online. There are all sorts of games, playable 24/7, and built to suck you in and make you never want to stop playing. They range widely in type, with something for everyone, of every age. There are realistic, fantastic, violent, peaceful, competitive, educational, narrative, nonsensical, simple, and complicated games. Usually, they are well-designed, with impressive graphics or three-dimensionality, and seductive, fun, and super addictive. They are often built with clever reward and incentive systems to keep the players interested, motivated, and playing. Depending upon the game, a player can play alone, as a group, with friends, or with strangers at remote locations. Many games are competitions or violent, and involve surviving deadly virtual threats. Being the last-man-standing at the end of a game is a common theme in the design and point of many games.

Hundreds of millions—maybe billions—of males play the games. Many boys and young men—especially ages 14 to 21 or so—get seriously compulsive about playing online games, to the point where they neglect much else in their lives. They become isolated from normal life. They stop going outside. Some get totally addicted.

There are now even professional gamers, guys who become proficient playing recreationally, and then decide to make a career out of it. There are actual internet platforms dedicated to the live streaming of games being played by the professionals, and there is a whole advertising and sponsorship infrastructure that has been developed for the gamer world. As with all the other hype and spectacle online, gaming has developed its own stars and its followers. The best gamers become known to millions of fans who watch them play. The gamers talk entertainingly while they compete and they develop online personalities as they comment about their play and other random things. The audience can also talk in real time with the gamers. The professionals, like the influencers I described earlier, sell their sponsors' products; the sponsors and the internet platforms pay them appearance fees for each live-streamed game.

Gaming is a bizarre and unhealthy way to make a living. A professional gamer must sit in a chair nonstop for 10 to 16 hours a day, play the games attentively, sell products, entertain the audience with chatter, and stay at it seven days a week. The fans demand it; they are young, need constant stimuli, and will easily abandon a gamer who's not online enough. And for every successful professional (there are relatively few), there are hundreds of thousands of young men who are working—by playing the games themselves—to take his place. Yes, the gaming pros sometimes make a good living, but it's a job in the gig economy—temporary, insecure, without benefits, and ultimately unsustainable for a number of reasons. And like so much on the web, its lifeblood is advertising, and selling dubious products—like sugar-and-caffeine energy drinks—to an increasingly impressionable and mostly young audience.

The grip that Webworld has on the young is both vaguely bewildering and unknown to many adults. In addition to the unorthodoxy of watching other people just play video games, some Webworld participants have reached such a point of passivity that they will happily watch other people—people who are not accomplished or exceptional in any way—just simply live, as long as the experience is beamed out over the internet and onto their screens.

Just as professional gamers live-stream for fame and money, the formula for those who become "successful" at streaming their own lives requires the same commitment to sponsor and hawk products, interact with the audience, be available online nearly every waking moment, and give their personality some quirk, gimmick, or promise of entertainment-by-antic.

If live game-streaming is bizarre, just plain live-streaming is really strange. A live streamer is really making something out of nothing. A live-streamer takes the real world as a stage, and just acts and mugs and riffs on it. He usually pretends an ironic posture. But a live-streamer is just an erstwhile internet troll who decides to be a real-world troll. His fans—the audience—are equally vacuous and desperate, or they wouldn't be spending hours watching somebody (a nobody) try to invent reasons for watching him. Although a sense of community sometimes builds around a popular streamer, it is a community with the character and weaknesses of a cult. Its members are often loners, losers, angry, socially inept, nihilistic, or reactionary. Both the streamer and his fans are destined to disband eventually, and usually neither will have grown from the experience. Ultimately, the live-streamer is a con man, and like so much in Webworld, has preyed on internet users (and human nature) who lack the strength or judgement to seek better alternative activities.

* * * *

In this chapter on Webworld, I have outlined just some of the aspects of the internet and the online world that are negative and destructive all by themselves (such as content that is deliberately false), or that result in related, destructive consequences (such as addiction to gaming).

It is easy to spot and understand the blatant dark side of Webworld. It is often much harder to see and comprehend the slower, subtler damage that it is doing to people, institutions, and society. Additionally, for a lot of reasons, there is substantial resistance—from a lot of people—to critiquing Webworld and finding it destructive, perhaps more destructive overall than constructive.

It is the sum of all the parts of Webworld, and all the effects and consequences of those parts, that make it into a force. That force is changing longstanding, human habits of mind. Slowly, incrementally, unevenly, sometimes noticeably, sometimes unseen, but always for the worse overall, Webworld is changing our capacities for and postures toward patience, tolerance, cooperation, complexity, coherence, and the environment. It is changing, by degrees, our abilities for and approaches to seeing, learning, thinking, analyzing, synthesizing, understanding, writing, and speaking.

It is changing our attitudes about time, boredom, meaning, and truth. It is changing the ways we relate to each other. Really, it is no exaggeration to say that Webworld is changing nearly everything.

It is important to note that Webworld doesn't affect everyone equally, or change each of us to the same degree. Although I believe that it does affect the habits of mind of each one of us—almost no one can avoid it—certainly there is a wide variety in the individual human response to it. At one extreme, some individuals just disappear into Webworld in one way or another, while others hold it away at a great distance. Most of us fall somewhere in the middle. Webworld has been a net positive force for some individuals, and a destructive force for others. But overall, when the collective consequences of Webworld are tallied up, I believe their destructive effects outweigh—and are continuing to outweigh—the considerable good that Webworld has done.

In this book, as I describe the many forces affecting society today, and identify the degree to which each is unprecedentedly consequential and new, it is Webworld above all others that is shockingly powerful, and of course completely, 100 percent, new. Effectively, no part of Webworld and its dynamics existed just 25 years ago. And solidifying it as the force above all forces, its frameworks, operation, economies, and reach extend over and dominate all of the other forces and features and possibilities of society.

Webworld is reducing our attention span, changing our definition of and tolerance for "boredom," and altering our abilities to "wait" or to be alone with only our thoughts. With laptops, tablets, and smartphones constantly at hand, we have been conditioned to desire constant stimulation. We cannot "wait" anywhere without scrolling for information, texting, playing an online game, or listening to music that we select. At any interregnum, we must be digitally entertained. Hand in hand with that, the nature of so much online content—short, sensational, trending—and the dynamics of the way it is presented, erodes our attention span. Instant messaging, tweeting, commenting, and texting all lead to short, punchy communications and content, and we get accustomed to that. Even within the website of a traditional newspaper, the reader is constantly offered links, moving graphics, video segments, advertising, sponsored content, reader comments, opportunities to comment, and other distractions.

In related changes, our capacities for patience, for accepting complexity and uncertainty, and for cooperation and empathy are being reduced.

We are becoming less sophisticated in many ways. Over time, if we use the internet a lot, most of us inevitably get guided into mental silos of information that challenge us insufficiently. The algorithms that largely determine what is placed in front of us on our computer screens—and that are largely based on our clicking history—too often show us information that we will probably enjoy. And mostly that means material that in some way or another reflects us and who we are. Again, we are affirmed, confirmed, reinforced, and made more confident of our knowledge as a result of that process. Over years online therefore, we see less complexity, fewer viewpoints different than our own, and content steadily less challenging to our thinking and pondering faculties. By degrees, we lose the resilience in our abilities to entertain doubt, uncertainty, and complex, multifaceted realities, or realities that contain a blend of factors that are alien to our culture or experience. Without sufficient exposure to the wide range of thoughtful and healthy opinions and thinking on many subjects, we develop the idea that our perspectives—and even the mini-culture that each of us lives in and identifies with—are overwhelmingly correct. Living in these mental silos, our ability to converse and cooperate with others outside of our circles diminishes and withers. As the dynamic continues for years, as it already has for most people, even our capacity to feel empathy for those outside of our silos diminishes. (And, of course, from inside Webworld and our respective silos, it is difficult for each of us to accurately recognize and measure the degree to which we are being affected by its dynamics.)

Related to our loss of patience, our shorter attention spans, and the constant stimulation provided by online experiences, Webworld is reducing our quiet time and reducing both our time for reflection and our ability to reflect. For most people, screens are everywhere in their lives and daily travels. Screens are in our hands, on our desks, in our cars, and in front of us both at work and during recreation. They are ubiquitous in stores, stadiums, coffee shops, restaurants, airports, and every other conceivable location. We cannot tear our eyes away from them. Now, we cannot even pump a tankful of gasoline without enduring (or enjoying) a screenful of sound and motion displayed on the gas pump. With less quiet time in our lives, and less time spent thinking things over—things that are not work-related—we are losing the capacity and affinity for deep and critical reflection and introspection.

Additionally, with its emphasis on drama and the sensational—and its 24/7 emphasis on whatever is new and happening—Webworld tends to promote fragmentation, not integration. Obviously, the population is being sliced into silos, interest groups, listserves, political groups, and market segments. But more subtlely, Webworld fragments knowledge itself into pieces. It tends not to promote the integration of different subjects, or promote the big or long or deep view of things. It certainly doesn't encourage people to connect the dots about things. I'd go so far as to say that Webworld—for its success—needs people to be fragmented, dis-integrated, myopic, unwise, impressionable, and silly.

Webworld is a collection of fragments. Its sheer number of parts and pieces is overwhelming. It fragments our attention. Its on-screen distractions constantly attempt to lure us to other sites or links or content. Webworld's dynamics never rest, and it is never content to let us read just one article—uninterrupted and unsolicited—from start to finish. So much of it—blogs, comment sections, short videos, texts, tweets, memes, social messaging—consists of tiny little pieces of stimuli devoid of context that even its physical design and presentation are fragmented. As a vessel and a tool, the internet promotes the idea that meaningful learning, thinking, viewing, opinion-forming, and speaking can occur in 280-character fragments, 15-second videos, disappearing photos and messages, or other brief-but-accelerated interactions. Webworld is training people to be satisfied with fast and fragmented and superficial interactions.

The fragmentation of everything online, the dangling of lure-like links, the ever-changing screen content, and the constant and never-ending updates also act to eliminate any possibility of cognitive closure in the user's mind. Unlike reading and finishing a book, or completing some offline creative task or project, surfing the web is a never-ending activity; it cannot be completed. So it often feeds a nervous energy, anxiety, and vague distraction. The screen is always beckoning, as steady and present as electricity. It is insistent and infinite. We don't control it; we know it is "on" even when we are not looking at it. Because of that quality, the web further undermines composure, contentment, and peace-of-mind.

The dynamics of Webworld also implicitly promote the idea that we can and should all have opinions—or reactions—about everything. The ever-present comment sections, and like, share, smile, and emoji options distributed everywhere online, encourage us to react instantly, and decide hastily, about something we have just read or seen. There is an erosion of the idea that we may need to ruminate about something, or gather more information, before we react to it or feel competent to express an opinion about it. Webworld is quite happy with us if we jump to conclusions, dispense with nuance, see things in black and white, and generally opine quickly and sharply.

Slowly, steadily, by degrees, Webworld is changing our values. Because of the internet, we are exposed to more advertising than have been any people in any previous era. Advertising is constantly in front of us and around us—visually and auditorially—and its relentless presence impacts us. We are more materialistic today than we would be without Webworld. We purchase more stuff today than we would without the existence of Webworld. The internet and all its platforms and dynamics slowly turn our heads. The ease of online shopping, browsing, and buying, combined with many social media circles that encourage a sort of competitive image and life-style curation among users, catches-up many of us into an unhealthy consumerism. Again, the spending impulse is not new in modern American society, but the degree of consumption, the standards of living that we feel we need, and Webworld itself are all new.

The web's omnipresent advertising, complemented by social media's promotion of glitz and the celebrity life, works seamlessly with television, movies, and the fashion world to influence our culture and shape our values and desires and actual behavior. Without realizing it, we are losing the ability—or maybe the habit—to act or behave consistently in ways that reflect what is important, or wise. We are actually confused. Thus, for example, some individuals, taken in by the norms of our present-day culture, will purchase a large, hyper-sybaritic, $50,000 SUV when they have no rational need for such a vehicle. They may be single, have no children, and never transport anything large. They may even have to take out a 72-month loan to afford such a pricey vehicle. By any objective standards, and for many reasons, the purchase is stupid and destructive. The content of Webworld is not solely responsible for warping the buyer's thinking, but it helps to facilitate a materialistic culture that views his behavior as perfectly sane and perfectly normal.

Furthermore, we are influenced by Webworld into believing that efficiency and convenience trump nearly all other values and considerations. In the chapter on technology, I mentioned the threat to brick-and-mortar stores that comes with our increasing shift to purchasing items online. We are all aware that every book, clothing item, piece of furniture, or gift that we buy online represents one more sales loss to some physical store. And because we are being conditioned to expect and want nearly immediate possession of every item we purchase online, we are demanding quicker and quicker delivery of all merchandise directly to (or near) our doorstep. So delivery trucks are everywhere 24/7, the wasteful production of literally billions of new boxes and huge quantities of packaging materials is exploding (apartment building lobbies are filled with Amazon cartons and other delivery-service boxes every day), and we are killing our Main Street retail businesses. But in the face of this ongoing transformation in the physical environment (big-box stores 25 years ago started this threat), and this waste of resources, we simply cannot stop ourselves. We have elevated "convenience"—and a simple-minded notion of convenience, at that—above all other considerations.

It may be that the day will come when the physical environment and its quality and organization—and the experience of seeing it and moving through it—just doesn't mean that much to us anymore. This may seem an impossible development to people today who are 45 or 50 or older. But younger people, who grew up with computers and digital media, and whose epistemology is quite different from older generations, might not be alarmed with the disappearance of physical stores, public squares and public places, the substitution of a wide range of online experiences for "real" ones, and the rise of artificial intelligence and augmented and virtual reality to replace the non-Webworld life. Already, automobile navigation systems, helpful though they can be, are erasing the cognitive notions of landmarks, pathways, mental maps, and where places are in relationship to other places. And online worlds and virtual reality experiences promise to have more dazzle, excitement, personalization capability, coherence, and attractiveness generally as compared to the increasingly crowded, semi-chaotic, and financially challenged public-space sphere. These are certainly the directions that we are sliding in, with varying degrees of awareness, and little discussion.

In any discussion and assessment of technology and Webworld and their consequences, as I mentioned earlier, one of the big problems is the existence of faultlines through the population. People younger than, say, 30, use and experience Webworld—and are informed about its myriad facets—in vastly different ways and magnitudes than people aged, say, 50 or 60 or 70. Really, digital technology has progressed so far so fast—and continues to do so—that every decade has impacted the age groups of our population differently. A 20-year-old today has had vastly different exposure to the internet world—and for literally his entire life—than a 45-year-old or a 65-year-old. The epistemology of their lives—what has affected and shaped their attitudes and very conceptions and very being— is radically different. So their expectations of living in relationship to Web-world, and what they may find acceptable or desirable or not, are also radically different. It is quite possible that the worst effects of Webworld on the human mind—the ones that I have just outlined—will simply not be discernible whatsoever to young people whose earliest memories as infants and babies contain digital screens and devices.

Without difficulty, most of us—of all ages—can see how computers, the internet, robotization, and automation play large and integral and sometimes indispensible roles in the commercial and financial worlds. Webworld is woven into and straddles all segments of capitalism and the economy. We know it manipulates us, using our data. But in analyzing the social and cognitive consequences of Webworld, and the extent to which those forces are changing, shaping, and molding individuals (and thus society), many of us have, and will continue to have, difficulty.

* * * *

In this chapter on Webworld, I have focused exclusively on the web's negative effects. As we have seen, Webworld is a force that has had a myriad of bad consequences ranging from quite specific and observable to rather amorphous and more subtle. And the effects play out with varying degrees of severity among a population as large and diverse as 330 million Americans.

There are two additional closely linked outcomes that the Webworld juggernaut—with assistance from other factors and forces—is producing, and they may be the most significant consequences of all. Webworld is in the process of undermining both democracy and society itself.

For all the reasons, and in all the ways, that Webworld is affecting individuals—our thinking, values, behavior, priorities, skills—we are becoming less able to conduct our politics and minister to our democracy. Closely related, we are also finding it tougher to maintain an orderly, coherent, resilient, and fair society.

As the internet—shrill and mercenary—continues to make us myopic and reactionary, it is combining with the other forces I describe in this book to damage our capacities to act on behalf of everyone and on behalf of democracy. Many of our citizens, already scared and anxious over health, job, financial, or environmental issues, and then revved up to fractious levels by targeted online content, are behaving in juvenile and angry ways that are damaging to society. And many wealthier citizens, who may not have those same health, job, or financial worries, are nonetheless choosing—aided by their Webworld silos—to react in ways that are focused primarily on preserving their wealth and privileged place in society, perhaps at the expense of helping to create a fairer economy (and society) and a stronger democracy.

Webworld is a force that is balkanizing our politics, and thus our democracy and society. As we get sorted and divided by websites, blogs, podcasts, videos, and social media—all complemented and reinforced by cable TV and talk radio—we are losing most of the once-reliable touchstones that helped to tie our citizens, democracy, and society together. Webworld and its dynamics are eroding our common truths, experiences, histories, principles, values, perspectives, and even the importance of physical place. Webworld and its echoing media partners are destroying our definition of patriotism, the legitimacy of fellow citizens with whom we disagree, and our understandings of what democracies and societies require in order to thrive and survive.

Over time, and not always obviously, Webworld is making us stupid, self-centered, short-sighted, and eminently capable of acting against our own and our nation's best interests.

Egged on by Webworld's dynamics, we build our silliness, distraction, anger, resentment, paranoia, anxiety, opinions, or certainty until many of us are nearly too dysfunctional to participate in building democracy or building society. The worst of us rant about the politics of our fellow citizens, subscribe to intolerance and scapegoating, and are cognitively shut down to learning anything new or different than we already believe.

Others among us—more polished in manner and less openly retrograde—are just as convinced that others unlike ourselves have nothing to offer and are simply hopelessly ignorant. Politics—and thus democracy and society—become nearly impossible among a citizenry so divided and alienated. And every day, every week, every month, the operation of Webworld relentlessly feeds those divisions.

As I have described in the chapters on capitalism and technology, and as I will describe in the following chapters on politics and human nature, we are living at a time when the sharpness and synergy of many forces—including Webworld—are blending together with an unprecedented power.

The power of these forces and their threat to us cannot be understood unless one looks at them all together. Webworld possesses the power to divide us and destroy our democracy precisely because of the complementary set of conditions that are being established simultaneously by the other forces. It is a perfect storm of forces, and Webworld just exploits, maintains, and enlarges the storm.

CHAPTER 4

POLITICS

Among all the major forces challenging us today, and impacting us, is politics. It is a complex force—always changing and capable of anything or nothing—made more complex because we citizens are indispensably and by deliberate design woven into its operation and dynamics. Humans, of course, are part of every force described in this book, but in politics—more so than in, say, capitalism or technology or education—the bases for action and the directions our society takes are products almost exclusively of human drama. The fuels behind politics are emotion, ideals, fear, patriotism, and a host of other relatively intangible motivations and factors.

With capitalism, for example, we may be trying to produce a better automobile, or an efficient solar panel, or simply trying to get rich. With technology, for example, we may be trying to automate an assembly line. With education, we may be trying to teach a student what he needs to learn to become a doctor. There are, of course, other larger goals—and human drama—associated with each of those examples, but still there is a smaller, immediate, partly ideology-free purpose fueling those endeavors. That's not to say those forces can't contain a political element. They do. As we saw in the chapters on technology and Webworld, none of those forces have neat boundary lines; with the Silicon Valley technologists, for example, we know that their useful digital inventions stem partly from a desire to bring about their vision of a nearly utopian society.

But with politics, we have a large, explicit multiplicity of realities and goals—big and small—that we charge it with addressing. Not only do we assign it the responsibility of organizing and regulating the nation, democracy, society, capitalism, technology, education, and everything else (including every force described in this book), we also define it as the vehicle by which we'll work out our competing visions and aspirations for justice, freedom, equality, security, prosperity, and the good society.

Therefore, the force of politics arches over everything, and in a democracy like the United States, its health and stability are critical. There are other components of society—such as religion, family, and schools—that do offer guidance as we strive to craft a better nation and world, but it is with the tools of politics that we have agreed to sort out our differences, policies, and visions, both locally and nationally.

Politics has always been a major force in the U.S. Since the country's birth out of a revolution in 1776, Americans have always been conscious of the power of our representative politics to help define and guide this 243-year-old experiment. Over all those years, the health of our democracy, the performance of our politics, and the level of citizen participation in both have waxed and waned. There have been good periods, and absolutely terrible ones. The Civil War, the Robber Baron era, and the Depression years certainly stand out as particularly awful ones.

Today, we are in a terrible period of politics, perhaps as bad and threatening as any period in American history. The current state of our politics has been a long time building. Where things stand today in 2019 have taken 45 years or so to develop.

The American political system today has been badly distorted. Its operation, institutions, and representative quality and capacities have been damaged. Most ordinary citizens—of all political persuasions—see these damages and are dismayed and angry about them. Confidence in our government and its politicians—especially at the federal level—is very low.

Perhaps the biggest problem with the federal government today is its unresponsiveness to—and underrepresentation of—the ordinary citizen and his interests. Instead, over the past 45 years, a government has developed that is increasingly responsive to big business, big finance, and big corporations in general. With enormous amounts of money at their disposal with which to donate to Senators and congressmen, corporations and industry trade groups are able to wield considerable influence on the positions, actions, and votes of politicians. Congress is incredibly responsive to the corporate agenda, often to the detriment of the interests of ordinary citizens.

The magnitude of money in politics today is huge and unprecedented. Corporations, trade groups, and wealthy individuals donate hundreds of millions of dollars during each election cycle—totaling billions of dollars—in an effective attempt to influence the direction of American politics. The amount of money changing hands—and its corrupting role—are out of control. Bigger amounts than ever, and more unaccountable than ever.

Corporations and wealthy private citizens have an open field when it comes to finding ways to use their money to support and influence politicians. They aren't restricted to simply donating directly to politicians. There are many avenues available to funnel funds to a candidate or organizations supporting him. There are PACs (political action committees), super-PACs, 501(c)(3)s, 501(c)(4)s, 527s, state and national party committees, and other financial vehicles. Some of these options offer complete anonymity to the donor, and others effectively have no upper limits on the amount of money that may be donated.

All of these pathways for political donations do have some rules that the organizations and their operatives must follow. But the rules are largely a sham and are deliberately abused, skirted, and taken advantage of. And rules enforcement is weak, inconsistent, and mostly ineffective. For example, certain types of political committees—which are actually working on behalf of a candidate or a cause—can claim to be primarily "educational" organizations or non-profit "social welfare" groups, and can then avoid many campaign finance restrictions.

Many organizations, which may have a classification that requires them to be organizationally "independent" of any particular politician or candidate, can collect donations in unlimited amounts and effectively work in parallel with a candidate or a campaign. They are "independent" in structure and name only, and everybody knows it. Everybody knows which committees are working on behalf of which candidates. Donations are made accordingly.

The explosion of funds supporting increasingly large numbers of partisan committees and organizations has contributed to a more toxic political climate than has existed previously. During campaigns, huge sums of money are fueling non-stop political advertising, and because the identities of many of those funders are hidden behind the rules that govern committees, there is often a level of viciousness and deceitful attacks in the ads that is unprecedented. Lies and slander have always existed in political advertising, but today their presence and stubbornness are magnitudes greater than in the past.

And, of course, the internet repeats and magnifies everything that occurs in the "real" world and compounds the damage. As I outlined in the chapter on Webworld, political extremism and fake news and divisive ads proliferate online. So political donors and organizations have in the internet yet another explosive, potent vehicle for supporting their candidates, attacking the opposition candidates, and influencing both politicians and the electorate.

In addition to donating millions of dollars a year to the never-dissolved campaign coffers of Senators and congressmen, corporations and industry associations maintain legions of fulltime, well-paid, in-house and contracted lobbyists. These lobbyists have extraordinary access to the offices of congressmen, they possess large degrees of influence with both the politicians and their staff, and they often write and revise drafts of actual legislation that become law. Lobbyists for the big banks, for example, often write the rules and regulations that banks have to abide by; and lobbyists for the pharmaceutical industry often author the legislation that drug companies have to comply with. Yes, it's a racket.

So corrupt is the relationship between politicians and corporations and lobbyists that many Senators and congressmen become lobbyists upon retiring from, or being defeated in, politics. They may go to work directly for a corporation, or be hired by a professional lobbying firm that represents many corporate clients. Congressional staffers are also courted by corporations and lobbyists seeking favorable legislation, and so they too are provided with many job offers when they leave government. The reality of the dynamics of this "revolving door" of politicians and lobbyists is well-known on Capitol Hill, and it causes politicians to be circumspect about angering their potential employers. The entire setup is very cozy and reciprocal. During their time in office, congressmen and their staff will respond solicitously toward corporate agendas; in return they will receive corporate donations. Ultimately, many Senators and congressmen and staffers will take a job with either a favored corporation or a professional lobbying firm that represents some of the companies that they have helped. The old pols get a lucrative job, and the corporations—that have already received years of legislative victories—continue to have an inside track in the halls of Congress.

On both the Republican and Democratic sides, wealthy interest groups, individuals, and corporations also employ their money to pursue specific political agendas by supporting a wide range of think tanks and universities that are sympathetic to their viewpoints—and that want their money. There are entire think tanks, for example, devoted to promoting libertarianism or "free-market" theory. These organizations—funded by same-thinking benefactors—routinely produce "research" and white papers that buttress whatever ideology they believe in. And many universities, for the right price, will set up department programs or new professors to study and teach some cherry-picked, biased, academic approach or ideology.

Not all donations, and not all lobbyists, come from corporations and business interests. There are union, environmental, teachers, consumer, and general public interest groups in Washington, D.C. that maintain lobbyists and lobbying efforts on behalf of agendas that are not corporate at all. But taken as a whole, the number of lobbyists, their power, resources, intensity of effort, effectiveness, and amount of money mobilized on behalf of Big Business (in all its facets) is far, far greater than their counterparts on the general "public interest" side (not that business has no public interest component; it does).

An extra word needs to be said about wealthy individuals. Today, with an effectiveness and in magnitudes greater than in the past—even than during the Robber Baron era—many rich citizens can and do single-handedly exert enormous influence on our political system. As has happened frequently within the past decade or two, sole individual citizens have used their extreme wealth—totaling in the billions of dollars—to select and sustain candidates, select and sustain political ideologies, select and sustain legislative initiatives, and to otherwise hugely affect the operation and outcomes of our political system. They have also used their personal wealth to defeat candidates, ideologies, and initiatives. This is not a healthy development in our democracy. Like big corporations, many rich individuals today have weaponized their wealth—in ways that are often hidden, sneaky, selfish, and subversive—to obtain inordinate and unrepresentative power within the political system, and to act against the general public interest.

A number of factors have been involved in bringing us to the current condition of money in politics. First and foremost, over the past 40 years, there has been a slow, steady erosion of the rules and regulations governing the role of money, the place of donations, and the participation of donors in the political system. With deregulatory actions by the government, and with deregulatory decisions by the courts—including, most notably, the Supreme Court—many laws that once restricted the play of money in the political system have been either substantially weakened or removed entirely. Many limits on spending, and the transparency requirements around donors, have been lifted. And the invention of all of the spending vehicles—like 501(c)(4)s—that I have mentioned have also altered the campaign finance system in ways that give freer rein to Big Money. Today, effectively, campaign finance controls are a joke.

Another factor that makes the role of money in government unprecedentedly large today is simply the sheer magnitude of the wealth itself of corporations and private individuals. As I outlined in the chapter on capitalism, income inequality and wealth distribution within the U.S. in the past 40 years has skewed horribly. Corporations and the executive class—especially the top 1 percent of earners—today have just enormous amounts of money, and they can and do spend it to push their political agendas. Relative to the rest of society, and relative to decades past, they can buy better access, better influence, and more results for themselves.

Put all this together—the huge sums of donations, corporations, lobbyists, revolving-door jobs, wealthy individuals, the various PACs and other advocacy organizations, the lack of campaign finance regulations, and the lack of accountability and transparency—and what we have today is a thoroughly distorted political system. It works overwhelmingly on behalf of wealth and barely for the average citizen.

In the chapters on capitalism and technology, I described how developments over the past 45 years have led to the present state of affairs where too many ordinary Americans are struggling economically and living paycheck to paycheck. Too many Americans are barely making it while the top 5 or 10 percent of Americans are reaping a disproportionate share of the nation's wealth. As the forces of technology, globalization, automation, computerization, and deregulation dramatically changed the dynamics of the economy, American politics did very little to temper the damaging consequences for the ordinary citizen. The role of money in the political system is the main factor that, increasingly since 1980, has prevented our government from satisfactorily representing average Americans.

Look at who has done well since 1980 or so. The defense industries, fossil fuel industries, large banks and investment houses, the financial services sector, pharmaceutical companies, the insurance, agricultural, casino, technology, and legal sectors, and the telecommunications companies all have their agendas well looked after.

Those industries spread a lot of money around—with lobbying, donations, and jobs—and consequently they are treated well by the political system. They get the policies, subsidies, tax rates, trade frameworks, regulations (or deregulations), and the shape of capitalism they want.

The average worker, without the everyday access to congressmen that money buys, and without the megaphone that money buys, is poorly represented.

Another factor that is reducing the amount and fairness of representation that ordinary citizens are receiving across the U.S. is the practice of gerrymandering. It's a process that occurs when either party manipulates the shape and size of a congressional district—thereby altering the mix of voters in that and adjoining districts—in order to gain some advantage in the election of our congressional representatives.

Each state in the union is divided into congressional districts—there are 435 in total—and each district has roughly the same number of residents—about 711,000 today. Obviously, states with larger overall populations have more congressional seats, and therefore more representatives in Congress. Seven states—Alaska, Montana, Wyoming, North Dakota, South Dakota, Vermont, and Delaware—have such small overall populations that they each qualify for only one representative (thus with no possibility of gerrymandering).

There are various ways to gerrymander a district. The majority power in the state may want to pack all of its opposition into one or two districts, and thus reserve all of the other districts (and their congressmen) for itself. Or conversely, it may seek to dilute the power of the opposition by spreading opposition voters across all the state's districts. In either case (and there are other variations) the district borders are drawn deliberately (usually by the party in control of the particular state's legislature) to achieve the desired political advantages and desired voting results. This gerrymandering tactic often results in districts with startlingly odd and extremely irregular outlines, not anything resembling a rough rectangle.

Gerrymandering is very damaging to democracy because it gives disproportionate advantage to the party in control of it. Gerrymandered districts often produce election results and a state congressional delegation that do not fairly and accurately reflect the political opinions of the state. Additionally, gerrymandering produces skewed districts that are so packed with one party that the representative from that district will never be at risk of losing an election.

Gerrymandering is a blatant and disgraceful power grab. Yet it is common today across the country. Historically, both parties have engaged in it, although at the present time Republicans are far more frequently utilizing the strategy.

Republicans today are also far more guilty than Democrats in efforts at outright voter suppression. Claiming that there is significant voter fraud during elections—when there is virtually none across the country—Republicans in a number of states have passed laws that require additional or unusual measures by which a voter must prove his identification at the polls.

Republicans generally also have not been eager to restore voting rights to citizens with criminal records. And Republicans in a number of states have engaged in shady tactics to cull mostly Democratic citizens from the voter-registration rolls, and they have reduced early-voting periods in areas where Democrats are concentrated.

* * * *

The devastating consequences of money in politics today, and the lesser but still important effects of gerrymandering and voter suppression, are, of course, accompanied by many other significant developments that have occurred during the past 65 years or so, all contributing to and building the steady polarization we see today in American politics. For all of that time, the two major parties have been growing further ideologically apart from each other, and more homogenous within themselves.

During the civil rights era of the late 1950s and throughout the 1960s, the tacit deal that the Democratic Party had with its conservative—and sometimes outright racist—southern members started to fall apart. Prior to the activism led by Martin Luther King and other black leaders that began in 1955 with Rosa Parks and the Montgomery bus boycott, the Democratic Party had for decades mostly ignored the segregation and second-class-citizenship imposed on blacks in the southern states. But the transformation of the black struggle for equal rights into a wide-ranging, interstate, mass movement eventually allowed no politician or party to remain neutral. So the Democratic Party gradually began to advocate for civil rights and civil equality. With boycotts, demonstrations, sit-ins, the Freedom Rides, voter registration drives, and the 1963 March on Washington, ordinary black people—and their cry for justice—became a force to be reckoned with, and Presidents Kennedy and Johnson slowly—then powerfully—supported their cause. After Johnson pushed the Civil Rights Acts of 1964 and 1968, and the Voting Rights Act of 1965, conservative southern politicians increasingly aligned themselves with the Republican Party.

At about the same time during the late 1960s, and into the 1970s, other important issues arose which contributed to making the Republican Party more conservative and further divided both the American people and the two parties. The escalation of the Vietnam War between 1964 and 1969 (to 550,000 troops), and the student-led protests against it, reinforced the fault lines that the civil rights movement was opening in society. With a sharpness and a bitterness that was new (at least since the Depression), citizens were dividing into opposing camps—liberal or conservative, Democrat or Republican. With such momentous and consequential affairs at stake, anything resembling a moderate middle-ground tended to disappear.

Adding fuel to the fire, Richard Nixon, elected President in November 1968, used the "southern strategy" both in campaigning and in governing. The "southern strategy" was the practice of attracting conservative and bigoted Democratic voters into the Republican fold by using coded language that indicated negativity toward blacks. The language nominally disguised any intended prejudice or hostility toward blacks, but the phrases that were routinely and repeatedly used in the southern strategy came to be understood as communicating certain messages. President Nixon talked a lot about "law and order" and about "states' rights;" many citizens believed that those words were oblique ways of signaling disapproval of the advancement of blacks, and disapproval of federal anti-poverty programs, welfare programs, and affirmative action. The phrases, thematically, also came to be generally associated with disapproval of anti-war protestors, "hippies," and other "permissive" liberal groups and ideas.

Americans at that time even divided over the display of the American flag, as Republicans incessantly waved it, and claimed that they were the true patriots of the country for supporting President Nixon and the Vietnam War. Displaying the flag became so emblematic of right-wing passions and hostility toward liberals that a common bumper sticker of that period showed a miniature flag and the slogan, "America, Love It or Leave It." Another ubiquitous right-wing bumper sticker showed the flag with the accusatory statement, "These colors don't run." In response, many Democrats stopped displaying the flag altogether—whether on a holiday like Memorial Day, or in any other circumstance. From roughly 1969 to 1972, as it became clear that soon the United States would have to leave Vietnam—and leave as the "loser"—all of the issues of race, poverty, war, patriotism, and values, and even the nature of our culture itself blended into a large, nearly all-consuming, society-rending argument.

And when Nixon resigned in 1974 during the Watergate fallout, the nation was thoroughly divided and sick. A new and different kind of gulf had been opened between the political parties and within the citizenry. Some parts of this gulf never closed or healed. On many points of debate—in politics and culture—there had been no resolution, and many people on all sides of many issues were left feeling dissatisfied, cynical, bitter, betrayed, angry, or wounded.

Throughout the 1970s, as the Vietnam War faded a bit from the immediate forefront, other issues developed into prominent, heat-generating topics. Strong controversies and strong emotions erupted over abortion, women's rights, certain religious groups, and property taxes. In 1973, the Supreme Court's Roe v. Wade decision making abortion legal—with some restrictions—really precipitated the formation of a strong right-to-life movement. The "women's liberation" movement started in the late 1960s and gained strength throughout the 1970s. In response to the general and increasing "permissiveness" of American culture, many conservative religious believers on the political right reacted with a backlash of sorts. They became more politically active and injected their stridency or fundamentalisms (in some cases) into political and social debates. All of these issues strongly aroused and polarized people and were therefore often used somewhat disingenuously—mostly by politicians on the right—to keep attention off of more important economic, environmental, and geopolitical developments.

Lastly, the reflexive anti-tax fervor that today grips the Republican Party was born in the late 1970s. In California, in 1978, an anti-tax measure was passed by the citizenry using a ballot-box initiative petition. Called "Proposition 13," the measure lowered property taxes and severely limited the occasions and rates of future tax increases. Because of singular circumstances surrounding California's state finances in the 1970s, Proposition 13 stemmed from a genuine need for tax reform. But it was a flawed instrument, and ended up skewing the tax relief largely in the direction of corporate property owners and the wealthiest homeowners. Proposition 13's causes and effects were complicated, but a big (and unfortunate) part of its legacy is the idea that government spending is wasteful, taxes are always too high, and the citizens—however uninformed or misguided—know best.

Proposition 13 and other tax revolts, the growth of hot-button social issues, the various "rights" movements, and the defeat of Nixon and the Vietnam War all contributed to a growing politics of resentment and populism on the right. Traditional Republican conservatism was starting to be replaced with something rawer and less sophisticated.

In that vein, in the late 1970s, Republican congressman Newt Gingrich almost single-handedly led a transformation in the tone and behavior of congressional representatives. Perhaps unusually ambitious and ideological, even by political standards, Gingrich introduced a level of take-no-prisoners partisanship that was new and starkly cynical. His methods required Republican congressmen—with hyperbolic rhetoric—to attack their opponents, attack the institution of Congress itself, and delegitimize both.

Gingrich's scorched-earth tactics happened to coincide with the introduction to Congress of C-SPAN in 1979. C-SPAN cameras filmed gavel-to-gavel coverage of House proceedings, and Gingrich and his fellow acolytes took advantage of this free publicity to deliver regular speeches which unfairly characterized Democratic representatives as unpatriotic, anti-religious, soft on communism, and corrupt. It was a level of demagoguery that had rarely been seen (not forgetting Father Coughlin, Huey Long, and Joseph McCarthy) and its intent was malicious and manipulative. Gingrich's goal was to make Congress itself appear inept and corrupt so that voters would throw the incumbents (mostly Democrats) out.

The legacy of Gingrich's time in Congress (1979–1999) was a heightened partisanship that pushed the two parties apart and raised the levels of hypocrisy, ideological stubbornness, false accusations, and anger that always threaten to engulf politics. After Gingrich, in the 2000s, for a variety of reasons, Congress continued to founder.

Concurrent with much of Gingrich's tenure was the presidency of Ronald Reagan. Although milder in his conservatism when compared with today's Republican Party, the one immoderate note—and a very significant one—in his political rhetoric was a disdain for government. Taking office in January 1981, he spent eight years roundly attacking the very idea of government, saying that government was the problem, not the solution. Reagan's attack on government, and the people who depend on it, was not nuanced or complex; it did not attempt to point out where government could be improved and where it worked well. It reflected a simple-minded and inaccurate view of the public sector and it did a lot of damage to the country. It further divided the citizenry. It eroded public support generally for taxes. It eroded support for the idea that we are a society deliberately vouchsafing something called the common good, and not just a happenstance collection of individuals going about our private business. And it helped pave the way for the politics and economics that followed.

As I described in the chapter on capitalism, the 1980s, 1990s, and 2000s also saw steady deregulation in the business, finance, and industrial sectors. Philosophically, in the minds of many citizens, the private sector gained in recognition and legitimacy while the public sector diminished in value and reputation. Ironically, while the very idea of taxation itself was called into question by so many Republican officeholders, and by so many citizens, the tax code indeed became less progressive. Over the 37 years between 1982 and today, tax rates have been generally altered in ways that hurt the average worker and greatly—disproportionately—benefited the wealthy. And as Republican officeholders—far more than Democratic officials—generally promoted the idea of the "free market" (which wasn't free at all, but highly designed by legislation), big corporations and globalization looted the Treasury and workers' paychecks.

All of these developments took 45 years. At the same time that Republicans were hammering the idea of government, casting aspersions on the concept of taxes, and deregulating business and industry wherever they could, developments in the media world were aiding their long campaign. As I mentioned in the chapter on Webworld, the repeal of the Fairness Doctrine in 1987 and the subsequent proliferation of radio talk shows and cable television had the effect of further dividing Americans. Instead of watching three major network news shows, and thereby holding a common set of facts and realities (for better or worse), the citizenry gradually broke up into many groups, each watching whatever news, entertainment, and gossip that appealed to it.

There was one particularly poisonous outcome of the multiplication of news outlets, and that was the birth of extremely conservative and reactionary and hyperbolic radio talk shows. In the late 1980s and early 1990s—continuing through to the present—quite a number of immoderate right-wing radio hosts gained in popularity. These are hosts in the Gingrich style of rhetoric—exaggerating, accusatory, self-righteous, certain, and against compromise. They view Democrats as barely legitimate, perhaps un-American, socialist, and elitist. Daily and weekly, they have tens of millions—something like 50 or 60 million combined—of devoted listeners and they deliberately misrepresent complex political realities in a cynical campaign to anger and incite their audience. They are an amazingly large force on the political scene, and there is nothing analogous—either in quantity or influence—on the liberal side of the dial. Many people of either political party who are centrists or moderate, and who don't listen to these hosts, would be shocked to hear the content and hyper-partisan tone they broadcast in. Four examples—among many— are Rush Limbaugh, Mark Levin, Sean Hannity, and Howie Carr. They routinely disparage or ridicule anyone they perceive as insufficiently conservative, and they present events in ways that will leave their listeners incompletely informed about important aspects of current affairs. Perhaps most damaging, they help to normalize a posture of dogmatism and anti-intellectualism that then spreads to their audience. That contributes mightily to the divisions among people in society and makes much more difficult the building of solidarity among ordinary citizens—a solidarity that should exist even while we will disagree about many things.

In addition to reactionary talk radio, Fox News came along in 1996 to feed its viewers a steady diet of anti-government, anti-taxes, and anti-Democrat stories. It was the first of many cable-news stations that constantly advocated for political positions and agendas and mixed straight "news" reporting with opinion. Over time, it could and did literally brainwash its audience. It further divided—and is still dividing—Americans.

Perfectly complementing the growing partisanship, shrillness, oversimplification, militancy, intolerance, and demonization of all opposition that was occurring in politics in the late 1990s and the early 2000s, the introduction and growth of Webworld added a new vehicle that would be used to expand and broadcast destructive political messaging on a large and unprecedented scale. As I described in the chapter on Webworld, political operatives—particularly on the extreme right—use the internet to disseminate political untruths, promote conspiracy theories, bully and tear down innocent people, and generally divide people. Although there are unreasonable partisans on all sides of American politics, it must be said that the Republican Party, in the past 10 or 15 years especially, has become more rigid and uncompromising than the Democratic Party. For the Republican—and especially for the alt-right—arguments against compromise, the internet has been a godsend. In actual typical everyday use, the dumbing down of nearly everything that appears on the internet is a perfect match for those who would oversimplify, deceive, confuse, mislead, manipulate, and un-educate citizens. And ultimately, because of the ways that Webworld is most commonly used by almost everybody today, it is the perfect tool with which to divide and fragment the population.

Many ordinary citizens of both parties, who may not visit the most poisonous political sites and videos and blogs on the internet, have no idea of the degree of extreme content available online. They may not have an appreciation of how reactionary and destructive it is. But a good number of their fellow citizens are looking at the content, and believing it and internalizing it.

For the reasons I outlined in the chapter on capitalism and technology, many ordinary workers are struggling mightily to survive financially. For 40 years these workers have been misled and lied to. These workers are rightfully angry, and many of them are ready to believe the destructive messages—lies themselves—that are promulgated on the worst websites and in the falsest social media posts.

In some of the rural areas of America especially, where factories, mining, farming, and other once-viable occupations have disappeared, entire towns and entire populations have been devastated by the changes in the economy. Essentially abandoned by industry and large-scale commerce, and then further victimized by the subsequent closing of the many small businesses, suppliers, restaurants, stores, and service centers that normally characterize a thriving community, residents and workers in these areas have been left isolated and nearly helpless to revive their towns and lives. In many cases, having no other options, they are forced to move. And many people, stuck with a home or a mortgage they cannot sell, and perhaps in debt, cannot afford even to do that. In Appalachia, the Rust Belt, and many parts of rural America, hollowed out towns and hollowed out people are all too common. It's no accident that the crises of opioid addiction and destructive anger have hit hard in areas where workers have become disposable people.

For 40 years, nobody told these workers that globalization, technology, automation, computerization, capital mobility, executive remuneration, Wall Street practices, and the tax code (with its subsidies, deductions, rates, and loopholes) were all arrayed against them. Nobody told them that unions, industry pensions, company healthcare, and living wages were all under sustained and deliberate assault and would eventually disappear (or close to it). Nobody told them that income inequality would rise to shocking levels. Nobody told them that the Wall Street meltdown of 2008–2009 was coming, and that never again would they have economic or job security.

No, in fact, the contrary was the case. Over the past 40 years, neither Republican nor Democratic lawmakers covered themselves in glory, but Republican officeholders have been particularly responsible for misleading ordinary Americans. Republican congressmen and Presidents since 1980 have told the country the false narrative that I have already mostly described. That narrative, which had the benefit of being simple and easily repeated, was—and is today—that the government is sketchy, wasteful, wants your "hard-earned" tax dollars, overregulates everything, and generally gets in the way of the private sector, which is the sole source of initiative, creativity, wealth, job generation, problem-solving, and the applied attitudes of liberty and freedom.

Most narratives have some truth in them, and of course so does this one. But it is inaccurate, vastly oversimplified, and ignores the complexities, simultaneous realities, balances, and much else at play in our society and economy.

To promote this narrative, and to further unify those who may believe it, the Republican Party since 1980 has also highlighted other issues which do not really relate to the core of the narrative, but which often serve to appeal to and reinforce an anti-government psyche. The right to bear arms, opposition to abortion, religious freedom, dislike of affirmative action, being "strong" on crime, and other positions on social issues have been—and are—often used by the Republican leadership to shift the focus of ordinary citizens away from any deep and meaningful analysis of its economic and political narrative. The social issues are real and important, but with cynical and manipulative timing they can be—and have been—often served up as distractions.

Much of the anger and alienation in the American citizenry today—especially in the more conservative half of the electorate—is a product of being told a narrative for 40 years that was largely a lie.

Many factors led to the election of Donald Trump to the presidency. Any one of them could arguably have been the "difference maker." But certainly one major factor in his victory was the anger and alienation of many citizens who voted for him. I dislike pretty much everything about Trump, but I am in sympathy with most of his supporters—those who are frustrated, confused, desperate, traumatized, underemployed, and betrayed. If you lie to people for 40 years, screw them royally, steal the country's wealth, and feed suspicion, paranoia, anxiety, and ignorance, this is what can happen.

Trump was a Molotov cocktail thrown by people who were at wit's end. He came along at the right time for them. Trump's supporters, revved up increasingly for decades by a perfect storm of Fox and similar cable news, conservative and fierce talk radio, and the poisonous echo chambers in Webworld, just detonated in the voting booth and expressed it all back in their vote.

And in addition to the juggernaut of right-wing media which has fed the distorted, oversimplified narrative that Trump's supporters hold on to, they were and are also fueled by the very real experiences and realities of their own lives.

For some voters, casting a vote for Trump was simple revenge. They knew correctly that, in some sense, they were victims, and somebody had to pay. They voted as much against history and the status quo as for Trump.

Unfortunately, Trump, of course, is not the vehicle with which to address the very legitimate concerns of his supporters. He is a small and unlearned man—devoid of character, devoid of an honorable or substantive core—and he has never had any intention of making this country healthy, just, sustainably prosperous, and whole.

Today, our country is in a terrible place. We are in a crisis, which is really the sum of many interlocking crises. Politically, we are a badly fragmented nation. The forces that have put us in this condition are still potent and operating and remain mostly unaddressed. We still have an incredibly destructive Webworld, a Republican Party without the leadership courage to be honest and balanced, a Congress fueled on all sides—Republican and Democrat alike—by money, an economy captured by corporations and a runaway and predatory capitalism, a tax code for the wealthy, a technology sector intent on automating as many jobs as it can, and a citizenry with its capacities limited by trauma, economic insecurity, the internet, a lack of knowledge and sophistication, and of course, its own epistemology and human nature.

Speaking of narratives and distractions, a word needs to be said here too about "Obamacare," undocumented immigration, Islamic terrorism in the U.S., and Hillary Clinton's emails. These subjects have been added to the list of topics that Republican officeholders sometimes use to distract attention away from any deep examination of the core Republican narrative that I described above. Especially during Donald Trump's campaign and presidency, these newer subjects have received considerable attention. While they are important and worthy of discussion, too often they are presented to conservative-leaning citizens as among the primary reasons for, and drivers of, the financial distress and anxiety that citizens feel. But every force discussed in this book—the forces that are indeed truly rocking the world of ordinary working Americans—has been developing for 40 years or more. The evolution and interplay of capitalism, technology,

Webworld, politics, media, education, human nature, population size, and global warming—and the destructive consequences of each force on our lives—have been wreaking havoc on our society and economy long before Obamacare, "illegal" immigration, militant Islam, and Clinton's emails were even an issue to us.

After all, neither Obamacare nor illegal immigration caused the decades of deregulation that helped lead to the Wall Street meltdown. They didn't produce predatory capitalism, automation, or globalization. Neither Islam nor Clinton's emails caused manufacturers for decades to send millions of factory jobs to China, Thailand, Vietnam, Indonesia, Bangladesh, and elsewhere. And none of those subjects—controversial that each may be—is responsible for the decades of the growing role of money in capturing our congressmen, or the decades of tax code revisions that steadily and increasingly empowered large corporations and the wealthy.

So, in our polarized country today, citizens are divided by narratives. We are all looking in different directions for the solutions to our problems. Among conservative or Republican citizens, their embrace of the myth that the "free market" is or could ever be actually free (of design) prevents them from seeing what has actually occurred for 40 years, and who is responsible. They mistakenly divide our population into "makers" and "takers," and incorrectly believe that the private sector holds good, egalitarian, "American" values while the government is constantly to be suspected of wanting to take their "hard-earned" dollars. In the past 10 years especially, many conservative citizens have been brought to a rigid, narrative-embracing fever pitch by Fox News, conservative talk radio, the right-wing side of Webworld, and Donald Trump. The right-wing multimedia outlets have worked hard to obscure the economic, technological, and deregulatory realities that are the main culprits behind the struggles of ordinary workers.

Among many on the right, their anger, alienation, anxiety, financial stress, threatened identity, lack of education, and lack of political sophistication leave them open to political manipulation, and it made many of them want to break Washington, D.C. So they voted for Donald Trump.

* * * *

The polarization among the citizenry that we see in the U.S. is evident across the world. Depending on the specific country we examine, the factors precipitating the divisions may be weighted differently, but the forces that I describe in this book—the ones rocking America—are similarly rocking the world. Look at Europe, Asia, the Mideast, and nearly everywhere else. Some combination of most of these forces—and sometimes all of them—is playing out in dozens of countries. For one reason or another, in many nations, pretty much everyone feels like a "stranger in his own land."

The globe is a tiny place now, and lots of people everywhere feel how little control they have over their lives. We are all experiencing the "disruption"—as Silicon Valley so euphemistically calls it—caused by unbounded capitalism, advancing technology, accelerating automation and robotization, job instability, and financial insecurity. Many of us—especially in Europe and Central Asia—are being buffeted by political changes, environmental challenges, military conflict, and large-scale refugee migrations.

In many countries, including the developed democracies, serious rifts are opening up in society and in politics. National cultures, religious denominations, political parties, classes, tribes, and other entities that people voluntarily (or by default) affiliate with—and that help to give citizens grounding and identity—are being threatened and fragmented. Political consensus is being shattered and societal attitudes are multiplying in number and varying widely. As all sorts of changes and stresses are being put on societies and governments, their cohesiveness and ability to respond effectively are being severely tested.

The European countries are being tested by the large numbers of refugees and migrants fleeing from multiple wars, economic privation, sectarian terror, and environmental deterioration. Europe is being tested by home-grown nationalism, right-wing authoritarianism, and a restless populace. Similarly, but not identically, Asian, Arab, and Islamic countries are being tested by wars, terrorism, landscape and community destruction, environmental devastation, cultural upheaval, and wracking dysfunctions in nearly every aspect of ordinary society. And arcing over and warping all nations and their specific challenges are the commercial, consumerist, technological imperatives that come not from any one country or culture but from the seemingly unavoidable, semi-anonymous, unaccountable forces responsible for that thing we sloppily call "progress."

(Semi-anonymous forces, yes, but because of their synergy with a sort of democracy-enforced, deregulated capitalism and their elevation of private-sector economic growth above all other gods, they are widely and accurately viewed as the products of Western societies.)

Concurrent with the tangible developments or disruptions that are shaking the economic security and the comfortable, longstanding, cultural identities of individuals and national societies, the biggest technological imperative and force arcing over everything is the internet. The dynamics of Webworld are enlarging anger, emotion, and polarization, and just wreaking havoc on people's facilities for discernment and equanimity. In nations across the world, whatever the specific threats to people's ways and identities, the web increases citizens' sense of besiegement, helplessness, paranoia, and loss. All of their feelings get stampeded into a politics of reaction.

The "progress" I am referring to above—of which the internet is just one part—is homogenizing, bullying, respectful of no tradition or culture, often reckless, and very rapid. Its very speed, in fact, is one of its most powerful, destructive, and disorienting properties. This progress— the sum of all the forces that this book is describing—is becoming the new global culture, and it is sweeping away much that it encounters. It is sweeping away anything that contradicts it, opposes it, or that threatens its values or its dominance.

People everywhere feel this tide, and they feel how powerless and inconsequential they are in the face of it. They see and feel the changes occurring in their unique and particular cultures and in the landscapes and physical places that have long both shaped and reflected their lives. Universally, ordinary people across the world are increasingly angry and resentful about the changes and insecurity that the tide of forces is bringing. It is indeed "the age of anger." A good number of people also feel panic and dread at thoughts of what the future has in store for us.

In the United States, plenty of people feel alienated, but the mass of ordinary citizens only vaguely grasps the power and dynamics of this "progress" of forces, and the ways that politics and capitalism have been used to pave the way for it. We have some idea, of course, but mostly we are still taken with the standard of living that is possible here, the wonderful entertainments that are available on cable and in Webworld, and the still-amazing opportunities to have freedom, ambitious careers, self-actu-alization, and individualism.

In Europe, many citizens feel alienated and wary but—in contrast to Americans—have a better understanding of the forces of capitalism, tech-nology, politics, and globalization that are shaping their world. However, this has not made their responses any more unified or coherent than in the U.S. Just as in our country, the state of European politics is in flux, reflect-ing divided ideologies and a divided public.

In Europe and in many other parts of the world, one of the conse-quences of the toxic mix of the internet, a fearful or uncertain public, a distrusted economics, and in many cases an unwelcome number of immi-grants, is the rise of authoritarian leaders and far-right political parties. In Britain, France, Germany, Italy, Sweden, Poland, Hungary, Greece, Tur-key, India, Australia, Brazil, and the Philippines, there are either brand new or greatly strengthened right-wing movements that are growing or have taken power outright. And, as with the Trump administration, mostly these reactionary administrations or groups are not broadly or capably focused on either ordinary-citizen solidarity (across society) or addressing the root causes of global change.

In both the U.S. and Europe, we can observe how the issue of immi-gration easily confuses and displaces the bigger discussion needed regard-ing the largest forces threatening society. In the U.S., where immigration (authorized or not) is clearly not remotely a threat to our country, Presi-dent Trump nonetheless happily repeatedly places attention on the subject as a useful distraction from much more significant matters. Because he is not going to help American citizens understand their world—much less do anything about it—he uses "invading caravans" from South America and other specious threats to instill fear in Americans. A fearful people cannot think straight, and that suits Trump's purposes.

In Europe, unlike here, the issues raised by immigration, migrants, and refugees are real and significant. Over the past 10 or 15 years, the wars and conflicts in Afghanistan, Iraq, Syria, Libya, Somalia, Niger, and many other Saharan nations have resulted in millions of refugees and displaced people. Whether fleeing terrorism, civil war, chaos, ravaged physical com-munities, destroyed natural environments, or other existential dangers, people have had little choice but to seek safe places. Consequently, Europe has been the logical destination for those wishing to escape sickness, starvation, torture, rape, conscription, enslavement, and death. In Europe, this wave of "foreigners" causes legitimate concern, as there are fundamental difficulties in caring for and assimilating millions of diverse and already-struggling peoples. Under the best of circumstances—that is, if the receiving countries and their citizens were not already being wracked and distorted by the global forces I am describing in this book—it would be quite a challenge for any country to receive the mostly poor, traumatized, and culturally different populations that are currently seeking safety and shelter.

Hungary especially provides a clear example of these dynamics. Part of the European Union, the citizens of Hungary have been buffeted by the same forces sweeping across all nations connected to the global economy. Through little fault of their own, for a decade ordinary Hungarians were ill-served by their own inept government and then the Wall Street and global financial meltdown of 2007 and 2008 further victimized them. Hungary received bailout assistance from the International Monetary Fund, but the help was conditioned on "austerity" measures—again felt unfairly by relatively powerless and financially weak citizens. So in 2015, when hundreds of thousands of Syrians, Iraqis, and Afghans showed up along Hungary's Croatian and Serbian borders, the country's citizens were already resentful and wary. Now add to that mix Prime Minister Viktor Orban, Hungary's nationalistic strongman leader, and his increasing influence over the media and the conversation in the country. Like President Trump here, his rhetoric doesn't accurately explain how power has long damaged the world, but instead offers scapegoats and easy answers for citizens to focus their anger on. Now Hungary has built a fence along its southern border to keep refugees out. The country has a population of only 10 million people, so managing a significant influx of poor migrants would indeed have been a difficult task. But the lesson here—as in the United States and many other countries—is that today ordinary citizens are creating a politics and reacting to unfolding events with capacities and attitudes that are a result of what has been done to them—and what they have observed and experienced—during the past decades.

And if we can see the genuine issues surrounding immigration into Europe—challenges that face both the "home" population and the incoming refuge-seekers—then we can surely imagine some degree of the culture shock that is occurring around the world in many Arab, Muslim, Hindu, African, Central Asian, and other mostly non-Western populations. We are starting to see the shattering consequences of the forces of capitalism, technology, and Webworld on the developed world and on mostly Western populations. Yet, to a large extent, those are the populations that produced and promulgated the forces; if anybody could have "handled" their consequences, it should have been us Westerners. If we can see and feel—and eventually understand—our own anger, sense of betrayal, alienation, and sometimes bewilderment, one can only imagine the degree of those same feelings in the lives of the truly disempowered and dispossessed in many places across the globe.

* * * *

Throughout history, in times of confusion or flux or upheaval, there have been honest, courageous leaders; and there have been smaller men who have offered destructive pathways forward. Today, of course, we see examples of both. President Trump, as of this writing in mid-2019, has so far not looked for wise or relevant or broadly inclusive approaches to addressing the major forces of our time. He is content to promote immigrants as scapegoats, and to have citizens not understand the state of the world, and the way the world works.

In greater Europe, with all of its countries, there are many leaders, and they vary widely in character and intention. Some are indeed mostly forthright, upstanding, and collaborative, and would be thrilled to see all of mankind prosper and grow freely into a peaceful, cooperative world. Other current leaders are more authoritarian, and the pathways they offer might not safeguard everyone equally, and might not address all of the forces that are buffeting society and the environment.

By looking at Europe and its challenges, and at the Muslim countries, and at Russia, China, Brazil, and others, we can start to understand the stresses in the United States. Though each country is different, with problems that are specific to each, we can observe how each nonetheless has to deal with global forces that originate mostly not within its borders, but that span the globe. We can also recognize that humans and their cultures everywhere—regardless of their nationality—can be and are being shaken by the same things. That should help us to understand what are the most forceful and threatening developments across the world today.

Identifying a hierarchy—a ranking—of the most significant issues facing Americans today is a critical need for our country. Our populace is divided and extremely polarized partly because we have allowed ourselves to become distracted, undiscerning, and unknowledgeable. We have been led astray for decades. And we are continuing to be led astray by President Trump and many in the Republican Party who would feed us scapegoats and secondary issues in an effort to keep us unknowing.

CHAPTER 5

MEDIA

A NOTHER NOTABLE FORCE at play today is media. "Media" includes an enormous array of platforms, formats, tools, and technologies. The media consists of newspapers and magazines printed on paper, newspapers and magazines online, all the offerings of Webworld (blogs, websites, videos, influencers, and social media platforms and apps), movies, television (networks and cable stations), reality shows, radio talk shows, and even advertising itself.

The media as a force is often woven into and through some of the other forces we have already looked at, especially politics and Webworld. Many parts of the media are in fact inseparable from Webworld.

The media has long existed, and it has always been a force in and on society. It has had varying degrees of influence at various periods in our history, and it has held varying degrees of integrity, courage, and competence as well. During 244 years and more of American history, the press has exhibited many different loyalties, many formulations of mission, and many identities. In the lead-up to the American Revolution, and during the War for Independence, journalists took sides for or against the Crown. In later years, newspapers sometimes became shills for and organs of the political parties, and sometimes deteriorated into the most tabloid-like sensationalism. Later still, many newspapers aspired to more professionalism, and more independence from society's power brokers, and produced much formidable muckraking journalism. Today, many news outlets have grown into their role as the Fourth Estate (as though it were the fourth branch of government), that necessary, quasi-adversarial entity that is meant to exist permanently and equally—but privileged—beside the other public and private institutions of our nation.

But regardless of any specific moment in American history, and regardless of the waxing and waning of both the influence and performance of the media, the press—specifically—is critical to the frameworks and functioning of our democratic system. As I mentioned in the chapter on Webworld, traditional newspapers have a significant role in observing, analyzing, reporting on, and illuminating the daily operations of our governments and politicians. The press has been, and still is, indispensable to informing and educating citizens. The men who established the institutions, structures, and power relationships (at least conceptually) of our country knew that a free, independent, protected press could serve as a check on the abuses of power that almost inevitably arise in any large and eventually longstanding organization—in this case, an entire nation. The recognition and guarantee of a free press is written into the First Amendment of the U.S. Constitution.

Today, however, the many manifestations of the press and "news"— across all sorts of platforms—and their place in our society, and our relationship to them, are all in crisis. As citizens fragment into the many silos of Webworld, and as talk radio, cable television, and irresponsible politicians all combine to mislead and literally uneducate the American people, we are becoming increasingly incapable of the discernment and habits of mind and discussion that are necessary to participate constructively in building a judicious government and a wise country.

This is happening partly because of the diminishing role befalling the competent, professional press. The "traditional" press—the long-established and capable newspapers of the large cities and the many smaller communities outside of the metro areas—has been, and is, under constant attack. With the rise of the internet over the past thirty years, and the explosion of "media" sources that the web has brought with it, citizens and power brokers with a wide range of agendas have been able to bypass the editing and "gatekeeper" functions that were once (in pre-web times) the prerogatives of traditional newspapers. There are both positive and negative consequences with that change, but the negative effects are proving far more significant than what is gained.

And similarly and simultaneously, the creation of hundreds of channels of cable television, hundreds of "talk" and "reality" television shows, and thousands of talk-radio shows allowed, and allows, citizens, whackos, shock-jocks, poseurs, and power brokers to bypass once-monopolistic network news stations. And after 1987, with repeal of the Fairness Doctrine, neither talk-radio nor cable TV had to give any airtime whatsoever to viewpoints countering their own. Thus, the stage was set for many radio and TV shows to produce relentless, aggressive, ideologically-driven and colored content—24/7—that almost invariably did two things: it proclaimed without reservation the superiority of its opinion, and it attacked and delegitimized all other viewpoints and anyone who would hold them.

When the internet brought literally millions of websites, blogs, videos, chat rooms, social media platforms, apps, and an infinite amount of advertising messages, the number of media offerings available to every citizen became enormous. In just thirty years, a tsunami of media alternatives was created—in TV, radio, and online—that mostly overwhelmed the longstanding traditional press. And most of these alternative outlets recognized and practiced little concern for the well-established norms and understandings of ethics, mission, investigation, fairness, and integrity that guide the best examples of journalism. I have described much of this phenomenon in the chapter on Webworld.

The problems with this evolution of the media are many. First, as we saw in "Webworld," the internet stole most of the advertising revenue away from newspapers. Consequently, they had to cut staff significantly and they still struggle constantly to survive financially. The challenges that face mainstream newspapers affect all of them, regardless of whether they have liberal or conservative editorial boards.

Second, the mainstream media, whether online or in paper, is now shunned by a large percentage of the conservative and right-wing segments of the population, and they go so far as to think the press illegitimate, biased, fake, and elitist. The right wing and the alt-right do not respect even the most professional, serious, and ethical of the country's major newspapers. These segments of the citizenry have been essentially brainwashed by ten to thirty years of listening to poisonous radio and television talk shows and ten to thirty years of reading half-truths and misleading stories on the web.

Most of the "news" sources—whether TV, radio, or online—that the most conservative Republicans and the alt-right listen to are not rigorously edited, and they do not aspire to or adhere to best journalistic practices and standards. The sources are frequently irresponsible or professionally negligent. They often present extremely one-sided or greatly oversimplified news reports and arguments. Many of them—especially online—promote fear, paranoia, and conspiracy theories. They are filling the minds of almost half the citizenry with disinformation, resentment, and destructive perspectives. With that context—the deliberate dumbing of the audience—it is no wonder that many people cannot tell fake news from real news, and cannot accept facts that conflict with the propaganda that they listen to every day on their favorite show or website.

Another consequence of the multitude of alternative media offerings is the erosion of the very idea of expertise. As I described in the chapter on Webworld, when citizens can shop around online to find news sources that agree with them, and when they can—without the review of an editor—instantly post their own thoughts and reactions, however uninformed or unsophisticated, they begin to think of themselves as pretty knowledgeable. The study and training and thinking that goes into becoming an expert on something are alien practices to many habitual users of the web; they start to think that their web searches and clicking and linking are rigorous "research," and they are impressed by their own behavior. (Facility with a smartphone or laptop, surfing, viewing, and posting, can give anyone a false sense of agency.) They do not know that usually they are just moving within their silo and confirming the views and opinions (and "facts") that they and their silo siblings already share and promote. They do not know that they are not testing hypotheses or challenging their beliefs. They often do not know what arguments, facts, or circumstances are being overlooked by their news sources or their information searches. But despite those shortcomings in their silo-world, over time they become more confident, more sure of the rightness of their perspectives, and more dismissive of facts and narratives that don't align with their knowledge and viewpoints.

This leads ultimately to a very serious problem and predicament, one that we are faced with today. With people who have become thoroughly persuaded of holding the beliefs they hold, there may be no way whatsoever to motivate them to question their views or examine literature or media that will challenge their positions. They will not read and consider anything opposed to their political views and they will not listen to any speaker offering doubt about their ideas. They are impervious to thoughts that are new or different from their own. Such is the consequence of living in, and repeatedly affirming your ideas with, a media silo-world. While it has always been possible to use newspapers, literature, cults, or demagogues to become some sort of fanatic or simply a rigid, black-and-white thinker or believer, today the internet and Webworld provide unprecedentedly powerful tools and dynamics that work to produce those results.

So we are faced with a vehemently divided citizenry, and a division (and divisions) that is reinforced every day by the media choices and habits that nearly everyone makes. And the portion of the citizenry that is taking its news and information from the most strident sources on the web—and equally poisonous voices on talk radio and cable TV—is increasingly unable to countenance anything else.

It has taken 40 years or so for a sort of suspicious, wary, libertarian ethos to rise and come to dominate the thinking of many ordinary people on the right. The traditional mainstream media is a casualty of this ethos. We have reached the point where a President (our current one) of the nation can say, repeatedly, that the press is "the enemy of the people," and half the nation is not repelled by that statement. Because of 40 years of false narratives—promoted by right-wing politicians, donors, think tanks, and irresponsible media—we have a conservative portion of the country that understands almost nothing about genuine journalism and its place in our nation. It must be said that this damage has been perpetrated almost entirely by Republican opinion-makers and power brokers.

As I described in the chapter on Webworld, today we are in a time where citizens think they are journalists, think they are fact-checkers, and think they are as competent as professional, mainstream-media editors to sort and select their news diet. We are in a time where plenty of excellent journalism exists—easily sufficient to inform anyone truly interested—and tells the real stories about the whats and whys of our world. But the people who most need those stories are not reading them.

So, overall, increasingly for the past 40 years and as of today too, mostly we don't have a failure of the press to do a capable job, we have a failure of the American people to do the job required of a citizenry inhabiting a representative democracy. We have a failure of the American people to keep themselves sufficiently informed about whole areas of knowledge that are necessary to truly possess that identity called "citizen."

This is not fully the fault of citizens. We share some responsibility, of course, but as I explain in the other chapters of this book, many simultaneous forces and influences are constantly at work around us, competing for our time and attention, requiring our involvement, sometimes victimizing us, and sometimes immobilizing us in various ways. There are many factors to take into account when assessing humans and our condition, and our capacities for learning and performing. I have outlined some in the preceding chapters and I will describe others in the chapters on education and human nature.

While I criticize my fellow citizens, I have sympathy and solidarity-of-feeling for them. They are my brethren. I want my country to survive and succeed, and it cannot do that with a deeply polarized and neutered citizenry. I know all the reasons—and they are good and valid—why many citizens do not have the time, resources, skills, habits, background, health, resilience, safety, or luxury to read what a citizen would need to read in order to be informed. And I am not here referring at all to a citizen developing a liberal or conservative mindset. I am referring to building an emotional and intellectual foundation with which he then can be empowered to think about and judge all that goes on around him in the nation and the world. (In the journalism business, and specifically in the column-writing business that I was in, criticizing your readers as unlearned or uninformed is considered the third rail of journalism. I'm aware of that, but this is a book about how all of the forces and developments in society today are interacting to produce the crises that we're in, and actual humans with actual shortcomings are part of the story.)

Whether citizens can stay informed sufficiently to play their necessary role has always been a subject of concern in the country. The Founding Fathers worried about it, renowned journalists and public intellectuals have had extended discussions about it, and students of government and journalism have long debated the issue. Probably, there hasn't ever been a final answer, partly because we still have a country and it remains a muddling democracy. But we are now well along in the process of failing it.

* * * *

Many forces are at work in society today. When we think about "media" as a force currently, it is important to note that it is not monolithic. In fact, a certain part of the force—the traditional, responsible adherents to professional journalism and news—is losing its power and influence and ability to contribute to the education of the general citizenry, and especially the citizenry who could most benefit from true and honest reporting.

Conversely, the largest portion of the media force—the internet, Webworld, and all that goes along with it—is gaining in power and influence and the ability to sway people. Whether you are liberal or conservative, political or apolitical, you are increasingly likely to get your information and entertainment from an online source. Sure, you could simply be reading your traditional "newspaper" on its online website, but the chances are constantly increasing that you are reading something else.

So a distinction must be kept in mind; the potential of media for a constructive role in the present and future is great, but the actuality of the media that is winning today is destructive and negative.

CHAPTER 6

EDUCATION

SIMILAR TO THE FORCE we call "media," education is a powerful ele-ment in society today and it too is a two-sided phenomenon. It has a potential impact, and it has the actual impact that is in evidence every day. And, like most of the other forces described in this book, it is often wrapped into each of the others. Education is such an actual, integral component (for better or for worse) of these forces that it almost shouldn't have a stand-alone chapter. But I want to call attention to it as a force (or sometimes a missing or ineffective force) and also want to highlight some aspects of it that aren't covered in the other chapters.

The potential positive impact of a quality education—for each indi-vidual and then for an entire society of such individuals—is huge. To a person, we pretty much all believe that, and it is quite natural to feel that if only we could equip everybody with a full education—providing scho-lastic, vocational, and emotional aptitudes—then all our problems could and would eventually be solved. For isn't that a foundational belief of the evolution of Western thought? What the Enlightenment thinkers strove to show was possible? That man was, if not perfectable, pretty able to learn infinitely, and to create healthy, vibrant, creative, and successful societ-ies—societies that would continually advance, progress, and be always an improvement on those that came before.

Lots of people still see education as the first part of the answer to nearly everything. Today, there are amazing and significant and powerful schools, programs, initiatives, and people doing effective work to help both young people and adults become educated. And, of course, one is never done and "educated," as though it is some final status and resting place. What the best schools teach, in addition to subject material, and what the maturing students learn, are the habits of mind that enable lifelong learning. No matter how educated or smart we are, we had better have developed intellectual thinking habits that show concerns for evidence and proof, different viewpoints, cause and effect (connecting dots), hypothesizing, and why things matter. In addition, in our emotional development, we had better come to understand the importance of respect, humility, gratitude, compassion, and empathy. Being able to imagine life in another man's shoes is critical to participating constructively in a society and a democracy.

But, as with all the other forces I have described in the preceding chapters, I am not focused here on the positive aspects of education as a force. For those good aspects are not competing and producing adequately enough to counteract those parts of "education" (in all its forms) that are corrupting the thinking of many citizens and undermining our ability to address and solve our problems. It is the damaging aspects that are most powerful today.

Education occurs in a wide variety of places and ways across society. I've already referred to a big exercise of education that occurs in Web-world, cable TV, talk-radio, and politics. For the alt-right, the reactionary right, and for—increasingly—the Republican Party as a whole, those media venues have become complementary and interlocking vehicles for "educating" their audiences. For the reasons that I've already outlined in the preceding chapters, many adults are receiving a continuing education through this range of media sources, and it is an education that is often misleading, inaccurate, incomplete, and actually destructive.

As I've described, the education that comes from strident, right-wing media voices is more akin to brainwashing than an honest attempt to help people understand their world. These voices give readers and listeners a constant diet of half-truths, misinformation, omissions, emotion, and instructions that do not add up to "education." In fact, the worst right-wing media outlets violate the basic tenets of teaching, learning, and scholarly instruction. Again, I am not here referring to honest disagreements about issues or policies, and honest attempts to address them in all their fullness. And I am not referring to honorable efforts to develop ideologies or opinions that reflect a particular point of view. What I am referring to are methods and styles and substance of media that are pretending to be those positive presentations but are in fact dishonest or camouflaged, or distorted or unprofessional, or simply transparent ranting—all of which do damage to the idea and reality of what qualifies as rational, constructive education. Those outlets are modeling an anti-education.

Now there are certainly examples of anti-education on the left. If a liberal wants to, he can find media outlets that are echo chambers of some strident ideologies. But given the circumstances of the current time, the anger and alienation in the citizenry on the right, the misleading narratives that have been peddled to that portion of the citizenry, and the President we have, the media dynamics on the very conservative side of the spectrum are doing far more damage to the country's habits of debate and learning than excesses of the left are doing.

This is a matter of both degree and content. Both the left and the right can be fairly accused of being sometimes (or often) insular. But there are very troubling features of content and posture that occur on the right that rarely occur on the left. And President Trump—most prominently—both leads and follows these destructive themes and beliefs, thereby strengthening them, increasing their legitimacy, and helping to divide Americans.

I have mentioned some of these distortions and outright untruths in previous chapters. The most damaging belief, and one that is absolutely antithetical to sustaining a participatory democracy, is the idea that the political opposition—the left—is unpatriotic or anti-American, illegitimate, opposed to following the Constitution, and somehow hostile to the country itself. Accompanying that belief—that picture of liberals—is the complementary posture that, therefore, there should be no compromise with liberals. Conservative radio talk-show hosts especially promote this theme, and encourage holding absolute certainty about it. The listener need not entertain any doubt about the threat to the nation that liberals pose. This is by far the most damaging message that any political party or "side" could embrace because it divides ordinary citizens, not by highlighting honest policy disagreements but by questioning the validity of the other side as good Americans. This sort of poison prevents people from being able to talk with each other, to trust that we each hold the same good intentions for the country and that we in fact share very much. Ultimately, splitting up Americans by encouraging any group of citizens to think of themselves as the only "true" patriots is devastating to our chances of sustaining this country. Only if ordinary citizens—of all political stripes—can find solidarity with each other will we be able to address the most important and threatening problems we have.

There are other important examples of how right-wing media is miseducating citizens in major ways. Constant bashing of the "mainstream media" is giving citizens an incorrect understanding of the press and its role in our democracy. The term "fake news" is thrown around recklessly by President Trump and right-wing observers and they apply it to any news reporting that they don't like. They dismiss the nation's major newspapers as fake and biased and the "enemy of the people." This is what they are teaching millions of adult Americans.

Many conservative Americans—misled by right-wing voices—do not know the features of capitalism and socialism. Their media silos are teaching them that our nation is going to be either capitalist or socialist—there is no overlap and no blending of the two. Therefore, almost any strong criticism of capitalism, or discussion of, say, the income inequality in the country, must come from somebody who desires socialism. Talk of raising tax rates on the biggest income earners, or advocating for more regulation of the financial services industry, often elicits accusations of socialism. And for the right-wing media, any discussion of raising tax rates also brings on lectures about how wasteful the government is and what an obstacle it is in general for the private sector.

Another area where millions of Americans have been deliberately miseducated is on the subject of global warming (aka climate change). Here, Republican politicians, right-wing media, and large corporations have been shockingly successful. The science needed to understand global warming is not difficult, nor is it in doubt, but you'd never know that listening to conservative media or the paid lobbyists of the fossil fuel industries. Scientists cannot tell us the exact temperatures or exact consequences of global warming for a certain location on a certain future date, but they do know—with certainty—the patterns and trends and unfolding consequences generally that we can expect across the world in the decades of this century. But millions of adult Americans have been taught to disbelieve all of the scientific reports about global warming that in fact for about 35 years have only become ever more definitive, authoritative, and alarming.

More than any other topic, citizen reaction to the subject of global warming illustrates some of the many factors at play when we talk about both the present actuality and the potential of education as a force, especially (but not exclusively) in the adult population. What is happening when many citizens cannot or will not accept that global warming is a real, man-made, developing and serious crisis? There are a variety of answers. For some people, they don't want to accept what they view as a liberal cause. Other people, whose jobs may be in coal or oil production, and whose livelihoods depend upon the prospering of fossil fuel industries, are too scared about losing their continuing employment to admit global warming is real. And many people don't want society to have to pay for the very real costs of an energy transition to greener fuels.

Many people don't understand the actual science involved. They can't see the carbon dioxide in the air, and the whole thing is just too abstract for them. Perhaps they aren't well educated and perhaps they never had a chemistry class. But lack of an education is not necessarily always the explanation. For there are plenty of people with college degrees, completed science classes, and a "good" education who still don't accept global warming. Still other people may have religious and faith-based outlooks that put us in God's hands. And still other people believe that technology will eventually produce the ways to solve the crisis.

Even the level of trauma that someone has experienced in his life can alter or limit his abilities to accept or understand certain things, including environmental threats. People with past or present addictions or dysfunctions, or who have been abused or emotionally damaged, or who have suffered trauma in any of innumerable ways can find their emotional and intellectual capacities reduced or limited in certain ways.

Suffice it to say that there are many reasons why people do not accept global warming (and I didn't list them all). This points out a fundamental truth about education and learning—especially with regard to adults—and one that is fully at play today. It simultaneously highlights both the potential and limitations of education as a force, and it should temper our expectations of thinking that education—in any real world—could ever be an adequate solution to the challenges that face us today. For humans and what they believe—or want to believe—are the products of a devilish mix of factors.

How do we know what to think? How do we know what to believe? When faced with competing versions of the truth, or contradictory explanations or evidence, how do we decide between them, or otherwise make sense of them?

It's fascinating really: we all live in the same world, confront the same culture and society and economy, have access to the same pool of information, and observe with our own eyes the same current events, and yet we can believe widely different things, hold dissimilar interpretations, and reach diametrically opposed conclusions.

How is that possible? Well, of course, the reality is far more complicated than I outlined above. As Americans, we all live in the same country, and the same current events swirl around us. But we all see them imperfectly, experience the economy differently, reside in varying communities and cultures, and utilize infinitely varying sources and techniques to gather information and data with which to form opinions and make sense of it all.

In addition, although Americans proudly share a common set of big values and goals—freedom, liberty, equality, justice, opportunity, happiness—that consensus is quickly tested by our descriptions of what those words mean in practice and our disagreements over the extent to which each of those goals has been met.

And here might be the most significant factor—for most of us anyway—to explain our stubborn contentiousness and the stark divisions in our national perspectives, political beliefs, and personally-held narratives. Our personal experiences—the backgrounds, lives, families, observations, events, traumas, and blessings—that we possess are infinitely and often radically different from one another's.

At almost any age, but increasingly as we get older, before you or I witness a new event, or receive a new piece of information, we already have ideas and preconceptions about how the world works and how it should work. We know how we have lived, we have observed how others have lived, and we've drawn conclusions about what is effective, fair, sane, dangerous, and healthy. In short, whether we are aware of it or not, we've got a big set of strong opinions and coping strategies with which we navigate the world.

To some extent, we are prisoners of our own experiences. We are all apt to generalize, assume, and project, based on our experiences. And we're apt to push new information into narratives that we already hold. Or worse, ignore it.

Really, our capacity for blindness is infinite. As I said in the Introduction, it is so easy to mistake our personal horizons for the horizons of the world. One of the hardest things to do is look with new eyes at things and circumstances that we think we already understand. The totality of our life experiences—our epistemology—can be so circumscribed or constricting or traumatizing that certain perspectives and possibilities are simply beyond our comprehension. Maybe even beyond the active considering that must precede comprehension.

And remember, all of this epistemology occurs to us while we are both intellectual and emotional animals. We are not cool, dispassionate brains, able to think and analyze with unimpeachable logic about practically anything at all.

And layered across all of our attempts at education and learning is a set of simultaneous forces and influences competing for our attention, our minds, our emotions, and our very souls. As I have described in previous chapters, the forces of capitalism, technology, Webworld, politics, advertising, and media are constantly and powerfully—today unprecedentedly powerful—promoting their messages and their idea of education. They want us to be "educated" in ways that will benefit them and their agendas for society. The world doesn't stop while we are left alone to become "educated" in some neutral or ideal way. Our interactions with society, family, friends, and religion don't stop while we become empowered and formidable in our own right. At all times—whether young student or old adult—we live in a culture, and it both deliberately and by default never stops "teaching" us and conditioning us.

At the same time that we may be trying to receive a healthy, constructive education, there are many forces that are trying to misinform or miseducate us, or convince us to develop in a certain way. The worst forces—and I've already described many of them—teach us or lead us or encourage us to become dogmatic, or overly certain, or to embrace black-and-white thinking, and us-versus-them postures. As we look at the extreme divisions and extreme wrongheadedness just in the American population—never mind the world—there are forces with unprecedented power at work to deepen those dysfunctional states.

One of the realities of the forces that would influence us today is the skill with which they exploit human nature. We know a lot about human nature, and in addition, the past 30 years or so have seen us learn an extraordinary amount in the fields of psychology and neuroscience. Today, we have a keener grasp than ever before of the power and primacy and motivational force of emotions, and we understand human behavior, vulnerabilities, and the privileged place of epistemology as a human develops and ages and learns. Consequently, many of today's most powerful actors—corporations, technology companies, Webworld algorithms, casino and lottery managers, and radio talk-show hosts—have learned how to take advantage of human vulnerabilities and human nature. Slowly and steadily, especially as Webworld and digital technology metastasize over everything, we are losing the competition to design and own our thoughts, principles, desires, behavior, education, and way of being. I will have more to say about human nature in the next chapter.

* * * *

One of the more striking developments in the recent and current education of young people is the embrace of "STEM" learning. "STEM" stands for "science, technology, engineering, and math," and it is the name of a movement that began 7 or 8 years ago—and is now widely adopted—to increase the teaching of those four subjects from kindergarten onward through grade 12 (and beyond). The curriculum in the schools—both public and private—was modified and adjusted to enable more class time on STEM subjects. Adding more pure science and math to the schools wasn't difficult or controversial—those are traditional, long-embraced subjects. The biggest change to the curricula that had existed prior to STEM's advent was the addition of classes and entire courses devoted to computer science and to skills and knowledge related to building web-connected systems, apps, tools, and products.

This was quite a challenge for schools. Some subjects and activities had to be dropped in order to make room for the new computer classes. Introducing the "Technology" and "Engineering" parts of STEM programs was also a departure from educational philosophies that had previously governed most school curricula. Achieving in computer science is a vocational skill, and although vocational education has long existed, it had almost always been limited to the high school grades (not lower) and to students who explicitly desired to focus on a particular trade. In the 1950s, '60s, and early '70s, some junior high schools and high schools did offer "shop" classes for all students, but those were entry-level classes given with the intention of introducing students to the different trades. Only students interested in pursuing a trade continued in the vocational classes.

But today, in what has been a shockingly fast and shockingly complete transition, students across the country begin in kindergarten to use computers during the school day to both do their schoolwork and to learn how to use the computers themselves. Every day, especially as the grade levels rise, significant class time is devoted to teaching computer skills that are mostly vocational and not always broadly intellectual; they may, of course, get students thinking, but it is thinking in the petri dish of a web-dominated world, and it is thinking in service to furthering—and not questioning—that version of a world. Both elementary students and high schoolers are taught "practical" skills in coding, programming, and website and app design. They may learn computer-aided drafting, photo-shopping, graphic design, and 3-D printing. They may assemble circuit boards, learn the various computer programming languages, and build and program robots.

How did such a large change in pedagogy happen so relatively fast, and with such universal adoption? Well, a coalition of supporters—and the culture in general—made it relatively easy. Parents, teachers, school committees, students, and high-tech corporations all embraced the idea of computer science in the curricula. Parents—themselves robust computer users—see computer skills in their children as the kids' ticket to a good job. High-tech corporations view young people in a number of ways: they are future employees and present and future customers. Tech companies in fact compete with each other to provide laptops, tablets, and desktop computers to the schools. They also compete to provide email services, browsers, news feeds, apps, and a whole array of computer-related programs and services. The corporations see computer science classes as an opportunity to build brand loyalty to their hardware and software products. The schools are helping corporations build customers for life. Additionally, the corporations are thrilled to see the schools take on the task of training their future employees. The more computer skills that a graduate (of high school or college) has, the less employee training the tech companies have to provide (what an elementary student learns today about computers will be outdated by the time he goes to work but his digital mindset will stick with him).

The school committees—not immune to the general cultural embrace of digital technology—are seduced by the promise of free (or inexpensive) laptops and programs, and the need to keep up with other tech-equipped school districts. Similarly, teachers can receive free training and other incentives in return for recommending certain company products and services. While some teachers remain uneasy about the emphasis on computer use, they are less in number all the time, and will eventually be replaced. As for student opinion regarding the adoption of pervasive and mandatory computer-related curricula, they don't have a choice; they are powerless. That may be a moot point anyway; by the time kids today go to kindergarten at age 5, they've already been interacting with digital tech gadgets for 3 years. So it would be silly to expect students to complain. There has been an explosion of tablets, apps, programs, games, and other digital activities designed for children ages 2 to 5. And most parents allow their children extensive time on these web-connected distractions.

The relatively quick, widespread, and barely debated introduction of computer skills classes into the schools illustrates the hegemony of a certain mindset today. Mostly, we are gaga over all-things-tech, and we cannot and will not take the time to examine—with any real, sustained seriousness—the consequences of this posture. That it was into our very educational system that we fully injected computers and what amounts to cheerleading for a digital society, is all the more telling. We are unequivocally endorsing the growing use of computers, digital automation, and artificial intelligence, and we are willing to put the imprimatur of our children's schools on that message. We should hardly be expressing dismay at the long hours our young people spend online and on social media; and we should hardly expect that they will ever question the use of tools that we invented and require them to use. And when not actually requiring them to use their smartphones and devices, we create an entire Webworld designed to seduce them, advertise to them, and convince them that time online is better than almost any experience they could be having in the offline world.

CHAPTER 7

HUMAN NATURE

IN THE PRECEDING CHAPTERS, I have described some of the powerful forces in society today. I argue that the people responsible for inventing, managing, directing, and in some cases simply unleashing these forces have learned—more effectively than ever before—how to take advantage of human nature and to exploit it in deliberate ways in order to further their agendas and their vision of the good society.

Human nature has always existed; well, it has existed as long as humans have existed. And although we aren't used to thinking of it as such, it is every bit as much of a force as all of the other forces outlined in this book. We take human nature for granted—we don't think about it much—and so it can be kind of a stealth force. Certainly we become mostly integrated with and acclimated to our own personal expressions of human nature, and thus it recedes as an active item of consideration in our thinking about the world. Similarly, again without ever thinking too much about it—we are used to the reality that we share homes, workplaces, town halls, stores, bowling leagues, and all of society with other people, all of whom have distinct and varying "flowerings" of their human natures. We may sometimes think about people's occupations, education, health, race, religion, ethnicity, and even personality, but rarely do we consider their core nature—their human nature—that we all share. Across all people the world over, the attributes of human nature are our common denominator.

Unlike all of the other forces I am describing, human nature hasn't changed much in 15,000 years. It certainly hasn't changed much in the past, say, 400 years. While the practices, powers, and reach of capitalism, technology, education, and politics have changed dramatically and become much more "advanced," human nature has remained more or less what it's always been.

It is important to consider human nature here for a few minutes because it is a major backdrop, context, or "playing field" in which or upon which all of man's activities occur.

We can safely sketch some general statements about human nature, and about the attributes that it encompasses. Mostly, man is a social animal, often living with a sexual partner, and forming groups and communities. There are certainly hermits among us, and those that live alone in isolated places, but they are not typical. Man is also an organizational and political animal, meaning that we build ever larger communities—like towns and cities—and structure them with rules and laws. Whether at the individual, family, tribe, village, city, or nation-state level, we create, build, set goals, organize work, and seek order.

Complementing our general industriousness and desire to build and order things, we are a story-telling animal. We live by narratives and we seek integration and coherence; we can connect dots. Our narratives help us make sense of the world and the events that we see around us. We are a meaning-seeking animal.

Complementing our social nature and our tendencies to form groups, cities, and entire cultures, we exhibit a behavior called "homophily," which describes our tendency to associate with individuals who are similar to us. They can be similar to us in one way or many ways.

We are, of course, rational, irrational, and emotional beings. We all have capacities to be in any of those states, or blend them, balance them, or move back and forth between them as circumstances, the environment, or our moods and psyche change. It is probably fair to say that most of us are more emotional, and rely more frequently on our emotions, than we imagine we do. (But today, unlike in the past, two things are true. One, we are learning just how important and ever-present emotions are, and how nearly inseparable they are from healthy—and unhealthy—reasoning. And two, the new existence of the internet magnifies all of the dynamics involved with emotion.)

We can be selfish or altruistic, consistent or contradictory, and good or bad and can be all of those ways-of-being in any combination and to various degrees and for various lengths of time. We possess the capacities to love and to hate. We have a tendency to copy others, and we possess the ability to imagine. In our core, each of us is to some degree egotistical.

All of us can be laid low by trauma, and all of us could be plagued by mental illness, insanity, depression, or other unwelcome psychological condition. Yet too, most of us are capable of personal growth, maturation, emotional and psychological health, and continuous learning.

But, in every one of us, as I mentioned in the preceding chapter, our epistemology—the sum total of our experiences, cultural influences, and thinking and learning—becomes more and more powerful as we age. The older we get, usually the more we are consistent in behavior and thought with who we have become. And human nature being what it is, we just plain forget how we are put together. When we move through the world, reacting to myriad events and people, we hold our personal orthodoxies dear, value our experiences over those of other people, and are quick to dispute or discount what we don't understand. We can then have difficulty generating empathy, tolerance, flexibility of mind, and the ability to walk in another man's shoes. Over time we let our epistemology become our identity; the two are close and related, but they are not the same thing. If we cannot see and make the distinction in our daily lives and interactions, we are apt to become defensive and close-minded; we must defend our ideas and our political opinions vigorously because in our minds they have become the same thing as our identity.

Within every one of us, our personal epistemology is a super-powerful force: it develops slowly and incrementally, over years; it develops naturally and by default, without needing our volition or effort; we don't notice it, and are even apt to deny its hold on us; and it is incredibly hard to change it, adjust it, or rise above it. It is also difficult to fully understand all of the many aspects and features of our own epistemology. We are all full of ideas, opinions, assumptions, prejudices, fears, ignorances, strengths, weaknesses, idiosyncrasies, and other content. No matter how good an anthropologist of ourselves we may try to be, it's just hard to see oneself completely and objectively.

* * * *

Looking over that entire outline of the shared features of human nature, and notwithstanding our genes and the instructions they hold, we are then, if not quite a thoroughly blank slate, pretty malleable beings, open to being molded. The attributes and potential faces of human nature are shared, yes, but each of us has a personal and unique profile or character when it comes to how our nature expresses itself.

A little more discussion of being "good" or "bad" (or "good" and "evil") is warranted here. It would be the rare person who didn't contain within himself the potential to be either good or evil, or both, either simultaneously or at different times, and perhaps under varying conditions. Depending upon who you are, and a whole spectrum of the circumstances surrounding your life at a moment in time, you may be articulating positive thoughts and words and engaging in "good" behaviors, or you may be expressing poisonous thoughts and acting in negative or destructive ways. And, of course, there are all shades of gray between these two extremes. My point is to emphasize that each one of us is fully capable of evil, or short of that, a whole range of anti-social behaviors. Each of us is capable of selfishness, prejudice, meanness, greed, unfairness, irrationality, dishonesty, irresponsibility, stupidity, cruelty, and immorality or amorality.

Sometimes tied to our capacities for choosing from among the spectrum of behaviors, the human being is a pleasure-seeking animal. We exhibit this trait in an infinite variety of ways—from sex to food to entertainment to spirituality—and it is a powerful piece of our make-up. Similarly, we are also impressionable, and we can be manipulated.

* * * *

All of the traits, possibilities, and vulnerabilities within human nature are today fodder for many of the other forces described in this book. The human animal can have the best in him brought out by his life and the environment, or he can have the worst in him drawn out by his life and the world around him (and, of course, degrees of good and bad in between). Here, I am focused only on the forces and developments that are actively fostering or circumstantially causing the worst expressions and faces of human nature.

Without a doubt, as I discussed somewhat in the chapter on Webworld, it is the internet and many of its parts and culture that are the most damaging forces in America today. For all the good Webworld does, its negative impacts on and interplay with human nature are devastating.

It is not an exaggeration to say that Webworld preys on us by exploiting the attributes of our human nature. The Silicon Valley designers of the internet, social media platforms, apps, devices, games, and the whole ecology of the online world understand parts of us well, and they offer an infinite spectrum of digital content to keep all of us engaged and clicking.

For the political animals among us, Webworld offers a banquet. We can find news 24/7, view opinions and comments, immortalize our own tweeted reactions, and do it all for free. Most of us feed our desire for affirmation and our belief that we're right by slowly selecting and falling into a silo-world of like-minded political thought. Webworld's algorithms speed this sorting process along seamlessly, invisibly, and seemingly benignly. But, as I described in the chapter on Webworld, Americans are being divided by this process. Webworld pushes us into our ideological corners, reinforces our belief systems and stubbornness, and tricks us into thinking that we are quite reasonable. We come to know less and less about our fellow citizens, and that extends to their thinking, their jobs, and their lives. At our very worst, we become extremists, or we think that all those who oppose us are the extremists. Today, as political conversation between camps barely exists, and as hostility and bad feelings across political society continue to grow, our democracy continues to deteriorate. Webworld is playing a significant part in this.

By nature, man is a storytelling animal. I have already mentioned that we all hold narratives by which we organize our thinking and make sense of the world. Naturally, many of us believe substantially different narratives; that is inevitable and okay. But if we hold them too tightly or too unequivocally, or they are completely wrong, we need to be able to recognize that and take steps to modify them. Webworld often prevents both the recognition and the modification; it puts us at the center of our own media production and it reliably feeds us the ingredients, facts, opinions, arguments, and reporting with which we build an impregnable, unassailable worldview. Any fact, event, or testimony that would counter or challenge our narrative simply bounces off of our mindset.

With regard to politics and forming our personal narratives, Webworld is doing severe damage. It is taking advantage of the natural human desire to be right, to understand the world, and to think that our way of being in the world is the best one. With an effectiveness that no force has ever had previously, Webworld relies on aspects of our human nature to keep us browsing and clicking. And as I described in the chapter on Webworld, we are becoming less patient, less reflective, less wise, less broad-minded, and less able to function usefully as political citizens of the country.

Webworld is diminishing us in other ways too. It is in our human nature to be rational and emotional, and sometimes we struggle with hitting the right proportion of each state (there's no constant, "right" balance appropriate for all occasions). But Webworld thrives best—meaning it keeps our attention—when its content titillates us. It thrives most when we are primarily emotionally engaged. We are drawn to drama, sex, action, violence, spectacle, the sensational, over-simplification, affirmation, reinforcement, photographic and video presentations (rather than text), and a whole slew of other stimuli and entertainment. When Webworld gets us excited, we are more apt to stay engaged with it and generate reactions to the content in it. And the nature of Webworld and the algorithms that build its dynamics invariably prod us to react quickly, emotionally, and often carelessly. But revved up and stampeded, we don't see that. We are just satisfied to be "participating." On the web, the bar for participating is low; it is sufficient just to have reactions and to say how we feel.

Webworld encourages and conditions us to be mostly emotional. The internet won't help us understand those emotions, it'll just feed them. It'll juice us up. As we spend hours daily or weekly on the web and social media, we are becoming sillier, more impulsive, and more superficial, and less able to maintain our attention on complicated, lengthy, and serious matters; and we are less able to wait for more information about anything, if more is needed.

Webworld seduces us away from confusing and difficult fare. It is hard work and sometimes boring to adequately study something, to consider all the aspects of something. Human nature needs only a little push to favor its emotional states, and for many people Webworld provides that impetus. It validates how we feel.

Emotions are a big part of the story that I am telling in this book because, globally, they have become significant factors in helping to shape people's reactions to unfolding events and circumstances. Across the world, in country after country, economic, political, technological, environmental, demographic, and population changes and developments are being seen increasingly through emotional filters and narratives. Rocked by the forces described in this book, people are feeling anxiety, anger, fear, resentment, humiliation, and insecurity. Especially in the developed world, it is becoming evident to ordinary people how much they have lost, are in the process of losing, and how much remains to be lost—perhaps even financial viability, democracy, and civilization itself. Compounding the true and legitimate reasons that people have to be afraid, irresponsible leaders in many Western nations are multiplying and fanning these fears by citing specious factors and arguments that are in reality wrong-headed distractions, manipulations, and scapegoats (this is part of the reason we are seeing such inordinate fear of immigrants).

The actual state of the world, and the state of leadership in it, are triggering dangerous emotions in large parts of society, emotions that threaten to take on a power that may expand out of control. These negative emotions continue to afflict growing portions of the developed world's population. They will play an increasingly prominent role in circumscribing the range of actions that nations may take toward current and future events.

Many of us, especially the young, want to be cool and hip. Our presence and profile online is becoming one arbiter of that measure. Webworld exploits and magnifies our desire to be liked and popular with ways to be "followed," liked, retweeted, and friended, and with other tools and gimmicks to generate attention. The web brings out our narcissism, egotism, self-centeredness, and smallness. With the aptly named "selfie," we record our every move, location, experience, and interaction for posting on our personal web pages or on various social media platforms.

As I mentioned in the chapter on Webworld, we are steadily becoming a more materialistic culture. Advertising surrounds us every minute that we are online, and it is having its way with us. We are silly to expect that human nature won't be seduced by the constant showcasing of beautiful people, objects, places, experiences, entertainment, success, and other things for sale. Almost all humans desire some of those things and that life. And if they don't, well, we'll keep showing them ads until they do.

Here, Webworld and capitalism complement each other nicely, because capitalism too requires dopey, impressionable, grasping customers. Our version of capitalism is built around a model that requires citizens to keep shopping and spending imprudent and inordinate quantities of their money on stuff; about 70 percent of the value of our gross domestic product is fueled by consumer spending. That's a big job for consumers, who might slow their pace of spending if not continually courted and encouraged onward by the neighboring Joneses, advertising, and now the internet. Webworld helps to keep citizens in the right frame of mind—credulous, emotional, and desirous—to keep buying things. And now, with online shopping and faster and faster delivery, the concept of delayed gratification is slowly being phased out.

Remember, the primary goal of the big internet companies is to make money. They do that most successfully when they can maximize internet traffic and clicks. The more time online that we spend, the more data the platforms collect, and the more—and more accurately targeted—advertising they can show us. The advertisers pay the tech platforms in direct proportion to the number of eyeballs on the ads, and the amount of clicks the ads generate. Consequently, in pursuit of our attention and our clicks, Webworld's designers and managers exploit every weakness and vulnerability and tendency in human nature. Today, human nature and the internet are combining in ways that are threatening to the sustainability of society, democracy, and the natural world, and they are doing it with a power that has not been seen before.

* * * *

Humans are both resilient and fragile. Our human nature, with its capacities for both reason and emotion, and our frequent struggle to satisfactorily balance the two, is open to disruption, fragmentation, confusion, and dissolution. The combination of our very strong desire for coherence and our capacity to feel intense emotion leaves us vulnerable to being affected by dishonesty, chaos, cruelty, abuse, betrayal, and other experiences that we know or feel or perceive to be beyond the pale of normalcy or outside our gauge of what's "right." Anyone who's grown up in a culture—and that's nearly everyone—knows what's "right;" it is the long-accumulated total of shared honor, trust, fairness, care, values, expectations, and social and moral conventions that comprise the moral universe of that culture.

An individual can become traumatized when violence is done to him, to loved ones, to people and things he values, to his (or the) environment, to society, to the world, to the ideas and narratives that organize his world, and to meaning itself. The severity of trauma can vary in degree, and in the length of its duration. It can last months, years, or forever. Some people, often with skilled help, can leave it behind; some coexist and cope with it;

and some are permanently disabled in one way or another. No matter how one fares with it ultimately, it usually remains in scars of some sort, which can be useful and healthy or not.

Trauma may be a simple term, and it can be defined with reference to common principles and a range of recognizable effects, but it can occur in such a wide variety of experiences and conditions that in some cases we—focused on the conditions—forget or almost overlook the traumatizing consequences of them. Globally, buried within bigger crises, there are an infinite number of types of trauma, and we aren't used to focusing on that aspect of current affairs.

For example, less frequently labeled as trauma, and perhaps not examined as often or deeply as, say, the type of trauma represented by the specific, personal, physical abuse of my friend described in the Introduction, are the broader and more public traumas that become almost normalized across entire societies.

People in countries that are experiencing long-term famine, repression, economic desperation, dislocation, or civil war, for example, are living in conditions that are traumatizing them. Every day, every week, every year, they are experiencing abuse and privation and injury that are damaging them in the present, and that will have a scarring legacy on their future. But neither they, nor we, are in the habit of saying that they are living in trauma. But almost everything about their lives is an existential duress. When all of life becomes indistinguishable from trauma, we—and they—just call it "life." Calling it trauma is accurate, but it can seem to put an oddly obvious fine point on it.

The point here is that—from the United States to Britain to China to Ukraine to Afghanistan to India to Dafur—the global population is experiencing significant degrees of trauma, and those traumas are real obstacles to gaining the full capacities of human beings.

Today, a large percentage—maybe as much as 50 percent—of the American population possesses some degree of traumatization, past or present. This number will no doubt shock many readers. I daresay that somebody who hasn't personally experienced any trauma in his life will have trouble believing the number. But in the past 30 years or so, we have made immense strides in identifying, understanding, and talking about trauma. We have come to recognize how commonly it occurs, and we have largely removed the stigma and even judgement that once surrounded trauma victims and often prevented them from speaking about it. We have also developed our understanding of how broad and diverse is the range of possible causes of trauma.

Many people who have experienced trauma have mostly reconciled in some satisfactory or adequate way with it and are functioning well, or reasonably well. They may never talk about a past trauma, and they may feel no need to. Other trauma survivors run the gamut from healthy to incapacitated. But what the vast majority of them carry inside themselves is some effect or consequence of the pain they experienced. There can be positive effects: if an individual endures trauma, comes to understand its cause, can see that he wasn't responsible for what was done, "recovers" his wholeness, and can share his story with others, then sometimes he becomes an exceptionally empathetic, perceptive, and open person. The trauma, his recovery, and his gratitude at once again being healthy—after the low perhaps of contemplating suicide—lead him to see the trauma and hurt in so many others. This is partly what leads so many trauma survivors into work that helps others; and to become valuable, wise, constructive citizens no matter what line of work or activities they're involved with.

With other survivors, there can be negative consequences ranging from mild, mental blind spots to terrible dysfunctions. Even after participating in therapy, some trauma victims fight lifelong anxieties, fears, anger, resentment, depression, or demoralization. Other survivors are not as visibly or constantly or seriously affected, but they carry their injuries or their scars in ways that can be touched or accessed by certain commonly-encountered circumstances or situations. A partially healed or unhealed trauma survivor may have developed unhealthy attitudes, prejudices, partially dysfunctional or distorted narratives, and social behaviors that don't serve him well. Again, varying in degree and magnitude, his trauma may have left him with permanent limitations, with permanent diminished capacities and competencies. This can essentially put a ceiling on both his emotional and intellectual development. And it may be that a society with enough limited citizens cannot advance beyond a certain point emotionally and intellectually as well.

We are seeing evidence of this dynamic today. We have talked about how Webworld and social media prey on human nature and its vulnerabilities and tendencies. Webworld, politics, and media often prey on our anxieties, insecurities, resentments, prejudices, homophily, and worst selves. To the extent that a significant percentage of our population has trauma-related limitations, then our society as a whole collective may effectively have those same limitations.

I believe that today in the United States, drawn out of us and made worse by the long-building circumstances of the present and the combination of the forces that I am describing in this book, we are seeing the expression of the traumas (old and new), limitations, and ceilings of millions—maybe 100 or 200 million—of individual Americans. Taken together, these limitations and liabilities result in a serious handicap afflicting the population; it results in a ceiling on the positive measures our society is capable of.

Human nature is such that most people have a tougher time putting their best foot forward when they are under stress or duress of some type. The stresses can come from trauma (past or present), depression, humiliation, fear, financial problems, family conflict, medical issues, and many other things. Many of us are less generous, less empathetic, and less resilient when we are struggling personally. We are also apt to be angry, impatient, and cynical under those conditions.

A big part of the story that I have told here is the screwing of the mass of ordinary people. They have many reasons to feel anxious, angry, depressed, impotent, humiliated, or fearful. Today, with ferocity and openness, citizens are registering their trauma, sense of betrayal, and distrust. This state of emotion is rendering many citizens politically dysfunctional; their capacities for sophisticated thought, reflection, and introspection are overwhelmed or erased.

When we take human beings with unresolved personal, psychological experiences (say, a strict authoritarian upbringing) and we layer on another whole set of external stresses or misfortunes, the mix can be explosive. There is a limit to the resilience of people. Many citizens today are hostile, and many are enraged. Some of Donald Trump's supporters fit into this group, and he deliberately encourages their angry and resentful emotions.

Trump himself obviously has psychological problems. That he could imagine himself as prepared to be President is only one of them. His pathological lying and his deliberate efforts to increase the divisions in the American citizenry also reveal a damaged man. And as many citizens accept and embrace him, our society becomes sicker and more unstable. For all members of our society, there is a cost to all this emotion, and our need to cope with it. Whether you are expressing constant anger, or constantly just observing and understanding it, the destructive rawness takes a toll on our mental health. Our mental health is not growing, it is being diminished.

Just as the combination of unhappy individual experiences, personal emotions, and the biggest forces in our society are bringing out the alienation and anger in citizens, so too they can engender another result in a different group of citizens. A significant portion of the population is depressed and demoralized. While serious alienation from one's culture can trigger either aggression or depression (or both), and while these two "groups" sometimes overlap and are not sharply, neatly defined, they each illustrate different emotional responses to our world today. Through the preceding chapters, I've explained how the forces acting on society understandably provoke a lot of anger. And anger, often being loud, active, combative, and energizing for its owners, gets noticed and discussed. Certainly, both around the world and here at home, we are recognizing the anger and common denominators that are electing authoritarian or right-wing parties in democratic countries.

Depression or demoralization, on the other hand, is not given its full due as being a consequence often of the forces acting on us. Depressed people typically withdraw somewhat from society, become quiet and passive, and don't usually form into political movements and citizen activists. It is the very definition of demoralized people to feel powerless, helpless, hopeless, and paralyzed.

I have described how the poisonous content on Webworld, the meanness and dishonesty in right-wing media, the march of automation, the destruction of the natural environment (in the next chapter), and many other dynamics of today's world are just hammering people's psyches. Many people feel assaulted by so much that is occurring. As a web-dominated digital world is layered over everything, and increasingly we are required (without choice) to filter and navigate more and more of routine life through it, we feel the loss of control that this entails. And furthermore, we aren't asked to participate in selecting the paths that connectivity will impose on us.

We also feel a loss of control in the tempo, superficiality, and triviality of debate in the political sphere. As tweeting, sound-bites, and 24/7 online chaff steadily degrade the possibilities for meaningful discussion and sustained thoughtfulness, we observe this and are damaged by it. For many people, it is depressing, and it engenders a feeling of helplessness. There are lots of reasons for our political dysfunction—donor money in the system, for one—but a large one is the difficulty of conducting large, serious conversations about the most important issues we face.

Automation, robotization, artificial intelligence, and the elimination of jobs—present and future—cause anxiety and foreboding in many people. It is another area where many feel that we have no control over our lives. Who gets to decide which 10 or 20 million jobs will be automated and eliminated over the next 20 years? Who outsourced or eliminated the gone jobs of the past 40 years? Well, not you and I, the ordinary workers. Some people respond by getting angry, some become resigned, others become depressed.

Another area where many of us feel helpless to alter the path of technology, capitalism, and society is in the natural environment. As I'll describe in the next chapter, we are moving steadily—with resolve even—toward absolute catastrophe in the natural world. Our industries, economics, energy systems, resource use, living standards, and much else are all largely designed and operating in ways that bear no sane relationship to living on a finite planet. Unequivocally, we are on a path to a horrible, painful future, in this century. Some of those citizens who can see this are demoralized and depressed. Many are still working hard to make changes to society that might alter this outcome, but their efforts and successes are small compared to the forces—and their dominance—that are yearly bringing us closer to various, serious ecological collapses.

Another thought about Trump needs to be inserted here. As he speaks and behaves in a manner that displays his lack of concern for what's right—the honor, fairness, care, and moral contracts that we mentioned earlier—he elicits feelings of shock and betrayal in many citizens. That betrayal—Trump's shredding of long-trusted social and moral conventions—is profoundly shattering to individuals and society. It is alienating friends from friends as we divide into camps where one group is horrified and repelled by Trump's character, and the other group appears to accept it (whether reluctantly or explicitly). Our shock at his lack of honor is compounded by the unnerving effect of watching citizens with whom we thought we shared certain patriotic baseline credos and decencies, make excuses for his behavior, or shrug their shoulders, or give rationales for why it's necessary to overlook his polarizing words. If you're not a Trump supporter, there's a good chance that you're making some sort of adjustments to protect yourself—your psyche, spirit, beliefs, and expectations—from the disappointment of the betrayal you feel. Whatever the nature of your adjustments are, it is almost a certainty that they involve a suppression or depression of thinking and behavior that you used to engage in without hesitation. And again, this is diminishing society as a whole.

For many reasons then, it is an alienating world, and whether you are on the right or the left, and whether you suffer anger, resentment, depression, or withdrawal, or you simply can't cope with the speed, hype, craziness, irresponsibility, and dishonesty saturating nearly every aspect of our society, you are most likely diminished in some way. Your energy and motivation may suffer; you may sleep poorly; you may be overweight, unfit, unhealthy, or obese; you may be lonely; you may not trust people or institutions; you may sometimes feel empty or hopeless or even full of dread; you may question the value or truth of things you have long believed. In the most literal ways, you may be participating less, or less effectively, in society, at work, or in the duties of a citizen in a democracy.

If citizens were not human beings—if they were emotionless, hyperlogical beings—we wouldn't have to factor human nature into our thinking about society. We wouldn't have to understand human nature as a force in its own right, and also as a force that is acted upon by other forces.

But we are dealing with people and their emotions, and they are the actors and agents that are one of the coins of society. It is humans—not bots—who respond or not, who are seduced or not, who create solutions or not, and who both affect and are affected by the forces of society. As we observe and assess the dynamics today of capitalism, technology, Webworld, politics, media, and education, we would do well to keep in mind the potential, the limitations, and the current expressions of human nature.

CHAPTER 8

THE ENVIRONMENT

WHILE THIS BOOK acknowledges that most of the forces acting on us today are not new, it does maintain that their impacts now are unprecedented and—acting together—large and lethal. Whether we consider capitalism, technology, Webworld, or donor money in politics, all of it is substantially out of control and substantially whipsawing us. The accumulating effects are damaging us and society and, not least, the environment.

As we damage the natural world—and have been damaging it increasingly for 300 years or so—it is being degraded and destabilized to a point where it soon will no longer be a supportive or safe environment in which to live. We are rapidly approaching the time when planet earth will no longer support the large societies and civilizations that are spread across its surface. It will no longer be hospitable to billions of humans.

In some ways, the environment as a force and as a danger will come to trump the dangers of the other forces. It actually probably already does. After all, when human societies can't survive on the planet, it won't matter that, say, income inequality has reached obscene levels. But at the moment, it is the aggregated total of all the other forces and their consequences that are playing the major role in sustaining human destruction of the environment, and in preventing us from addressing and reforming our suicidal practices. Literally, it is the combination of out-of-control capitalism, rampant technological advances, the poison dominating Webworld, and the financial capture of politics that is retarding any meaningful action on global warming and environmental deterioration. So while a natural world in chaos will be our ultimate undoing, at the moment it is all of our behavior as embodied in all the "non-environmental" forces that is the biggest threat.

There are many human-caused impacts on the environment. The most damaging one today involves the amount of carbon dioxide that we are placing into the atmosphere. Since the beginning of the Industrial Revolution approximately 270 years ago, our burning of the fossil fuels of wood, coal, natural gas, and oil has steadily released increasing amounts of carbon dioxide into the air. Our power plants, industrial processes, heated and cooled buildings, trains and motor vehicles, airplanes, and ships all exhaust literally billions of tons of CO_2—a waste byproduct of combustion—into the atmosphere every year.

Initially, during the early decades of industrialization, this was not a global problem. In the absence of regulation, local communities and regions did become heavily polluted, but not sufficiently to become globally connected. In the 1800s, the relatively clean atmosphere could absorb and cope with the comparatively small quantities of carbon dioxide being emitted. And the human population, its industries, and the areas of developed land were all still manageable in comparison to nature's size, cleansing capacities, and resilience.

But today, the situation has become quite different. We have had two centuries of spreading industrialization, urbanization, and progress; a whopping population increase of 7 billion people (from about 1 billion in 1800 to nearly 8 billion today); the loss of millions of square miles of trees and greenery; and the introduction of "modernity" and its material lifestyle into nearly every corner of the globe. Today, the atmosphere (and other parts of the natural world) is being stressed and overwhelmed beyond its ability to safely digest or shed man-made CO_2.

We have reached the point where the chemical composition—the mix of gases—of the atmosphere is warming the earth excessively and destabilizing climate conditions across the planet. Specifically, the amount of carbon dioxide in the air has climbed to a new high level that is increasingly affecting (negatively) the balances and equilibrium of many of the important soil, water, chemical, weather, and climate patterns and cycles around the world. This sounds incredible. How is this possible? Man is so small, and the sky and the planet are so huge.

Well, it turns out that the "sky" is not so huge and what we call "air" is not so infinite. What we usually mean when we refer to the earth's "atmosphere" is the lower layer of air and chemicals that encircle the planet. This layer is only 60 miles or so in thickness, and critically, it doesn't mix much with the upper layers of the atmosphere located above it. So, effectively, any CO_2 or other pollutant that we put into the air stays in this thin lower belt. And all weather, climate, and atmospheric behavior and conditions are generated by the dynamics within this 60-mile layer around the earth. This layer also acts like an insulating blanket—letting the sun's energy in and then trapping it next to the earth—keeping our planet warm. (This is the "greenhouse effect" you've heard about, and some amount of it—within a proper balance—is necessary to keep earth's temperatures habitable for man and organisms.)

Most people, who rightfully perceive the sky as something "big," are astounded to learn just how thin it—the lower atmosphere—really is. Compare our 60-mile-thick sky with the diameter of the planet—7,900 miles or so—and you can get a sense of what a narrow band it is. The sky—the part of the atmosphere most relevant to us—is really just a thin shell surrounding the earth.

Above our sky-layer shell is the upper atmosphere. It is stratified into nearly pure, low-density layers of oxygen, helium, and hydrogen. This is not "air" remotely as we know it. These gases each weigh progressively less, and are held in place by the earth's gravitational pull. The hydrogen layer, the band furthest from the earth, eventually blends seamlessly into what we call "outer space" at an altitude of roughly 30,000 miles. In fact, outer space is practically indistinguishable from the top layer of our upper atmosphere as both are composed primarily of widely-spaced hydrogen particles.

I mentioned that carbon dioxide exhaust gases are constrained to remain in the lower atmosphere. They are not free to just drift "upward" indefinitely and diffuse harmlessly into infinite outer space. Instead, they are accumulating in the lower atmosphere—our sky—and increasing the concentration of CO_2 in the air. Now here's a difficult part of the global warming story to imagine. At best and at worst, the amount of carbon dioxide in the atmosphere today is tiny—about four one-hundredths of a percent. Most of the air is composed of nitrogen, oxygen, argon, and water vapor. About 78 percent is nitrogen, 21 percent is oxygen, and 1 percent is argon. That's about 100 percent already, before adding in trace amounts of hydrogen, helium, neon, krypton, xenon, radon, and carbon. The carbon can be in the form of methane, carbon monoxide, or carbon dioxide.

The CO_2 portion of the air today is equivalent to about 410 parts per million. That percentage is increasing every year by about 2 parts per million. At the start of the Industrial Revolution around 1750, CO_2 comprised roughly only 275 parts per million. So man is on the way to doubling the amount of this gas in the air, and therein lies the trouble.

Although carbon dioxide constitutes a very small proportion of the air, it is extremely effective at absorbing heat and containing it within the lower atmosphere. Briefly, what happens is this: incoming solar radiation penetrates the atmosphere and strikes the surfaces of the earth, warming them. They then re-radiate that solar warmth, but they do it with heat and light wavelengths that are longer than those of the incoming solar light and heat. The carbon dioxide gas molecules readily absorb these longer wavelengths and thus trap and concentrate the heat in the air, helping to keep both the earth and the air temperatures warmer.

And although CO_2 comprises a very small percentage of the atmosphere's gases, it is still a formidable quantity in absolute numbers. And man is adding approximately 35 billion tons of it per year into the sky.

Another atmospheric chemical factor that will increasingly come into play as we approach 2040 or 2050 or so is the effect of releases of methane gas. As the planet warms dramatically, especially in the northern hemisphere, huge areas of permafrost—permanently frozen ground—will begin to melt. In parts of Russia above the Arctic Circle, for example, temperatures in the past 30 years have risen 4 degrees Fahrenheit and have started to soften the permafrost; by 2050, temperatures there are expected to climb another 8 to 10 degrees F. In Alaska, all the permafrost will be gone by 2050. Arctic permafrost contains the remains of dead, barely decomposed plants that centuries ago froze and became buried. As the plants thaw out, microbes will start to process this organic matter, and carbon dioxide and methane will be released. Because there are enormous quantities of permafrost, and because methane is many times more effective than carbon dioxide at trapping heat in the atmosphere, this additional gas will accelerate the speed and impacts of global warming.

* * * *

The consequences of a warming planet and atmosphere are starting to be felt and observed, and they will continue to worsen. Already, around the world, we have seen changes in regional climates, in climate stability and norms, and in the expressions of weather. Generally, we are seeing a severity and frequency of storms, extreme temperatures, rainfalls, droughts, and other conditions which are atypical and unrepresentative of the regions where they are occurring.

With the global average temperature setting a new record high nearly every year, or consistently ranking among the hottest years, we are seeing a host of related events. More frequent and more deadly hurricanes, more frequent and more severe forest fires, longer and hotter droughts, and more intense rainfall downpour incidents are occurring as a function of the destabilizing climates across the globe. The colossal ice sheets and glaciers of Antarctica, the Arctic north, Greenland, Iceland, and the mountain ranges around the world are melting at increasingly faster rates. The glaciers of the Andes, Himalayas, Europe, and the northern countries are melting steadily and those located at altitudes lower than 15,000 feet or so may ultimately disappear (there are exceptions; the glaciers of the Karakorum Range in Central and South Asia, for example, are mostly remaining stable). In some areas, especially in the northern latitudes, long-covered permafrost and peaty grounds are being exposed and melting, and threaten to emit huge volumes of methane gas. The melting and destabilization of glaciers also disrupts long-established patterns of seasonal water runoff, drinking-water supply, and the irrigation of agricultural lands and natural vegetation across large areas and populations of the world.

On many continents, wildfires, topsoil loss, desertification, shrinking aquifers, polluted lakes, and extended heat waves are becoming more common. In India, China, and Bangladesh especially, air quality is poor, with pollution from power plants, industry, motor vehicles, and the burning of fields and vegetation all contributing to smoggy skies.

Here in the United States, in the past 10 years we have seen devastating hurricanes and incredible rainfall and flooding. We are seeing evidence of a warming and rising ocean. We are seeing hotter summers, less snowfall, and longer forest-fire seasons. In the western states especially, the hotter seasons are wreaking havoc on biomes and ecological systems that have long been stable. The great forests of the west are under assault from unusual heat, insects, forest fires, lack of water, and soil erosion. As the annual temperatures steadily move upward, the western mountains and forests receive less snow and have fewer sustained periods of below-freezing temperatures. As a consequence, there is less quantity of spring-season runoff, and also less water in the summer. All of these changes, which are gradual and often not apparent to the casual observer, nonetheless represent meaningful disruptions to the normal patterns that maintain healthy and resilient plants and landscapes.

The enormous forest fires in California in the last few years provide an example of how global warming contributes to and feeds off of the fragility of the existing balances in nature. Many factors contribute to these fires, which have occurred naturally for centuries, but which now have become worse and more frequent as a consequence of man's activities. With inappropriate land development in natural fire corridors, the building on floodplains and in chaparral country, excessive fire suppression (leading to an accumulation of incendiary dry vegetation), and the steady acceleration of carbon emissions into the air globally, we are damaging nature's resilience and stability. The special California conditions that feed its wildfires—intense heat, prolonged periods of drought, extremely low air humidity, forest dryness, and increased winds—are all exacerbated by a heating world. In fact, so bad has the fire risk become in California that now almost the entire state is vulnerable, and the fire seasons—which used to occupy distinct time periods—are practically year-round. What we are watching there now—the infernos, the mass evacuations, the deliberate interruptions to electrical power—will continue to expand until much of the state becomes uninhabitable in any normal sense. The only reason that residents there can survive what is already routinely occurring—week-long power outages—is because the temperatures generally are not especially cold, and because temporary support comes from outside the burning areas.

Another example of degradations in the environment can be seen in the Rocky Mountains. Changes in winter temperatures there are causing infestations of the pine beetle, which drills and destroys trees, to become much worse. The beetle population used to be kept in check when most of its larvae would die during long winter freezes. Today, most of the larvae survive. The trees are weak or dying, the soils are drying out, and the frequency and intensity of forest fires are increasing. Large swaths of forest have been devastated.

Across the world, as the population grows and development spreads, we are continually reducing the amount of land covered in natural vegetation, trees, wetlands, rainforests, and wild habitat of many types. This development lessens the capacity of the natural ecosystem to absorb carbon dioxide, and it simultaneously produces new CO_2. The loss of habitats also stresses the populations of many wild animals, birds, insects, pollinators, fungi, and plants. In many species, the total number of organisms is declining dramatically, and in many cases outright extinction is occurring. This is an emergency that will only become worse in the coming decades. Non-stop habitat loss and depletion of species pose risks to the integrated operation of the biosphere. Nature as a whole becomes less resilient.

The increasing levels of CO_2 in the air are also ominous for the oceans. As the air temperature rises, so the ocean temperatures are rising. And a considerable amount of CO_2 is absorbed directly into the seas. Warmer water is detrimental to many species of fish and it is harmful to coral reefs. Already, located in the warm southern waters, corals are dying and bleaching out in large swaths. Carbon dioxide emissions, warming waters, and ocean acidification (from absorbing more CO_2) are all endangering the reefs, home to something like 5 million different species. We don't even know the full consequences of threatening an ocean biodiversity that large.

Another product of the warming oceans is the unwelcome explosion in global jellyfish populations. Jellyfish thrive in warm seas, and in water that has less oxygen. They also magnify global warming damage, consuming the copepods and other plankton that are helpful—through photosynthesis—in removing CO_2 from the atmosphere and oceans. As we over-fish or kill many species, damage the complicated, interconnected ecosystems of the oceans, and thereby damage the predators, organisms, and other natural biological checks on jellyfish blooms, they surge out of control.

It is important to note that air and sea temperature increases are not spread uniformly across the world. Although we may say that the "average" global temperature has increased 1 or 2 degrees Fahrenheit, in reality different locations experience different increases. In some regions of the northern latitudes, for example, average annual air temperatures for many years have been 3 to 7 degrees Fahrenheit above normal. And as this causes an inordinate loss of sea ice in the summer months—almost disappearing entirely in the Arctic Ocean, for example—it exposes an atypically large area of dark-color water (darker than white ice), which then absorbs more sunlight, which then further accelerates the warming anomaly. These sorts of destructive circular feedbacks are occurring in various ways and places around the world.

This points out a central feature of nature and ecological systems. The natural world is not just a diverse collection of plants, animals, and geography. It is a complex, living, balanced mosaic of interwoven and interconnected organisms, physical conditions, and relationships. The environment and its inhabitants are all part of unbroken biological, chemical, physical, and geological cycles that are critical to nature's equilibrium and functioning. These processes are sensitive to the temperatures, salinity, atmosphere, precipitation, winds, pollution, seasons, and conditions of the environment.

Really, the ecosphere is just a big petri dish. Everything is connected to everything else, and altering one organism or chemical or physical characteristic will inevitably affect something else in the dish, some way. The essential quality of ecosystems—above all else—is their interconnectedness.

By injecting carbon dioxide into the sky in massive and unprecedented quantities, and at rates like nothing in natural history, we are conducting the world's biggest—and biggest-ever—uncontrolled experiment. It is a certainty that the CO_2 is precipitating reactions and changes in the organisms, environments, and cycles around the world. Much of that process is silent, invisible, gradual, and relatively slow, and we are only now starting to recognize some of the largest and obviously destructive impacts.

* * *

For a long time—maybe 40 years or so—scientists have been looking hard at global warming. The basic science involved has been understood for a much longer period—maybe 100 years—but it was the recognition of just how rapidly and relentlessly we were filling the skies with carbon dioxide that really triggered the scientific community to focus on CO_2's warming effects. Now, there remains no doubt about the forces that we have put into motion, and the events that they will precipitate. We may not know the precise timing of each consequence, but we know that they will occur—are occurring—throughout this century. By 2045 or 2050 (and beyond, of course), many parts of the natural environment will be damaged, and entire ecological patterns, cycles, and systems will have become disrupted and will be breaking down. With our industry, transportation, cities, and sprawl, we are causing a whole slew of reactions which will make the average global temperature rise by about 8 to 10 degrees Fahrenheit by 2100. Some parts of the globe will get hotter faster than others. Nonetheless, wherever we live, the increase will be catastrophic.

Some estimates of global warming have predicted a less dire temperature increase. Most climate scientists have offered a range of possibilities. But here's an important thing to know. For at least 30 years, scientists have been offering descriptions and predictions about climate change, its likely effects, and its possible future temperature increases. Understandably, it's been difficult to project with precision every environmental change, loss of ice, level of ocean warming, amount of drought, number of severe storms, and all of the other numerical and date-tied consequences of an overheating planet. So, for 30 years, scientists have issued warnings that have almost always included a range of possible temperature increases and a range of possible dangers (like really bad hurricanes) and have accompanied them with a range of timetables. But for 30 years, a pattern has emerged. Consistently, either temperature increases, or negative weather events, or adverse developments (like collapsing ice shelves) have been occurring ahead of schedule. By that I mean that the developing global warming dynamics are consistently hitting the marks outlined at the more pessimistic end of the predictions.

So we should take no comfort from the somewhat gently-offered "ranges" in which the full variety of disasters might play out. The scientific process—and the data to date—demands the couching of predictions in these ranges. Three other factors are at work here, which restrain the scientists. One, the ecological system is so complex, with such potential for the as-yet-unknown consequences of warming, that scientists have no way to definitively integrate those dire connections and negative effects into predictions. Two, scientists cannot quite believe that we are going to do nothing—effectively—to mitigate our destructive practices. So almost every prediction-report comes with a range that lays out scenarios based on various levels of constructive societal response. And three, neither scientists nor the public can bear to look fully in the eye of the planet of 2100. It would be terrifying; it is terrifying. A categorical statement from the entire (essentially) scientific community about what we will face in 2100 would some day—if not today—cause terror and maybe panic. What we will face in 2100—and well before—is so horrible as to be almost beyond the capacity of a modern Western mind to really believe, or dwell on.

By 2050, at almost every location in the world, what had once been that area's longstanding, normal weather and climate will be undergoing significant change. And simultaneously, societies around the world will be breaking down too. For a variety of reasons—which I'll explain in later chapters—I expect the worst to occur, both environmentally and societally.

The most devastating effects are going to come from the combined consequences of intense heat, drought, lack of potable water, and coastal flooding. Many regions of many countries will have sustained heat waves. Many locales—that don't experience this now—will for the first time experience weeks-long or months-long periods of daytime temperatures above 90 or 100 or 110 degrees Fahrenheit, and elevated nighttime temperatures that will not offer satisfactory cooling-off relief. Some regions of the world—those that are already very hot in the summer—will experience daytime temperatures that for weeks may be over 110 or 120 degrees or so Fahrenheit. These locations—where millions of people live now—will actually become nearly uninhabitable, or uninhabitable.

I live near Boston, Massachusetts. Currently, we have roughly 12 summer days when the temperature exceeds 90 degrees Fahrenheit. Sixty years ago, that number was 5 or 6 days. But by 2070, daytime temperatures in Boston will exceed 90 degrees on 90 separate days. That is basically the entire summer. Many days will be over 100 degrees. And nighttime temperatures—maybe in the low or mid-80s—will not drop enough to permit any natural, non-mechanical cooling and relief. Additionally, at night, as the city's buildings and streets re-radiate the sunlight-heat that they absorbed during the day, the hot conditions will be and feel relentless. During the summer, the mostly-masonry urban neighborhoods will become nearly unbearable; the inner-city climate will be life-threatening for many people. The city, its residences, its cooling systems, and its power supply are not prepared to endure a climate of sustained heat.

In parts of Africa, India, and Central Asia, where hundreds of millions of people live, by 2050 there will be extended periods when the daytime temperatures exceed 110 to 130 degrees Fahrenheit. Nighttime temperatures will be high and offer no respite from danger. The heat waves will be made worse by extreme water scarcity. Actual permanent drought is likely in Southern Europe, the Mideast, Iraq, Syria, and parts of China, India, Africa, Australia, and South America. These locations will become nearly uninhabitable.

Intense global heat will continue to melt glaciers, sea ice, and the ice sheets of Antarctica and Greenland. There are approximately 150,000 glaciers in the world, and almost all of them—from the Rocky Mountains to the Andes to the Alps to the Himalayas—are melting today at alarming rates. As a result of that steadily increasing discharge of water into the seas, and the fact that the ocean waters expand as they get warmer across the globe, the ocean level along the coast of Massachusetts will quite likely rise 8 to 10 feet by 2100. That will result in catastrophic flooding of one-quarter to one-third of the city of Boston. But long before 2100, many storms, many severe high tides, and substantial flooding will have already created chaos, panic, and immense financial loss to the city. Mass migration out of the city will begin long before 2100, and probably before 2050.

The same dynamic will occur in countless other American towns, suburbs, cities, and regions along our coasts. Along the entire eastern shore especially, millions of people will be displaced. New York, Atlantic City, Baltimore, Norfolk, Charleston, Savannah, Jacksonville, and Miami will all be severely flooded, just to name a handful of communities. The entire bottom third of Florida, where 7 million people live, will be flooded.

Across the world, well before 2100, hundreds of millions of people will be forced to abandon their homes because of rising seas and salt-contaminated drinking supplies. London, the Netherlands, Shanghai, Mumbai, Basra, Bangkok, Osaka, Jakarta, Rio de Janeiro, Alexandria and the Nile delta, and Bangladesh are just a few examples of coastal locales that will see deadly flooding. In Shanghai alone, where almost the entire city will be submerged, 20 million residents will be forced to flee. In Bangladesh, 30 or 40 million people will be pushed out by the rising water. The chaos, profound unmanageability, and outward-extending shock waves of these massive migrations will be unprecedented. On every continent, by 2050, we will start to see the movements of hordes of refugees.

In addition to the rise in sea level, the character of the water itself is changing. By 2045 or 2050, the oceans will be much warmer and much more acidic because of all the CO_2 they will have absorbed. A more acidic ocean will make it more difficult for clams, oysters, mussels, scallops, shrimp, lobsters, copepods, corals, and other shelled organisms to build their carapaces and hard shells. Shell material is made from calcium carbonate and more acidic (lower pH) oceans make it far more difficult chemically for organisms to assemble their shells. Nobody knows for sure what quantity of mollusks will die off. But it is a certainty that—between hotter waters and acidification—all of the coral reefs in the entire world will be dead by 2045 or 2050. This will surely trigger many serious negative consequences in the oceans, including the deaths of many entire species of fish and marine organisms and other horrible cascading effects throughout the connected ecologies of the seas. Hundreds of millions of people rely on reef fish for food, and they too will suffer.

Food production across the world will plunge. As extreme heat and drought spread across the globe, they will most damage the areas of the world that now harbor the best and largest croplands. Lack of rain and irrigation water, combined with temperatures that are too high for optimum crop yields, will dramatically lower the amount of food we can produce globally. Aquifers everywhere are being drawn down at rapid rates. In the United States, the Great Plains farmlands will see drought conditions many times worse than those that occurred during the Dust Bowl in the 1930s. By 2050, or earlier, many parts of the Ogallala Aquifer, which lies under eight states in the flat middle of the country and which supplies the irrigation water to our wheat, corn, soy, and cotton crops—as well as to cattle ranching and oil and gas drilling—will be effectively empty. This aquifer makes possible the bounty of grain produce that we use to help feed the United States and much of the world's people. But here and abroad, simultaneously, food production levels will decrease significantly, and that will contribute to the overall environmental and societal crisis.

Across the world, as temperatures rise and rainfall becomes more storm-deluge-driven but less in annual quantity in many regions, soils will degrade and become less fertile for farmland use. Erosion, vulnerability to wind and drying, and desertification will occur in increasing numbers of areas. Good soil, which like the lower atmosphere comprises only a thin shell on the surface of the earth, will become relatively scarce everywhere.

By 2045 or 2050, other dangers will be present and rising. Infectious diseases will be ascendant and spreading into geographical areas that have

rarely seen these plagues. The southern hemispheres will have huge out-
breaks of malaria, yellow fever, typhoid fever, dengue fever, zika fever,
and even diphtheria, and these illnesses will not stay confined there. As
destructively hot and violent weather prompts the migration of both people and insects—especially mosquitoes—and as the volume of refugees
causes breakdowns in medical treatments, protocols of many types, and
order itself, disease transmission will spread and grow. By 2050, five billion people—half the world population then—will live in zones where
most of these illnesses will be present and thriving.

By 2050, the air in most places around the world will be far dirtier
than it is today. It will contain more ground-level ozone—resulting in
smog—and it will contain more soot and particulate matter. Increased forest fires around the world, the continued burning of fossil fuels, the loss of
vegetated lands to development, and the burning of woods for small-scale
fuel and crops (by individuals) all will contribute to deteriorating air quality. Rainforests everywhere will come under increasing pressure from both
man and climate conditions. Across the globe, we take down rainforests
to harvest their commercial woods and to create farmlands and livestock
grazing areas. In places like Sumatra, Borneo, Malaysia, and Indonesia, we
remove rainforests and replace them with palm oil plantations. As these
special, lush forests are reduced in size, their destruction results in large
CO_2 releases into the atmosphere, less climate stability, and less pho-
tosynthetic oxygen production. Eventually, as they shrink, dry out, suffer drought, and generally become less resilient, they could themselves
become vulnerable to the kinds of massive forest fires that now affect more
temperate-area forests (such as California's).

The Amazon rainforest, an enormous nature reserve that spans parts of
nine South American countries, is inconceivably large. It is so big and ecologically influential that it is critical to the stable functioning of the global
climate. It is so huge that it generates its own rainfall and weather, and it is
tied into the wind and ocean currents of the globe. Yet man, since 1970 or
so, has already removed the natural vegetation and tree cover from about
one-fifth of it. Today, it continues to be threatened unrelentingly by a slew
of man's activities. The modern world's demand for wood, gold, beef, and
agricultural products—and what it will pay for them—creates irresistible
pressures on native populations to clear the forest to provide those goods.
In the Amazon consequently, there is extensive mining, cattle grazing,

farming, and logging. The indigenous peoples of the region, increasingly exposed to outsiders, drug money, and contemporary life, and the pleasures and conveniences and electronic devices that accompany it, cannot defend the forest. On the contrary, they are actively burning it. And the governments that are charged with protecting it are also too often seduced by the profits of exploiting it. By 2050, it is quite likely that one-third or more of the entire Amazon rainforest will be destroyed. By 2050, shocking though it seems, the rainforest may very well be in the process of becoming a desert or savannah—drought-stricken and thoroughly dry. In combination with all of the other environmental crimes that will unfold by then, the global climate will be destabilized and polluted beyond recovery.

In addition to the burning of the rainforests, northern forests around the world are increasingly vulnerable. Already, there are unusual, significant blazes in Alaska and Siberia. Often these fires expose and burn peaty land, which sets in motion further carbon dioxide releases. By 2050 or 2070, as societies and order break down, large fires may rage unchecked across wilderness areas on every continent.

Keep in mind that all of these negative environmental developments are occurring against a backdrop of a world population that will increase from around 7.8 billion today to around 9.5 billion in 2050. After 2050 or so, for a variety of reasons, the global population may climb, dip, or plateau—it can't be predicted with assurance—but we do know we'll reach at least 9 or 10 billion anyway.

The implications of having 9 billion people on the earth are terrible. All of the awful environmental conditions that I've described in this chapter will be accelerated and made worse by 2 billion more people. It is humans that are placing loads on the environment, despoiling it, eliminating it, polluting it, and exhausting its natural resources. Humans need to eat, stay warm or cool, play, travel, consume, entertain themselves, kill other living organisms, and dominate nature. Like no other time in history, we are concentrating in enormous, sprawling metropolises, and we are—with rapid globalization—reaching and paving and developing nearly every part of every continent (except Antarctica).

* * * *

Although I have been writing this chapter as though "the environment" is a discrete element that today is deteriorating, in fact it is a factor that is interwoven with all of the other forces described in this book, and inseparable from them. The deplorable condition of the environment today is a direct result of man's activities over the past 300 years. It is our industry and societies that have created an atmosphere containing more carbon dioxide than at any point during the last 650,000 years. This is a new and unprecedented development, with no historical parallel during modern man's tenure on the planet.

Simultaneously, while man warps the environment, it is gathering-up to lash us. This too—during man's time—has no historical parallel. Our entire economic system, our technologies, our transportation systems, and every piece of the many elements of our societies are based on and rely on the realities and patterns and stabilities of nothing less than planet earth. Our capitalism, our human settlements big and small, our material progress and civilizational order all depend upon earth's resources and eminent habitability. Throughout human history, right up to the present, in the most foundational and profound way human life and prosperity have been facilitated by 15,000 years of nearly unbroken ecological health.

That benign span is now ended. As the human-damaged ecosphere manifests—today and into the future—all of its interrupted or distorted cycles and its abnormal (but now normal) climate changes, those new environmental realities will collide with the old assumptions of our economics and technologies. As I mentioned in the chapter on capitalism, we have designed an economic system that requires ever-expanding growth and consumption, and an ever-growing utilization of the earth's natural resources. That actually never made sense even when the planet was healthy—since the planet is not infinite—but now that the ecosphere is gravely damaged and getting sicker, we will really witness the disconnect. As the diminishing water supplies, poorer soil quality, excessive heat, acidic oceans, imbalanced atmosphere, and horrible climate changes all create ecological conditions that we cannot cope with, our economic, technological, food production, and other globalized systems will collapse. Simultaneously, our political systems and societies will collapse.

Although there are a plethora of dependencies and vulnerabilities that characterize the globalized world that we here in the developed nations have made, it is difficult to predict exactly which one—or set of ones— will fall apart first. There are too many possibilities that lead to catastrophe. We have created a prosperous First World, but one that is now precarious and fragile.

It's possible that environmental conditions will become so bad that they set in motion a cascade of unraveling. If droughts, hurricanes, typhoons, hailstorms, floods, polluted air, forest fires, rising oceans, and heat waves become increasingly frequent and significant, they may cause mass population migrations and also trigger economic crises. They could cause massive crop failures, interrupted supply chains, resource scarcity, panic, civil war, and conflict between nations. These events may easily occur before 2040 or 2045 or so.

It is worth emphasizing the unavoidably global nature of the coming dissolutions. Because intense heat, drought, water shortages, and soil exhaustion may initially be worse in the southern and equatorial nations, some Americans may be under the impression that those countries alone will deteriorate and descend into chaos, while the nations of more northern latitudes—such as Canada, Scandinavia, and the United States—escape society-rending disruptions. That is wishful thinking. The collapse of southern and mid-latitude areas will halt global supply, resource, labor, production, and demand chains, will send hordes of refugees all over the world, and will produce civil war and violence in spreading waves. The global economy, and the American economy, will collapse. There will be no safe harbor as the environment explodes.

Another possibility is that technological breakdown, or various financial crises, or political dysfunction or extremism may precede environmental disaster. The hyperconnectivity—with the web and the Internet of Things—of our globalized capitalism and globalized industries makes these possibilities just as likely as the collapse of our ecosystem. These outcomes too will probably occur by 2045 or so.

But the common denominator behind whatever path we take to societal collapse is the ongoing contradiction between the ways we have organized our progress and the nature of the ecosphere. Fundamentally, our entire technological system and our entire economic system have no relationship to the most primary realities of the physical, biological, and chemical world. For centuries, we have been able to get away with that contradiction. Now, equipped with an array of unprecedented, enormous, and powerful forces, and bestriding the earth with nearly 8 billion people, we are in the midst of colliding with almost all of earth's natural cycles and patterns.

CHAPTER 9

HUMAN POPULATION

O F ALL THE FORCES DESCRIBED IN THIS BOOK, "human population" is the simplest and easiest to understand. It refers to the total
number of people on the planet. Yet, along with "human nature" it is perhaps not discussed enough, not really given its due as a major factor when
we consider the problems of the present and the future. Our population
total does not receive enough attention.

Today there are 7.8 billion people on earth. We have multiplied pro-
digiously; in 1800, there were only 1 billion of us. And by 2050, we will
be approximately 9.5 billion strong.

One of the points of this book is to assert that the collection of forces
that faces humanity today has a power, size, interconnectivity, and impact
never before seen. Well, it's a certainty that mankind has never attempted
to have 7.8 billion people (let alone 9.5 billion) on the earth before. So the
sheer magnitude of human beings on the planet today is unprecedented.
And that will continue to be the case right up to 2050 or so (beyond that,
we aren't sure population growth will continue).

Humans are certainly having an impact on the planet. The primary
consequence of the total human presence—combined with our activities—on the planet is appalling and unsustainable damage to the natural environment. We are polluting the land, rivers, lakes, seas, and sky.
Our towns, cities, vehicles, industries, recreation, and consumption are
devouring the raw materials and natural resources of the planet. And our
emissions, byproducts, and wastes are overwhelming the natural cycles
and systems and resilience of the ecosphere. We constantly violate the

healthy ecological processes of the physical, biological, chemical, and geological cycles of nature.

As I described in the chapters on capitalism and the environment, our modern societies are organized around principles that bear no relationship to the limits and realities of a finite planet. In the developed world, our system of economics especially remains bizarre. It cannot work and thrive unless citizens purchase goods and services at an extraordinary pace. In the United States, for example, unless consumer spending relentlessly maintains a magnitude that can fuel 70 percent of the gross domestic product, the economy will drop into a recession, with all of the negative consequences that would attend that. Of course, while we manufacture and buy consumer products at a frenzied rate, we trouble ourselves little by wondering how this economic model will resolve itself on a planet of fixed dimensions.

When we talk about the human load on our natural world, it is important to understand the role of our modern standard of living in determining our impacts on the environment. Across the nearly 200 nations of the world, there are enormous differences in the levels of development and technological and material progress. Not all of our 8 billion earthlings live at the same pace, consume at the same rate, or corral and oppress the natural world to the same degree. Even within one country, there can be vast differences in lifestyle and consumption.

In the developed world—like the United States—a successful, affluent person lives like a king, surrounded by comfort and plenty and wanting for nothing. He has more than enough to eat, has heat, air conditioning, and humidity control, and may have more than one home. He has two or three cars, drives where and when he wants, takes vacations, travels, has recreational pastimes, and selects and buys whatever he desires from a veritable cornucopia of consumer products. He has computers, tablets, big-screen TVs, and an array of digital gadgets. His entertainment possibilities are endless. If he lives in or near the city, he takes advantage of its cultural offerings and social possibilities. If he lives in the suburbs or a more rural town, he may take pride in an impressively green lawn, spreading fertilizer, pesticides, and weed killer to maintain it. The lawn may receive regular watering from an automatic in-ground sprinkler system. Our prosperous American possesses lawn mowers, weed whackers, leaf blowers, power tools, snowblowers, boats, all-terrain vehicles, and snowmobiles. In the summer, he may water-ski; in the winter he may downhill ski. He has pets. His lifestyle, his comforts, and his standard of living are ensured by an endless supply of light, power, fuel, and energy. He need deny himself nothing. Lastly, he has good health, good medical care, and physical safety.

The American's footprint on the planet is enormous. His consumption, his energy use, and the waste his household and activities generate are huge.

Now, take a rural, subsistence citizen of a Third World country anywhere in the world. In an undeveloped nation, that citizen—who is one of billions on the planet—may have nothing, and may fight every day just to stay alive. His food supply is unreliable, his water supply is unreliable and contaminated, and he may breathe unhealthy, polluted air. His health is terrible, he is exposed to horrible infections and diseases, and his lifespan will be many years shorter than our affluent American's.

If he has migrated to the city, he is living in a sprawling shantytown on the urban edge. He probably left the countryside in the hope of finding a job, but he may not have found one. His material conditions are no better than they were in his rural village. Either way—city or country—his level of consumption, energy use, and waste, and his footprint on the planet are negligible. An inhabitant of a developed nation has an impact on nature that is literally hundreds of times greater than that of a Third World resident.

Of course, in both developed and undeveloped nations, there are billions of people who fall between affluence and abject poverty. These are the ordinary workers of the world, and their standards of living, energy use, and habits of consumption vary widely.

It is powerful to acknowledge the vast disparities in the lifestyles, material conditions, and ways of living among the global population of 8 billion people (never mind 9.5 billion). For we are already severely trashing the biosphere and its processes with this population load when only roughly 2 to 3 billion people are reaching any significant level of consumption. And maybe only half of those live at the standards of middle-class Americans.

The ecosystems of the planet already cannot absorb the burgeoning consequences of the economic activities of the inhabitants of only the First World. Yet the developing world is eagerly pursuing the standard of living of the developed West. How could the earth possibly parry the environmental assault that would result if another 1 billion, or 2 billion, or 3 billion, or 4 billion citizens—who are on the earth already—obtain the material conditions and consumption levels of America? It could not.

Yet, that is the plan. And it requires no conspiracy or ill intentions. Multinational corporations, Silicon Valley tech firms, the Wall Street financial sector, Webworld, the fossil fuel companies, and all of capitalism itself are designed for infinite growth, ever-increasing consumption, and speed. All of those business entities—which make up the reigning economic orthodoxy—see the whole world as one big market opportunity. When it comes to creating new consumers—and grooming and conditioning them into one homogenized, globalized, materialistic culture— corporations and advertisers make no distinctions between First and Third Worlds. They are vested in selling as much stuff to as many new consumers as possible, and as quickly as possible.

Capitalism as currently designed possesses no mechanisms for moderation, for checking itself, for self-regulation, or for reflection. It contains no internal way to assess damage to the environment, assess the quality of life, or gauge the wisdom of its practices. In fact, so foreign to the dynamics and calculus of capitalism are considerations like that that many conventional economists still think of them as "externalities," though they may be more discreet than to voice that long-used label out loud today. Capitalism is designed to value money, profit, production, speed, efficiency, and a host of other variables that have nothing to do with the health of the planet. Instead, it is filled with incentives to produce and reinforce human behavior aligned with its primarily mercantile values.

So China and India—with 2.8 billion people between them—and dozens of other developing nations are working hard to mimic the standards and practices of the consumer nations. As globalization for 40 years has steadily integrated and homogenized both the economies and cultures of the world's nations, they are inevitably adopting the version of capitalism that the U.S. uses.

Long before another 1 or 2 billion people reach an American standard of living, both society and the biosphere will collapse. There is not enough soil, water, air, and raw materials to support a global population of 3 or 4 billion people (never mind 7 or 8 billion) living like Americans.

We are living in an American economy and a burgeoning global economy guided by the greatest hoax of all time. Our governments, politicians, lobbyists, corporate leaders, corporations, advertisements, Wall Street financiers, and capitalism all predominantly support—with their behavior and the operation of the market—the idea that increasing prosperity for all peoples and nations is possible. This is not remotely possible, and it is fraudulent to promote that goal.

* * * *

There are other problems, secondary to man's impact on the environment, that a global population of anywhere from 8 billion (at present) to 10 billion people creates. One is the problem of finding jobs for that many people. There isn't enough paying work now for billions of people, and the job shortage promises only to get worse with automation, robotization, and the advancement of artificial intelligence. As I described in the chapter on capitalism, the developed countries have sent overseas many formerly good-paying manufacturing jobs, and have automated many others within the domestic factories that remain. This has had the effect of lowering wages in the developed nations; and while it did sometimes introduce additional work in the Third World nations, it was often at exploitive wages that were marginal in terms of lifting the living standards of the workers. Furthermore, over the past 10 or 15 years, there has been considerable automation even within the Third World countries. Many of the jobs that remain in both First and Third World nations are hourly, contract, temp, gig, or service-sector jobs. Most are low-paying, insecure, and without benefits. Corporations and the tech sector will continue to work hard to automate and eliminate workers, and this bodes ill for a global population of 8 to 10 billion.

Additionally, growing urbanization across the world exacerbates the gap between the number of jobs and the number of workers. There is a steady migration—especially in developing and Third World countries—of poor people from rural and farm areas into the cities. As environmental degradation and the structural enlarging and industrializing of agriculture push small and poor farmers off the land, and as diminishing or damaged (with excess salt or pollution) water supplies afflict other rural inhabitants, they move to the city. But as the teeming shantytowns around the world bear testament to, there are not jobs enough for all of the people in cities (that are rapidly becoming megacities) either. The condition of the humanity and the natural environment in those places can be described only as desperate. That is the present, and it is the future.

Another problem made bigger by our new global population size relates to Webworld and its dynamics. Brand new on the planet, the internet—now connecting roughly 4 billion people, and growing every single day—is a unique and unprecedented thing. As I described in the chapter on Webworld, it has the power to affect or influence many of us in ways that are harmful to ourselves, our societies, and democracy. Never before have so many people been able to connect with each other, relate to each other, learn about each other, and react to each other—and all of that instantly and constantly—as we can today. Obviously, that reality contains the potential for advancing knowledge, understanding, and tolerance, and plenty of people use the web for those positive goals. But as I've described, huge numbers of people are misusing the web, or being affected negatively by its influential dynamics. I believe that Webworld is like the carbon dioxide in the atmosphere—a huge runaway experiment without any controls. Effectively, Webworld is to the human mind what CO_2 is to the atmosphere.

We have ample evidence that the internet—Webworld—is damaging human society. We cannot control its poisonous parts and their effects on society and democracy. Not all web users mean harm, and not all fall under its seductions. But a critical mass of people do, and their number—and the web's dynamics—are sufficient to render moot the many positive aspects of the internet.

So it is shocking that we have already connected 4 billion people, and are intent on connecting the rest as fast as possible. We have no idea if we'll be able to control or contain Webworld's effects. So far, we cannot. Since some percentage of the population uses Webworld either as a narcotic or to tear other people down, and some percentage is manipulated, seduced, deceived, abused, or made stupid by the web, the sheer enormity of the number of people on the planet ensures that very large numbers are available to perpetuate the negative dynamics of Webworld. Our global population is unprecedented in size, and still growing rapidly. The number of people getting their "entertainment" and "information" from the web is unprecedented, and still growing rapidly. Put those two realities together and we've got a disaster in the present that promises only to get worse.

Similarly, another problem accompanying an enormous global population is the sheer number of people who have—or will develop—either trauma or depression or both. In the chapter on human nature I described the damage to society that occurs when citizens suffer from trauma, depression, demoralization, alienation, or withdrawal. Although these injured people always constitute only a percentage of the human population, they form a significant number of people in absolute numerical terms. Like the critical mass of people who spread poison on the internet—and the equally critical number of people who are affected by it—the number of traumatized or depressed (or otherwise damaged) people exerts a powerful effect on the dynamics of society. Damaged people can act as a ceiling—a limitation—on what is possible in terms of the development, emotional advancement, and enlightenment of a society.

Furthermore, as the global population grows, and as many conditions deteriorate in the decades ahead, the number of traumatized, angry, depressed, or otherwise limited people will increase, and their impact on society—restraining its emotional growth, resilience, flexibility, and maturity—will only grow greater. The future will hold many reasons for people to become even more depressed, more fearful, and more emotional than they are now. With an ever-expanding global population being forced to process ever more troubling developments, we can expect the citizenry to become less rational and less capable.

At any one time today in the United States, there are probably 40 to 50 million people who are suffering some significant degree of depression or emotional turmoil. Some have years-long depression. Others may be experiencing a 6-month affliction; they will eventually improve, but their places will be taken by new patients. The emotional moods, conditions, and psychic turbulence of all of these people play a role in determining the collective direction our society takes. And that same dynamic plays out in the populations of every society and nation in the world. In a frightening and deteriorating world, fear and emotions will come to dominate the responses that people everywhere will bring to planetary-scale breakdowns.

Another more prosaic but nonetheless important consequence of a very large population is the road traffic that it creates. With the epic size of modern cities, and the concentration of citizens within them, the number of vehicles on the roads today has become a major factor in the experience of people's daily lives. Traffic has many deleterious effects on the natural environment, on the beauty of built places, on our sense of place and landmarks, and on the quality of our lives. In the next chapter, I will describe these effects.

In general, the large populations of individual nations, and the enormous global population, make more difficult almost every problem we have. The forces and problems described in this book are magnified, and the dynamics around them become more unmanageable, as the world population grows.

* * * *

So there is no confusion about the various issues surrounding human population, what is most critical is the total impact of all the people on the planet. What is critical is not some magic (or ideal) total number of earthlings, but what quantity of natural resources we use, how much pollution and waste we generate, and the degree to which we upset the important balances and cycles of the biosphere. These factors are the relevant considerations regardless of the total population or how it is distributed among the nations.

At least for the present, it is misguided to think in terms of trying to identify some optimum number of people that the earth could support. Because we are currently so far from anything remotely approaching a sustainable model of economic life, we could destroy the planet with either 3 billion people or 10 billion people. Conversely, if we were to redesign everything, we could live sustainably on it with 3 billion or 10 billion people. What matters are our practices and consumption and compatibility with nature's systems. For various reasons, the West got a head start on development and modernization before the Asian nations were able to fully industrialize, and so it raised its standard of living and its output of pollution well before Asia, the Third World, and one-time colonial nations. Now that China, India, and the developing nations are catching up to western-style footprints, and contributing their fair share of resource depletion and carbon dioxide emissions, we can see how wastefully and recklessly the West has been living. And as all the nations of the world—increasingly viewed by capitalism as one giant market opportunity—buy into modern consumption and "progress," the natural world is being wracked beyond its ability to maintain its necessary equilibrium. Any of a number of ecological collapses and catastrophes await.

CHAPTER 10

TRANSPORTATION

TRANSPORTATION ISSUES don't affect every American, at least in the sense of direct, day-to-day experiences. For the resident of a rural region, who works reasonably close to home, and who may visit a nearby city only occasionally, commuting and traveling by car can be an easy, convenient, pleasant, and even relatively economical activity. Large swaths of the country are sparsely settled, the roads are good, and the passing landscapes are attractive. Americans in these areas don't encounter traffic congestion problems and so transportation as a concern and as a force in their lives—unlike all the other forces described in this book—doesn't exist. They may have many problems, but transportation isn't one of them.

But the vast majority of Americans—who live in cities, suburbs, metropolitan areas, and the land areas adjacent to those conurbations—are today experiencing roads and highways with truly impressive, unprecedented amounts of traffic. Across the country, in spreading areas, traffic congestion is becoming severe, and for longer periods of each day than ever before. Traffic jams occur routinely now in locations where they never did in the past.

In and around cities, and in the endless sprawl of suburbs, malls, and office parks, people commuting to and from work now often face 1-hour—and longer—drives each way. And the quality of that drive is often horrible, with long stretches of stop-and-go traffic, and random, unpredictable delays. Daily, people cannot count on their commutes to take a knowable, plannable, fixed amount of time. Because so many roads during the ordinary rush-hours are filled to (and beyond) their design capacities, any accident, bad weather, or other unusual event can create extraordinary backups. And in many metropolitan areas, there is no evening "rush-hour;" traffic begins mid-afternoon and doesn't subside until 7 or 8 at night.

For those commuters who daily rely on trains, buses, and subways, often their experiences are not easier than the people in autos. Many mass transit systems are struggling. They may have old equipment, inadequate maintenance, and insufficient capacities for the number of passengers trying to use the systems at rush-hour. The heating and cooling equipment in the cars and buses often malfunctions, and delays occur in many routes. Many cars are overfilled and passengers are forced to stand for long periods of a trip (or the entire trip).

Ticket prices and monthly passes for many mass transit systems are not cheap, and many riders of low or modest incomes struggle to afford them. Fare increases occur on a regular basis and oftentimes they result in a reduction in total ridership. Many transit systems nonetheless are struggling financially. Their annual budgets usually require state assistance, and that can be a hard sell to taxpayers from the rural areas. Automobiles, on the other hand, are universally owned and loved, and so roads and highways are more easily supported by state and federal budgets, and by the taxpayers. Despite that support—or perhaps because of it—gas taxes are kept relatively low.

Adding to the woes of both automobile commuters and the transit systems, the invention and introduction of ride-hailing services such as Uber and Lyft have increased traffic congestion in the cities and have stolen ridership away from the buses and subways at the same time. Initially, because these services so obviously cut into the patronage of conventional taxis, we thought that that was the extent of their unintended (or intended) consequences. But we are now realizing that the ride-hails also draw significantly from public transit ridership. These added trips just further clog the city streets.

* * * *

Commuters have no choice but to endure either the daily traffic of the roads or the daily struggle with a mass transit system. For everyone the consequences are bad. Let's take a look at the toll on drivers.

Sitting in a car and fighting with traffic congestion is unhealthy. Physiologically, it is bad for us. It affects our heart rate, blood pressure, and adrenalin levels. The biochemistry of the brain is affected; traffic increases the production of stress hormones while it reduces the presence of healthy, calming, brain chemicals. Traffic and our negative reaction to it suppress the production of beneficial neurotransmitters such as oxytocin, dopamine, and serotonin. Consequently, we literally feel worse; we may feel somewhat depressed or anxious. We may return home at an end-of-day commute and bicker with our spouse. We may be more likely to "need" an alcoholic drink. And sitting in a car two hours (or more) a day, regardless of traffic stresses, is sedentary in the extreme. It is two hours of sitting motionless. Yet it drains us physically.

Psychically, commuting daily in traffic is destructive. It is dispiriting, alienating, frustrating, and angering. It can be boring and tedious. If traffic is making us late for an appointment, we are anxious and impatient and tense. Traffic can make many drivers aggressive, rude, and even drive dangerously. At times, on overcrowded roads we all struggle to cope emotionally.

Traffic wastes our time, energy, resources, and money. Millions of stopped and idling and intermittently moving cars increase the smog and pollution levels beyond what would occur in the absence of traffic congestion.

There is another aspect of traffic as a negative force that is giving it a role in preparing us for an advancing technology that will only worsen our relationship to mobility. I am referring to the slow but steady installation into cars of all sorts of computerized driving aids. Nobody had requested these "nanny" devices, but Silicon Valley and the car manufacturers dreamed them up. We may like them or not, but accept them we will, because we will not be given a choice by the market. And remember, the market favors private cars over public mass transit, and is working to make cars and traffic more acceptable to us. Semi-automated cars (and hybrids and electrics) are part of that effort.

Bearing that in mind, let's consider our love-hate relationship with the car, our responses to traffic, and the unfolding battle between private automobiles and public transportation. This contest is at a critical point because the levels of gridlock on the roads are becoming so threatening to the economy, general mobility, and the quality of life. Especially in the cities, heavy and regular traffic makes obvious the insanity of having neglected more capable and more widespread mass transit. Put drivers in stopped traffic long enough and frequently enough, and they'll start to demand better public transportation alternatives.

At the moment, traffic can make us feel powerless; we become angry at the congestion, and then we become angry at the politicians and leaders who have done nothing to prevent jammed roads. Yet, improvements aren't coming, so we are forced to accept longer commutes. We make adjustments, adapt to congestion, get used to it, adopt some degree of resignation, and stop imagining that conditions will improve.

But our cars—through technology—are starting to cope with traffic. Equipped with sensors, radar, lidar, and numerous exterior-facing cameras, many models (and more every year) can now brake and accelerate automatically, and stay in their lanes, in moderate, low-speed traffic. These semi-autonomous vehicles are still being developed, but car manufacturers, tech companies, Wall Street, and just about every other conventional financial interest in the world are hoping that continued technological advancement will eventually produce a car requiring minimal driver involvement, at least in commuter traffic. Achieving that goal would allow drivers to work or play on a smartphone or laptop on the way to work. They'll be able to spend two more hours a day online. Thus engaged or distracted, they would not mind a longer commute, or be upset by traffic. Demands that the state address traffic would be less urgent (maybe even diminish or disappear) and the personal car would retain its status as preferable to any form of mass transit.

This "solution" to traffic congestion would be terrible for the planet, but would continue business-as-usual for global corporations. It's no accident that cars and SUVs today are now nicer than the homes of most people. Even an average new vehicle comes with an interior comprehensively equipped with luxury features, conveniences, and materials that are nearly astounding. Inside a car or SUV, with food, drink, perfect temperature control, leather seating, phone, and full internet and social media connectivity, an occupant feels good. He understands that he is in an environment that was put together deliberately and thoughtfully, with him in mind. He feels respected, acknowledged, catered to, important, and empowered. What is fascinating is that, while traffic congestion and gridlock make our commuter feel disrespected and impotent, the steady evolution of cars from basic transportation to luxurious, supremely comfortable, affirming personal pods is sufficient to checkmate the traffic negatives. The experience and sensation of being coddled in a beautiful, perfectly ergonomic interior compensates for putting up with the traffic. And as cars become partly autonomous, especially in the mind-numbing conditions of low-speed stop-and-go congestion, allowing the driver to ignore the traffic and instead focus on the affirmations available on his laptop (or the car's web-connected computer screen), the automobile will continue to be the transportation mode of choice for innumerable citizens both here in the U.S. and across the world.

Additionally, as billions of drivers and passengers, sequestered in their automobiles for billions of minutes, talk, type, scroll, work, and surf online, they will generate reams of data about every aspect of their lives, health, thoughts, jobs, behavior, and interests. Monitored audibly and visually by the cameras, smart computers, and AI embedded everywhere in their cars—and no, not "defeatable" or opt-out-able—they will provide the auto manufacturers and the tech companies with a treasure trove of information. This data will be weaponized to create more advanced software, to further automation, and to influence and direct our behavior. The harvesting and surveillance of our data taken from our time in automobiles will be no different than that which occurs when we are sitting at our desktop computers.

Some cars already have interior-facing cameras in them. The cameras focus on observing the driver's eyes and his head position. If the camera detects that the eyelids are too frequently or for too long closing, or the head is drooping, the dashboard emits warning beeps and displays flashing lights and causes the steering wheel to vibrate in the driver's hands. Similarly, the computers in the car can detect when the driver's hands are off the steering wheel for a certain period of time, and again trigger lights and audible alarms to startle the driver. The steering wheel has sensors in it that can also read the pulse-rate of the driver. These automatic systems are marketed to us as "safety" or "convenience" features, but in reality they are a necessary part of semi-autonomous cars, and semi-autonomous or eventually fully autonomous cars are part of the Silicon Valley agenda. Despite the claims of auto manufacturers and tech companies that they are motivated by concerns for our safety, their true motivation is the money to be made by their partnership—from both the expensive computer hardware and software now required in the auto, and in the mining of the nearly infinite, new data collected as we ride in our vehicles. At some point too, the insurance companies will increase their access to the reams of data and camera footage as they seek to monitor drivers and vehicles more closely and reduce company costs and risks.

Another consequence of the continued dominance of cars as transportation, and their increasing web-connectivity, is a gradual and perhaps subtle diminishment of the idea of landscape and the idea of physical places. Roads, cars, traffic, pollution, congestion, and development sprawl already degrade both the beauty and the experience of the landscape. Slowly, we are required to accept that. We either look at it and try not to repeatedly acknowledge and process the ugliness, or we don't look at it at all. As a coping mechanism, we choose not to see it.

And now, inside beautiful cars, surrounded by a bubble-environment tailored to us, and engaged via screen to any part of Webworld we like, we are even less likely to look out the windows. (Oftentimes we don't well know where we are anyway, since we rely on navigation systems to direct us.) So landmarks, beautiful places, parks and trees, good architecture, and orderly man-made environments become less and less important to us. Slowly, we will value them less, and so we won't defend and protect their existence. This gradual erosion of the idea of "placeness," here furthered by the isolation, pleasure, and distance available inside a car, is complemented by the advance of connectivity in all sectors of society. As I described in the chapters on technology and Webworld, there are innumerable ways that the development of digital technology and the web are changing our attitudes toward physical places and undermining both our need and respect for them.

With cars so attractive and luxurious, and becoming partially self-driving, the pressure to improve mass transit systems gets reduced, both here and abroad. And of course, in China, India, and the developing world, car manufacturers are working steadily to inculcate the driving habit in billions of new users. The car sales market in China and India alone—with more than 2 billion potential buyers—has auto manufacturers and computer technology companies very motivated to achieve influence there. As I described in the chapter on capitalism, there is currently no economic model in use that would permit car companies and computer companies to deliberately slow down; deliberately state that increased development of mass transit would be better for China, India, the U.S., and the world; and that the ongoing warming of the atmosphere demands it. Even if those companies see the looming ecological catastrophe coming, they are prisoners of an economic system that cannot permit the consideration of such an eventuality. Regardless of every serious, large, and indisputable environmental factor, the automotive and computer industries are compelled to view every Chinese, Indian, Cambodian, and African as not more and not less than an eventual customer.

Given the population of the United States and the world, its concentration in cities, and our long awareness of pollution and energy issues, it is almost shocking how inadequate our mass transit systems and their capacities are. Ideally, our transit systems would have been thought of as logical, indispensable solutions to the problem of moving millions of people around in densely settled communities. If the development and expansion of public transportation had kept pace with the growth in population and the expansion of real estate development, there would be a spider web of rail trolleys throughout the cities and suburbs, and we would be far better off today in a myriad of ways.

However, once the automobile was invented, the very idea of mass transit was put on the defensive. The auto industry and its related oil, rubber, road-making, and parts industries have long fought against the existence, expansion, and maintenance of transit systems. The history of National City Lines, Pacific City Lines, and American City Lines bears vivid testament to the ruthlessness arrayed against all forms of mass transportation. Those three companies were put together or financed by General Motors, Standard Oil, Firestone Tire, and other automotive-related interests for the purpose of purchasing and shutting down streetcar and trolley systems across the country. Between 1936 and 1950, those three companies—holding companies really—bought more than 100 streetcar systems in 45 cities. Upon closing the deal in each city, the companies would immediately cease trolley operations and immediately—sometimes literally the next day—commence to ripping the streetcar tracks right out of the streets. The companies would initially replace the electric trolleys with buses—which were manufactured by General Motors, rode on rubber tires, used the public roads, and burned gasoline or diesel fuel. Eventually, the automotive consortium behind the companies would reduce the number of bus routes, and then sometimes halt service altogether. They would often sell the systems to other companies that would then buy their buses from General Motors. Commuters found the buses to be a poor substitute for the streetcars. It's no wonder that commuters in many cities and suburbs ended up in automobiles.

Few Americans today know the story of General Motors and National City Lines and the other G.M. subsidiaries, but it is a tale of one of the most significant events in all of American history. It created realities on the ground and had consequences across the nation that we are still coping with today. Too late, some observers saw the enormous and shocking damage being done, and they attempted to halt General Motors. In 1949 the company was found guilty of criminally conspiring with other automotive interests to eliminate streetcar systems and replace them with buses. But the federal courts imposed only minimal fines on G.M., and the company continued to convert trolley systems to buses until 1955. By then, approximately 90 percent of the nation's streetcar network had been destroyed.

In the United States, people who must rely on the public mass transit system are often at a disadvantage, compared with citizens who have the option to drive. If people are too poor to own a car, they can be severely constrained when it comes to employment opportunities, educational opportunities, medical appointments, shopping, and all sorts of necessary activities. Finding a route—even with transfers—that can get you from one particular location to another particular location is often simply impossible. Without a car, one's mobility and possible connections are held hostage to the range, effectiveness, and reliability of public transportation. In addition, the significant levels of income inequality within the American population are often expressed in—among other ways—the demographics of who has no choice but to depend upon mass transit. This can sometimes stigmatize mass transit as a second-class ride, and it certainly diminishes the political clout of its advocates. We can see this demonstrated clearly on a windy, rainy day when we drive (in our cars) by a bus stop without a shelter and see people waiting there exposed and getting soaked. That simply would not be allowed to happen if public transportation and the people who have to ride it were respected. Daily, weekly, monthly, the commuters who must rely on buses and subways endure conditions that tell them, "You are nobody, and your time and frustration and well-being are of no importance." Just as occurred throughout the twentieth century, mass transit still struggles against capitalism's bias in favor of the private-market automobile.

Compared with the forces of capitalism, technology, Webworld, and politics, transportation might seem a relatively small force to contend with. But its power and effects are both obvious and subtle, and its dynamics exist as both real and pervasive things. Like Webworld, it is diminishing us—almost all of us—and limiting society's capacities with steady, incremental duress, and it is softening us up to accept and continue the dominant technocratic approach to problem solving. It is training (or conditioning) us to be passive, and it is training us to look forward to more of the digital world.

There are many examples of the outright insanity embodied in the ways that we have structured so much about society. There is a wealth of examples to choose from. But the thinking and attitudes represented by the recent evolution of the private automobile, the SUV, and the "recreational" pickup truck, in the face of the intersecting issues of traffic, energy use, population size, land use, resource allocation, environmental degradation, and sustainability generally, might be among the best examples of our insanity.

Our relationship to traffic and our vehicles captures so much about us and the forces of capitalism, technology, politics, and human nature. For those forces have built our transportation system. For our part, without much choice really, we have contributed mostly passivity and endorsement. As I've pointed out, it doesn't take a lot to seduce and manipulate us. So, as the world deteriorates in every conceivable way, everywhere we go we drag with us 4,000 pounds of steel, glass, plastic, carbon fiber, wiring, and computers.

We are headed for the abyss alright, but damned if we're not going in anything less than the biggest, fanciest Nissan Armada. I mean, c'mon, it's going to be all-electric.

CHAPTER 11

MISCELLANEOUS FORCES

THE WORLD TODAY is one hyper-speed, noisy place. In the preceding chapters, I have described the major forces at work in American society, and to a large extent those are the forces at work across the globe in a critical mass of countries and areas. But there are many other forces and factors everywhere that are challenging us too. I rank them as second-tier forces not because they are unimportant, but primarily because they do not in the present or immediate future (say, the next 20 years) appear to have the power to precipitate the breakdown and collapse of civilization itself.

Instead, they are themselves indicators that all or parts of societies (across the world) are breaking down; they are the results, not the cause, of breakdown. In some cases, they are developments that indicate either a dysfunction or an inability in addressing old or new problems. And most of these "miscellaneous" forces are in reality pieces of the larger forces that I have already identified and outlined. As such, they add to the complexity and difficulties characterizing those larger forces.

The forces that I will briefly discuss here—immigration and refugee migrations, terrorism, black-white relations, health care, student loan debt, gene editing, war and nuclear war, and religion—are all very significant, and they pose terrible problems (or possibilities) for millions of people, but their repercussions are unlikely to change the course of entire human societies. That said, however—make no mistake—these "second-tier" forces can be life-or-death factors for the people for whom one or more of these items is really the only thing that matters right now in their lives. Some of these forces afflict significant numbers of people with a power sufficient to cause trauma or death. If you're sick and dying today without health care; if you're a black man shot by the police; or if you're a sweatshop worker in danger of being deported back to El Salvador, you have existential problems that are more urgent than the possible failure of capitalism 20 years from now.

IMMIGRATION AND REFUGEE MIGRATIONS

The issues of immigration and refugee migrations—here in the United States and across the world—are receiving enormous and deserved attention. Large population movements are a force with many varying causes and circumstances. There is the mass migration of refugees from conflicts in Syria, Libya, Sudan, and many other countries. There are refugees fleeing the gang violence in Honduras, Guatemala, and El Salvador. There are millions escaping destitution, starvation, sickness, and danger in Venezuela. There are people everywhere—Bangladesh, India, Australia, Africa—leaving the increasing environmental catastrophes of drought, floods, cyclones, forest fires, and other threats. And there are the millions of people who are migrating simply to find economic opportunity and the ability to provide for themselves and their families.

In a world with plenty of sustained violence, environmental deterioration, repression, and poverty, it is inevitable that large numbers of people will want to escape those conditions. The United States itself was created and populated by immigrants and refugees. That has worked out very well for this country. Immigration continues today, and although some number (approximately 11 million) of people from other countries are undocumented, their contribution overall to our nation is positive.

However, President Trump and some of his supporters are very hostile to immigrants and refugees from Hispanic and Muslim countries, and they want us to feel scared and threatened by those migrants. In his desire to sow fear in the American citizenry, Trump especially has been irresponsible and dishonest in his public statements about immigrants. This has made immigration into a far bigger and more controversial and emotional issue than it should be. It also makes American citizens less informed and more reactionary; it works to obscure the truth about the larger forces today that make any person's life a bleak one, whether he's a Guatemalan or a citizen of the U.S. The Mexican or Central American who is fleeing to the U.S. is just running from an extreme version of the same corrupt political and economic conditions that have been slowly squeezing American workers for 40 years. We don't have the shockingly brutal and widespread gang violence that plagues El Salvador and Honduras, but we've got—in a slower, more subtle, velvet glove—a substantial amount of the political corruption, economic injustice, and struggle to make a decent living that plagues the southern migrants.

If the U.S. wanted to reduce the flow of southern migrants to this country, it would work to improve the conditions of their lives in their native countries. Admittedly, that's a slow and difficult process. But instead of increasing foreign aid and program assistance to the governments, NGOs, and people of Central America, President Trump ordered the complete cessation of aid.

Ironically, Americans here should recognize that kind of response. For it's what's been done—very slowly—to Americans for 40 years. More and more, over the decades, American workers have been told, especially by the private sector, "You're on your own." Perhaps if President Trump announced that what the people of El Salvador, Honduras, and Guatemala really need are good jobs, a government that represents them, and safety, American citizens would realize that that's what we need too.

But instead, Trump uses immigrants as a scapegoat or a distraction, wanting his supporters to be so riled about them that they remain uninformed about the real and significant forces in their own lives, and the real causes of their own disempowerment and financial disappointment. But as I described in the chapters on capitalism and politics, for 40 years the ordinary American worker has been victimized not by immigrants but by globalization, automation, deregulation, Wall Street financial chicanery, a tax code for corporations and the wealthy, income inequality, wage stagnation, and employment degradation. Those are the forces that have made—and are making—America what it is, and undocumented immigrants are responsible for none of that.

Did undocumented immigrants cause the 2008 Wall Street meltdown? Did Mexicans, Guatemalans, Hondurans, and Salvadorans in the 1980s and 1990s close American manufacturing facilities and send those jobs overseas to China and Vietnam? In the 1980s, did they hollow out the steel industries in what we now call the Rust Belt? Are illegal immigrants responsible for four decades of globalization, automation, and—now—robotization? Are they the Silicon Valley utopians currently developing—as fast as they can—the artificial intelligence to replace human workers? Are illegal immigrants staffing the corporate lobbying firms that designed the tax code and implemented the deregulations that turned capitalism into a predatory, winner-takes-all system? Finally, are there undocumented migrants occupying seats on the Supreme Court that has ruled repeatedly to remove the restraints on the role of big money in politics?

It is ironic to be building walls around the United States when the real enemies of the American worker are located here inside the country. Building walls on the southern border will not help American workers. Sure, there is some competition from immigrants for entry-level jobs here, but the lion's share of the difficulties besetting American workers comes from the political, economic, and technological juggernaut that is driving American and global societies. That is the story of our time.

Nobody should misunderstand here what I am saying when I label immigration as a "second-tier" force in America. For many of President Trump's supporters, it is a force of the first order. They believe his warnings that we are being "invaded" and "infected" by swarms of foreigners along the southern border, and that our country will be transformed for the worst by these people who are not like us. But just because Trump promotes that view, and just because millions of Americans believe it, does not make it accurate or true. In actuality, as one of the nation's many challenges, accommodating immigration is a problem that pales in both significance and difficulty when compared to the most important forces that I describe in this book. We must take the management of immigration and the worries of American citizens seriously, but currently the issue serves most to obstruct solidarity among American citizens.

In Europe, the tensions of immigration and refugee migration are much greater than here, and for good reason. Decades of conflict in Iraq, Afghanistan, and Pakistan, followed by eight years of war in Syria and numerous conflicts in Africa have driven millions of people out of those areas, and many of them have sought safety in European countries. Although the vast majority of Syrian war refugees are temporarily (or not) living in Lebanon, Jordan, Turkey, Egypt, and other Arab or Muslim countries, there are relatively large numbers also in Germany, Hungary, Sweden, France, and The Netherlands. Additionally, many refugees pass through—with some staying in—Greece, Italy, and the Balkan nations on the way to destinations further north, so nearly all countries are affected in one way or another by the migration. Because the refugees arrived in fairly rapid fashion, and because there are real challenges in assisting them and integrating them into new (to them) cultures, citizens of destination countries have legitimate concerns regarding these matters. Nonetheless, just as in the United States, some European leaders are fanning inordinate fear and hostility of the newcomers. And just as here, that can confuse ordinary workers into scapegoating immigrants and refugees for structural economic, technological, and political developments that have long victimized those native-born citizens.

It is important to note here that while at the moment I am classifying immigration and migration as a second-tier issue, over time it will rise to become a primary challenge to organized societies. As we neglect to address the major threats that are the focus of this book, societies and natural environments around the world will continue to deteriorate, malfunction, and break down. As a consequence of that, huge numbers of people—eventually reaching hundreds of millions or more within this century—will choose to or be forced to flee societal collapse and ecological devastation. If you think that Europe and the southern border of the United States have seen a lot of migrants and refugees in recent years, just wait until we have economic, technological, digital, or environmental failures within the next decades. When it comes to human migrations, we haven't seen anything yet.

TERRORISM

Another factor being exaggerated and misused by some politicians and other voices—mostly on the right—is the threat of terrorism. While it is a real and serious problem, it remains a second-tier issue when compared against the current and constant emergencies unfolding as a result of the forces that are the focus of this book. There have been terrible instances of terrorism in the United States and across the world, and terrorism occurs on a daily basis in many countries. Muslim and Arab regions especially are struggling with various identities of Islam, and extremists within those conflicts inflict shocking and fanatical violence indiscriminately. Within the United States and other nations, there have also been many cases of anti-Islamic, anti-immigrant, anti-black, and anti-dissident violence and terrorism. As anger, confusion, humiliation, exploitation, and emotional distress generally continue to grow, terrorism of various types may spread.

Although terrorism today generally is still a secondary force, there are countries in the world where violence, chaos, destitution, and danger have become the dominant realities that inhabitants there have to face. Like population migration, those realities may become more widespread as we neglect to address their root causes.

BLACK-WHITE RELATIONS

In the United States, another important force in the lives of many citizens is the bigotry and extreme prejudice against black people that still exists in the hearts and minds of many emotionally underdeveloped people. In recent years, with more attention being put on police forces and their occasions of brutality and lethal violence against blacks, and with the rise in visibility of white supremacist groups, the nation as a whole has become more aware of how extensive bigotry still is. The "Black Lives Matter" organization was formed in part as a response to the frequency and horrifying circumstances of too many incidents where policemen beat, subdued, or shot black citizens. And the sights of neo-Nazis and confederate-flag-bearing bigots marching and demonstrating in the streets, and forming communities online, are additional reminders that blacks still face extreme hostility—whether openly or in disguised form—from many in society. So while prejudice may be a second-tier force generally, it can be the primary issue for many a black person.

There is another aspect of black-white relations that is folded into the politics of the country. Because racism still exists, especially in the southern states, it is playing some role in national, electoral politics. Some number of Republican politicians, including President Trump, are speaking publicly in ways that give a subtle (or not subtle) affirmation to racism and racists. This is troubling and wrong and it further divides America.

And because of the way Webworld amplifies destructive and discredited ideas, and allows hateful people to connect with and encourage each other, racists and racism are quite visible today. We will see how this plays out in the 2020 elections.

Racism is a powerful force and it is a factor that has been woven—to the disadvantage of black people—into the structures and dynamics of our politics, economics, judicial system, patterns of incarceration, zoning and land development, and culture. In the 2016 election Donald Trump benefited from some amount of racism, but it is not a primary force on par with the others outlined in this book. Like prejudice against immigrants, it is enlarged and used by Trump and others as a distraction. If ordinary working-class Americans can be induced to blame blacks and immigrants for their troubles, then they won't look at the real reasons and forces that have victimized them occupationally, financially, educationally, and culturally.

Racism is poisonous because it destroys black lives. It also damages white lives. It contributes to an unhealthy culture that we all have to live in, and cope with. It also is an indication of serious ignorance, underdevelopment, dysfunction, or trauma in the lives of the racists. In the context of this book—weighing the story of our lives—it is a factor inseparable from the complexion of our politics and traumatized lives, but it will not be the cause of our eventual economic, technological, digital, or environmental collapse.

Finally, although I am labeling racism a "second-tier" force, there is a sense in which it is—like hostility to immigrants—part of a primary force. To the extent that racism is evidence of a sickness among people—a sort of limitation to their capacity to be their best selves, what I touched on in the chapter on human nature—then it becomes part of a primary force. In some sense, all of the factors that prevent the formation of ordinary-citizen solidarity are a force that prevents us from addressing the more tangible forces I have identified.

HEALTH CARE

In the United States, while we have made great strides in recent years in extending healthcare and health insurance to more and more people, we still have large, persistent problems in the health care system. The costs of care, drugs, operations, and hospital stays are enormous, and increasingly we struggle—as individuals and as a society—to pay for them. Plenty of low-income and working-class individuals still don't get the health care they need. Many people—something like 60 or 80 million—who actually have health insurance coverage struggle to pay the costs of high premiums and deductibles. Because of those costs, many people do not visit a doctor when something is wrong with them; and they may forego needed medicines and prescriptions because of the expenses of purchasing them. Many people have little or no savings, and any medical ailments create extra financial difficulties for them.

The crisis in health care costs is really a piece of the problems in capitalism today. As I outlined in the chapter on capitalism, with the steady globalization of jobs and the accompanying assault on labor, corporations have been able to take advantage of the desperation of workers in the United States and all over the world. Fifty and sixty years ago, American businesses routinely provided full health insurance coverage to their employees. But today, with the gigification of the economy and the widespread use of subcontractors, large companies are able deliberately to reduce the number of employees that they provide coverage to. And the health plans that they do provide invariably require larger contributions from their employees.

Lots of American workers are left with costly plans. And many of the workers who are self-employed, underemployed, employed part-time, or participating in the gig economy are left to find and purchase their own health plans. This has become a huge issue for tens of millions of citizens, and it is yet another illustration of the dysfunctions and economic injustices that are built into the version of capitalism that we have designed today.

STUDENT LOAN DEBT

The amounts of money that college students and graduates owe for the costs of their education are staggering. In total, roughly 44 million student borrowers owe approximately $1.6 trillion. It isn't unusual for graduates to have $30,000 to $40,000 of debt. And paying those balances back isn't easy when many jobs pay poorly—if a graduate can even find the right job—and when housing and ordinary cost-of-living expenditures compete for funding in a young person's budget.

Like health care costs, the exorbitant cost of higher education is a piece of the problems with capitalism today. We have designed an economy with skewed values and priorities, and we have chosen to subsidize the wrong things. And because good employment opportunities are so limited, and because corporations are automating and robotizing everywhere that they can, young graduates and students have very few clear career paths open to them. In fact, the future of employment generally is so bleak that Silicon Valley is advocating for a guaranteed annual minimum income payment. That is because tens of millions of Americans, within 20 to 25 years, will be permanently unemployed, replaced by digital machines. This will only make our capitalism even more dysfunctional, and it will surely not help students pay off their debt.

GENE EDITING

Although gene editing in humans is not yet a large force in society, it is poised to become a powerful one. With the advances in CRISPR technology, the process that allows removal of specific genes from the DNA of organisms, it appears to be only a matter of time before we humans start to modify both ourselves and much of the other life around us.

This could have beneficial results or absolutely disastrous ones. On the good side, potentially, we could use gene editing to modify human embryos that have harmful mutations. We might be able to alter the DNA for the purposes of eliminating, for example, Tay-Sachs disease, or cystic fibrosis, or sickle-cell anemia. If this could be done without triggering unintended consequences, it would be a positive, substantive medical intervention. Understandably, this work will likely remain a controversial subject.

Albeit with different procedures, we have for a long time used genetic engineering on food crops in order to breed them for certain traits. We have, for example, inserted the genes from one species into another species; we produce a variety of cotton plant that contains genes from certain bacteria so that the cotton develops a resistance to insect pests. We have bioengineered the DNA of corn plants to do the same thing. Although these strategies have undoubtedly increased farm productivities dramatically, they too are controversial; again, we can never be completely sure that they won't cause unintended consequences.

Many scientists are working constantly to try to improve the resistance of food crops to insects, viruses, parasites, diseases, and fungi. These are significant threats that global warming is making worse. In light of global warming, climate change, and deteriorating natural conditions, researchers have also been examining the possibilities of bioengineering crops that can survive drought, floods, high wind, and depleted or salty soil. These are worthy investigations conducted by reputable scientists, and the goals and results are publicly shared and debated.

The worry with CRISPR and other gene-editing processes, however, is the potential for rogue individuals—with malign intentions—to manipulate the genetic code of organisms. For example, bad actors could alter insects to carry infectious diseases or viruses that could attack plants, animals, or humans. Terrorists could create bioweapons by manipulating DNA, introducing it into the right cells, and have it produce a virulent disease that could be released into the general population.

These threats are intimately tied up with the internet. Increasingly, the materials, techniques, and instructions for re-engineering DNA—whether plant, animal, human, or insect—are proliferating on the web. Today, anybody can purchase DNA fragments, modified DNA, live frogs and other organisms, and the equipment and directions to put the experiments together. It is absolutely possible that a malicious biohacker will sooner or later create something biologically horrible and sell it online or unleash it himself somewhere in the world. As with so many other unfolding developments in today's connected world, time is not on our side.

WAR AND NUCLEAR WAR

If you're in Syria, Yemen, Afghanistan, Sudan, or many other conflict zones around the world, war is the force that is dominating your life. Whether you're fighting, a non-combatant, a refugee, or just trying to survive, war can make all other forces secondary.

But for us in the United States, and in other countries without open or ongoing conflict, war seems remote at the moment. American soldiers are fighting in many spots around the world, but because there is no draft, and because those conflicts seem tangential to our daily lives, we don't feel the urgency and panic that war engenders. So, speaking generally, measured across American society, war is not shaping our personalities, emotions, finances, choices, psyches, or thinking. Certainly not in the manner of the primary forces described in this book.

Of course, our annual military expenditures, and the trillions of dollars that we have spent in Afghanistan and Iraq, have affected us. They have required a significant portion of our tax dollars every year, and thereby left us with less funding for other priorities. The American invasion of Iraq in 2003 was particularly wrong-headed and wasteful of lives and money; it also made far worse the already-struggling relationship of Western hegemony to Islamic societies. Choosing—just bald choosing—to attack Iraq was an ignorant, careless, and reckless act. We—and the rest of the world—are still paying for it in many ways.

But, really, we don't spend a lot of time thinking about the military budget, so again, war isn't on our minds or affecting us noticeably as a force.

There have been times when the possibility of nuclear war has captured our attention. In the mid-1950s, the mid-1980s, and when President Trump and Kim Jong Un of North Korea had their short confrontation in 2018, we went through periods of anxiety and alertness to the nuclear threat. Aware that an exchange of nuclear missiles could devastate civilization, we felt fear and apprehension.

Today, I daresay, most of us do not spend any time contemplating nuclear war. Ironically, considering the huge number of nuclear weapons on the planet, and considering the lethality their use would produce, I consider them a less likely threat than the constellation of forces that are the focus of this book. I don't think that we'll die by nuclear war; I think that the interaction of the forces discussed in this book will produce our deaths, or lead to the breakdown of civilization that will then cause our deaths—one way or another. If nuclear weapons are used this century, it will be in response to the cascading failures of societies.

In any case, neither war nor nuclear war is perceived of as an imminent, pressing force for Americans (and plenty of other nationalities) today.

RELIGION

Considering the sheer number of people on the planet who—to one degree or another—have an association with a specific religion, you'd think that religion would be a primary force in society and in people's lives. But it isn't, especially in the United States.

We could be forgiven for hoping that houses of worship might act as centers of a new movement to help people understand our world, improve our values and perspectives, and develop brotherhood. This would seem to be a natural mission for religion. But that is not going to happen. In 2015, Pope Francis published an encyclical that was absolutely magisterial, diagnosing the ills that afflict societies across the world. It was a wise, inspiring call to every religion and every human on the planet to adopt—in response to the crises around us—a new, healthy, sustainable, and soulful (but not necessarily "religious") approach to remaking our civilization. And yet the book disappeared relatively quickly from the public focus.

Those who still think that religion might offer an effective path toward sanity also need look no further than the large evangelical Christian population in the U.S. It offers no hope either. While diverse and containing many constructive worshippers, plenty of its flock have embraced President Trump and his unchristian words and behavior.

There certainly are populations for whom devotion to a religion is paramount, and it truly guides their lives. The more orthodox members of any of the world's faiths are testament to that. Born-again Christians, ISIS Islamists, observant Hindus, strict Catholics, and Orthodox Jews are all groups with an obvious loyalty to a religion. Their lives and behavior may be deeply informed by their religious beliefs and what they see as their faith's tenets.

In the United States, religion is mostly not one of the primary forces shaping us. Other forces are bigger. Perhaps the understanding Americans have regarding the need to separate church and state plays the major role in tempering religion in our political, commercial, and cultural life. After all, we founded and enlarged this nation partly to have freedom from religious impositions. But we have plenty of churchgoers and religious people in the country. Their faiths shape them and inform them in some ways. Sometimes our politics on both the right and the left will explicitly make a call to our spiritual souls and our religious beliefs. Debates about abortion, marriage, the death penalty, and the concept of "just" war often make explicit references to what our religious beliefs say about these items. And of course, for many of us (like myself) who grew up within families who went to church or temple or synagogue and learned something of a religion, but who later—and now—ceased any overt, observable practice of that (or any) faith, religion is somewhere back there in the composition of our epistemology, forever contributing something to the person we are. (On a personal note, I often speculate about this with regard to myself. I grew up in a family that once a week—Sunday—went to a relatively open-hearted, Massachusetts, Protestant Congregational church. I attended regularly with my parents until I graduated from college and moved out on my own. I barely ever attended a church service after that. But I had loved the sermons. Our ministers—in my eyes—were like college professors. They gave talks that were intellectual, challenging, steeped in current events, and that thoroughly engaged me and made me think of ordinary things and ordinary life from all sorts of perspectives. The sermons weren't exactly "religious," but they contained material and messages that were meant to instigate our souls, spirits, values, and consciences. They form a part of my learning, and I'm grateful for that.)

But the evidence is all around us. Capitalism, commerce, technology, Webworld, politics, sports, hype, chaff, entertainment, and trends—those are the forces today that predominate. Those are the arenas where we find something to worship. Those are our relevant gods. For whatever our religion or faith or agnosticism, or atheism, we all have gods. But formal religion today is a secondary force.

CHAPTER 12

POSSIBLE REFORMS AND THEIR LIKELIHOOD

I HAVE DESCRIBED the major forces shaping both our individual lives and society. Again, though I've organized them into their own chapters, in reality each one is interwoven with all of the others. They are interconnected, interrelated, and in many important ways, inseparable. They are huge, complex forces, and fully understanding them and their power requires us to pay attention to the ways in which they associate with one another and depend on and reinforce each other. In fact, so tightly woven together are capitalism, technology, Webworld, and politics that changing any one of them in significant ways would require major adjustments to all of them. All of the forces are part of a culture. They are both producer and product of that culture.

Most of the forces are global, and most of the world population is experiencing them in one fashion or another. Obviously, nations across the world have real differences—physically, environmentally, economically, politically, historically, developmentally, and culturally—and so the forces operate with some variation. They may be altered somewhat in the societies of different countries, and they may exhibit modified expression in those and yet other nations. But their power, dynamics, and relentlessness are huge and inexhaustible and indefatigable, and they wear down other realities and ways. The forces, mostly Western in hegemony and values, have an homogenizing effect on the world; over time, other cultures are sanded down into the culture that the forces bring.

In the United States the forces are in their fullest, most unrestrained, most powerful, and most dominating states. Also here, compared with the rest of the world, they are at their most embraced and most unquestioned. However, simultaneously and somewhat ironically, because the American citizenry has become quite divided in many ways, a significant percentage of the population sees the flaws in the culture being produced today. Many Americans have many smart criticisms of the forces I've been describing, and they would support changes and reforms to improve the private sector, the public sector, and society.

CAPITALISM

We know what's wrong with capitalism today and we know how to fix it. What is needed are changes and reforms that will preserve the positive aspects of capitalism while reining in its excesses. It has become a rapacious, out-of-control system that is no longer serving the wide public interest or serving the vast majority of people on the planet. Especially in the United States, we have seen how capitalism has been distorted to serve a very narrow slice of wealthy people while neglecting the welfare of the vast majority of ordinary working Americans.

For the first time in history, the changes to capitalism that are needed exist simultaneously on two levels. This fact creates an incredible challenge that I don't believe we are capable of facing or responding to. While we could restructure much about our national economy to address income inequality, wages, automation, job loss, the tax code, executive pay, corporate behavior, the government budget, infrastructure spending, and a host of other relatively familiar and "conventional" (things that we are somewhat used to debating) issues, we must also overhaul the fundamental, long-used design of capitalism in light of pressing environmental and sustainability issues.

Think of it this way. If all we had to do was adjust capitalism to better spread the wealth—lift all boats, so to speak—we could conceivably find ways to do that. Those reforms would still provoke furious debate, but at least most Americans would grasp the basic issues involved. And in our country's history—say, during the reforms required by the Robber Baron era—there is precedent that we could refer to to reassure Americans that periodically capitalism requires tuning up. Those previous experiences with regulating it could also reassure citizens that tempering the free market is not socialism, is not unpatriotic, and does not stifle the creativity and entrepreneurial spirit that capitalism does so well to encourage.

But now add two totally new realities. Today, the task in front of us—adjusting capitalism—must be accompanied by a profound change in the very design of the system, and it must be accomplished almost immediately, certainly within five years, or possibly ten. Our economic system needs to be made sustainable, and sustainable for all of the nations of the world to be able to practice it. (One of the trickiest factors to accommodate in any program of reform to American capitalism is the reality that today the economy is thoroughly global. This would make it difficult—from the standpoint of both national competitiveness and saving the environment—to remake our economy into a totally green one if other nations do not follow suit. We already see this dynamic in operation in Third World countries where pollution and labor exploitation are ignored. Corporations run there and behave in ways that they can't in the U.S. So, to save capitalism, the seamless operation of a global market, the atmosphere, and the biosphere, the reforms we institute in America would have to be duplicated across the world.)

But first, let's take a look at what must be done to transform capitalism into a version that more fairly serves all Americans. Obviously, we've got to implement reforms that would more widely distribute the profits of large corporations. In general, workers' paychecks should be larger, and the inordinately high salaries and bonuses of corporate executives should be lower. There is an entire tier of businessmen, bankers, financiers, tech leaders, and other executives who receive remuneration out of all proportion to what is reasonable, and without any relationship to what is sustainable.

Millions of ordinary workers and laborers, whose wages have been nearly stagnant for 40 years, have fallen way behind. The modest wage gains of 2018 and 2019 are not profound. Ordinary American workers and households remain financially far behind where they should be. And with corporate profits so high, and unemployment so low, hourly wages should be increasing faster than they are. In addition, globalization and automation have made workers' jobs and their lives precarious. So reform must include responses that can literally slow those developments.

Globalization—among other things, a race to find the lowest labor costs—must be retuned to stop victimizing and exploiting workers, both here and abroad.

And automation and robotization—on course to eliminate tens of millions of jobs, here and abroad—must be restrained. The rapid pace of automation is lowering many wages, permanently rendering all jobs unreliable, undermining families and communities, and reducing tax revenue to the government. Automation has precipitated the gig economy and the reality that workers are on their own; corporations are destroying the social contract as they automate, outsource, and shed responsibility for worker pensions, benefits, and health care. So reforms would need to put back in place some corporate responsibility for maintaining a healthy labor force and a meaningful social contract.

To accomplish that would require changing the way Wall Street and the stock market bully corporate behavior and hold a relatively short-term and myopic vision of corporate success. Currently, a corporation's stock rises when it announces major layoffs, and its performance is measured overwhelmingly by its profits. Wall Street rewards corporations for automation, robotization, offshoring, breaking labor contracts, externalizing pollution and waste (again, into a Third World country with lax environmental laws), and generally behaving in narrow, antisocial ways. To change corporate behavior significantly then, also requires a major, simultaneous change to how corporations are valued by Wall Street.

To readjust capitalism, new regulations would be needed. Between 1975 and the present, deregulation has really hollowed out the moderating controls and restraints on the operation of capitalism. Wise laws and regulations on nearly every sector of the economy—agriculture, pharmaceuticals, media, telecommunications, financial, banking, insurance, technology, real estate, transportation, and others—have been repealed or rewritten in favor of business and the wealthy, and to the clear detriment of the ordinary worker, citizen, and consumer. Even bankruptcy law, contract law, and employee-rights law have been redone in favor of businesses and corporations. Campaign finance law and laws governing the place, role, and transparency of private-sector money in the government and in political campaigns have been gutted.

All of that deregulation would have to be examined and countered. Many federal agencies that monitor corporations and the private sector would have to adopt new rules and regulations, and Congress would need to write and pass a considerable amount of new legislation to implement new laws on acceptable business behaviors and practices. We would need to rein in monopolistic companies, predatory behavior, footloose globalization, worker exploitation, lobbying of the government, donations to politicians, the business-government revolving door of employment, tax sheltering strategies, and a slew of other destructive practices that are currently legal under our present regimen of capitalism and the market.

The tax code would have to be rewritten in many ways, with attention paid to an enormous number of provisions which govern business, corporate, and individual behavior. Currently, the code allows many specious deductions and encourages gaming of its rules. Its exemptions and taxation rates need to be reformed, with an eye toward broadening—fairly—the tax base and who is making what tax payments to the government. We should close tax loopholes, and we should introduce many more tax brackets governing what individual citizens pay in taxes; if there were 20 or 30 steps—instead of the current seven—we could more finely tune tax burdens to people's ability to pay (in 1971, the tax code contained 33 brackets). In general, given all of the circumstances in the country, the wealthiest American citizens should be paying higher taxes on their income.

Along with rewriting the tax code, we need to bolster the Internal Revenue Service with more funding and more staff. For many years it has been underfunded, and thus has been unable to perform adequately its auditing and enforcement responsibilities. Taxpayers and corporations have been able to deliberately underpay their taxes and have been able to get away with that. The U.S. Treasury has not collected billions of dollars of revenue owed it, as a consequence. A more robust, better funded IRS would more than pay for itself.

It is important to note that none of the reforms to capitalism that are called for here are calls for socialism, or calls for elimination of the "free market." No market is actually "free;" as I described earlier, all of our capitalist system and the ways in which it operates are designed. We write rules, laws, tax codes, trade agreements, credit regulations, banking protocols, and a lot else to organize and guide our economy and our capitalism. Whether we have more or less of the "reforms" that we are discussing here, we will always have an activist, involved government monitoring the private sector and regulating and enforcing. The government is the referee, enforcing the market rules established by the political process. The most pertinent focus is to understand who, or which groups and entities, are benefitting—and to what degree—from the design of the economy and the market.

Before I introduce the economic sustainability issue, I'd like to say that I don't think Americans can achieve the reforms I've outlined above, certainly not in any meaningfully timely manner. Currently, the political system at the national level is substantially influenced by lobbyists, corporations, and interests that would oppose these revisions. This is a huge set of needed reforms and it would take changes to much in society to enact it fully.

Think about what it would take to get corporations to pay better salaries—wages you can live on—to their workers and to pay their executive staffs dramatically lower salaries and bonuses. I'm not talking about federal or state minimum wages for the workers, but wages that allow them to save money, and not live paycheck to paycheck. And how do we convince private corporations to pay their executives, say, $1 million a year, rather than many millions? And to eliminate bonuses and stock options? These are absolutely necessary changes, but they are beyond the government to effect. Only boards of directors, shareholders, banks, and other private actors could force these reforms, and that is not going to happen any time soon. These reductions in executive salaries and bonuses would be shockingly large, but they (and many other reforms) are critical if we hope to have the funds to make a balanced and sustainable capitalism.

As far as restraining globalization and automation, again, the government is not going to enact meaningful reform on these fronts as long as it is dominated by corporate and lobbyist money and influence. The kinds of tax laws and regulations that would be required in order to discourage globalization are not going to be passed. And—corporations aside—we don't have anything approaching a popular understanding of and consensus on the pros and cons of globalization anyway. Same with the technologies of automation and robotization; can the government regulate the pace and content of technological innovation, artificial intelligence, and automation? Not any time soon. The public itself doesn't understand the magnitude and implications of the current generation of automation, nor is it informed about the capabilities and implications of the robotization that is rapidly approaching. There is just no chance that either society or politics is capable of any meaningful response—in a timely fashion—to these developments.

What about the corporations' sensitivity to their stock performance on Wall Street and their concomitant bias to the short-term view? There are few signs that this will change, and making it change would require revisions to many of the incentives, structures, relationships, and practices of capitalism and the market as they are currently designed. We would also need to impose taxes on all financial transactions and short-term speculative activities.

Can we re-regulate capitalism to counter the negative effects of the deregulation that has been ongoing for 45 years? This would be a mammoth undertaking and I think it highly unlikely to happen with anything approaching the speed, sophistication, scale, and effectiveness that is required. Too many circumstances are arrayed against it.

First, the political system at the federal level is a virtual captive of the corporate agenda, and the role of lobbyists and political donations keeps it that way. Additionally, the state of the Republican Party especially today also militates against reforms to temper the operation of capitalism. Just take a look at what occurred after the Wall Street meltdown of 2007 and 2008. If ever there had been a time and a set of circumstances that called out for new bipartisan regulations on the banking and financial sectors, that was it. Our entire financial sector, the mortgage industry, and the whole economy were in free fall. Everybody could observe that. With their unregulated recklessness, the big banks had precipitated a crisis, and the entire economy went into a staggering recession. It is instructive to look at the behavior of the banking industry lobbyists and the congressional Republicans as President Obama and the government tried to respond in the aftermath of the crisis. Spurred on by an outraged public, Congress wrote and passed the Dodd-Frank bill, which put in place some badly needed checks on the behavior of the banks. A new Consumer Financial Protection Bureau was also created. But only three Republican Senators voted for the bill, and Wall Street lobbyists worked hard to weaken the legislation's language. The promulgation of rules and regulations necessary for Dodd-Frank to be fully effective was slow and somewhat incomplete. Over the years since its inception in 2010, some of its powers have been reduced by Congress and President Trump. Neither the lobbyists nor the Republican Party accepted the need for regulation that would rein in bank practices. In fact, between 2010 and 2017, approximately 135 bills and resolutions were introduced into Congress by Republicans in an effort to diminish or eliminate outright the Consumer Financial Protection Bureau. As happens regularly after a crisis, once some initial legislation is passed and the public attention wavers, the permanent class of industry lobbyists is free to chip away at the details and enforcement provisions of any regulatory effort. Citizens have lives to attend to and jobs to go to and cannot maintain constant vigilance against forces that would influence and steer our government, but the permanent, paid, daily job of lobbyists is to distort the operation of democracy. And that Republican officeholders resisted a regulatory response even in the aftermath of a frightening freeze-up of the economy illustrates the fundamentalism of their free-market ideology. Today, when the economy is doing well by conventional measures, and when the threats to our society are much harder to see than during the 2008 meltdown, we can be sure that Republican Senators (even if Trump is not reelected) will be even more adamant against regulation than they were in 2010.

Second, the existence of the internet and the role it plays in misinforming and dividing the citizenry is a major force that acts to protect contemporary, predatory capitalism. The internet and social media promote—in large part—a certain mindless culture of ignorance, consumerism, and vague libertarianism, and this has the effect of ginning up skepticism of government regulation. Large chunks of the citizenry can be counted on to resist regulations meant to restrain capitalism's worst practices; and a divided electorate will not be adequate to push lawmakers to overcome corporate legislative powers and maneuvers. Remember, for 45 years the American populace has been given an increasingly false narrative as congress after congress, and presidential administration after administration, either actively enabled or could not halt the slow, steady morphing of capitalism into the beast that it is today. That history reflects a huge set of circumstances that will not be effectively reformed quickly—or perhaps at all.

We are in a similar position with the tax code. We know very well what reforms would help to make all citizens prosperous while at the same time strengthening capitalism. We could preserve the incentives and rewards of our market system while making it fairer, more stable, and less predatory.

But as with re-regulation, attempts to significantly rewrite the provisions of the tax code would be met with stiff resistance. Money in government, ambivalent politicians, corporate influence, the internet and social media, and a virulent, divided public will doom sufficient, meaningful reform.

But what about the differences between Democrats and Republicans? Doesn't it matter who is in power? If Democrats could be in charge of Congress and the presidency, wouldn't they initiate these reforms? Well, it certainly matters—a lot—who is in power. But if you look at the past 45-year record, you'll see that even Democrats were unable to adequately restrain the changing and charging forces of capitalism (and all the other forces discussed in this book). Democrats, while generally more inclined to support campaign finance reform and measures to temper the market, are nonetheless not immune to the corrupting influences of lobbyists, corporate money, the allure of corporate jobs after their political careers, and the zeitgeist and narratives of the country.

Some of this hinges on the results of the 2020 elections. Obviously, if a Democrat defeats President Trump, a Democratic administration would not be so hostile to regulations and monitoring the private sector. Trump has for three years been aggressively repealing regulations in many industries and areas, including those that affect the environment. He has also pushed coal mining, oil and gas drilling, more pipelines, and the expanded development of natural lands. Among Democrats in Congress, there is a growing awareness that deregulation and capitalism have become a free-for-all, so under a Democratic president there may be some efforts to rein in aspects of the market. Whether or not those initiatives would succeed would depend upon who controls the Senate. If Republicans maintain control of it, they would probably be able to block substantial reform; we should remind ourselves of the lack of progress under President Obama. If the Democrats win the Senate, any reform agenda they might support would face difficult impediments—embodied in structural and institutional realities, and in the popular will. It would not be easy to correct or reverse 40 years-worth of irresponsibility, hypocrisy, legislative malpractice, and bad-faith governance.

Furthermore, it is unclear how much change even the Democrats would propose to the technology, Webworld, and campaign finance sectors. There is certainly a widening knowledge of the abuses and flaws in the big internet-platform companies, and we are all talking about them.

There have been some substantial fines assessed to the platforms, and we may require better privacy controls. But there are big obstacles to restraining tech, automation, A.I., and the internet (see next sections). Campaign finance limits may get proposed, but the Democrats are far from united on this. And the Republicans and ultimately the Supreme Court are likely to oppose anything substantial. In the end, all of the potential changes will be resisted successfully to some degree by the players, institutions, and circumstances that are in place today. And again, the major point is: these reforms will not be big enough, significant enough, or fast enough to establish the differences that are needed.

* * * *

If all of that is not sobering enough, now let's add the need to remake the entire economic system in ways that recognize we live on a finite planet. In addition to all of the "conventional" reforms above, simultaneously we need to redesign capitalism and the market and their core operating principles and assumptions in ways that will strike many citizens as radical, shocking, threatening, unpleasant, socialist, un-American, and just thoroughly alien.

In the chapter on capitalism, I described the contradictions built into our current economic system of infinite growth. On a planet of fixed dimensions, with limited resources, we cannot indefinitely continue to exhaust those materials. Similarly, we cannot indefinitely continue to damage the air, sea, fresh water, soil, and natural habitats around the world.

We cannot safely sustain the material living standards already obtained by the most developed 2 or 3 billion people on the planet, never mind adding 2 or 3 billion more at those material standards. We would need the resources of 3 or 4 additional planets to do that. And not because we'd run out of oil or gas; we wouldn't. We've already found gas and oil deposits that'll last hundreds of years. No, the problems are—and would be—the rates of consumption of natural resources, a steady increase in land development (and corresponding loss in critical greenery), and the accumulation of devastating amounts of carbon dioxide in the atmosphere.

We cannot continue to operate a capitalism that requires citizens to fund 70 percent of our gross domestic product by purchasing goods and services. Meeting that goal every year requires us to buy too much stuff, consume too many resources, create too much waste, and be too ignorant and silly to be able to save the ecosphere and ourselves.

If we were going to redesign capitalism (we aren't), we'd need a new model that would function if citizens bought far, far less than they buy now. Consumers would need to focus primarily on basics and necessities and eschew other spending. Capitalism would have to be transformed into a sort of stable "maintenance-only" system that would be sustainable into the long future. If we in the developed world hope to live in an orderly society and on a peaceful planet in, say, 40 years time, we must create a global capitalism that can sustainably distribute the world's prosperity and resources across all the populations in the world. And again in the developed world, somehow this dramatic recalibration to produce and consume much less would have to be implemented without crashing the economy entirely.

For us in the United States and in the developed countries, almost every facet of life and society must change. The design of the market economy, our tax policies, the energy technologies we use, our habits of consumption, the patterns and sizes of our residential developments and homes, our transportation systems, our practices of recycling and waste disposal, our utilization of water, our entertainment, the foods we eat, the toys and conveniences we have, and our thinking about what constitutes "the good life" all would have to change. The costs and adjustments involved would be staggering and wrenching. Many well-meaning advocates for a sustainable capitalism talk about making an orderly transition to a green economy and green jobs; they rarely make any reference to how disruptive and expensive that would truly be. Many people think that they pay a lot of taxes now. People routinely complain about the expenses of living, and they desire to have better homes, nicer cars, bigger big-screen TVs, and more stuff. But if you think we pay a lot in taxes now, wait until we have to remake every aspect of society in order to preserve the viability of the natural world. In the future, one day, without a dime for affording anything beyond bare subsistence, citizens will look back at these days and wonder that they didn't recognize or appreciate how well we lived. Most citizens have no idea what sustainability—even to perpetuate civilization for the next 100 years, never mind beyond that—would require of us. And yet, there is no alternative if we wish for civilization to survive in any large, widespread, peaceful way.

* * * *

We aren't going to make these changes to capitalism. In the United States we are so surrounded by forces, influences, messages, distractions, and culture that support and pump up our current model of capitalism that we are mostly unable to entertain serious critiques of what is wrong with it. We certainly don't imagine radical alternatives to it. Surrounded by material lifestyles and goods to covet, used to unimaginable comfort and convenience, taking in constant advertising from every conceivable angle and source, and warped by 24/7 use of Webworld, we are largely helpless in the face of contemporary capitalism's power and effectiveness.

Having said all that, there are citizens and politicians who are aware of the need for economic sustainability and a transition to a capitalist system which is more deferential to environmental realities and ecological limits. These people are working toward improving our use of resources and reducing our damage to the planet. The Green New Deal, a carbon tax, and other initiatives meant to bake environmental sustainability into the very structure of capitalism are examples of a growing recognition of the flaws in our economic system. Certainly among Democrats, climate change is a primary concern. But the rate of progress we are making toward green energies, reducing waste, preserving forests and habitats, and saving the air and sea from carbon dioxide is pathetically small compared with what is required. We will run out of time, resources, water, health, and peace long before capitalism and the developed nations are transformed into sustainable models.

And, tellingly, very few citizens and scientists and economists—and not one politician, Democratic or Republican—are stating the obvious need to create a capitalism and a market not based on large levels of consumption. That is a message no one wants to give, and no one wants to hear.

TECHNOLOGY

As difficult as it would be to respond to the challenge of redesigning an obsolete capitalism, responding adequately to the contemporary force of technology is nearly impossible. And of course, capitalism and technology and the resilience of both are closely connected. We have only a limited understanding of the computer technologies that are now omnipresent, and we have only a limited grasp of how they are affecting us.

In the chapter on technology, I outlined the major issues that are arising from the use of computers and digital technologies. One of the biggest problems that computers and connectivity have created is that of dependency. And hand-in-hand with that is the problem of vulnerability. As we have computerized more and more of our life and work, we have created enormous dependencies on computers. At both the personal, individual level and business and institutional levels, we have transformed most activities and operations into digitally organized ones. Relatively speaking, there is very little entertainment, travel, scheduling, communication, work, or play that occurs without some digital connection. As a consequence of that, we are nearly wholly dependent upon smoothly operating digital devices and uninterrupted connection to the internet. If there is any problem with either, we are effectively paralyzed. Work, play, entertainment, communications, research, and the most mundane tasks of file maintenance and administration all come to a halt until the computers or connectivity are restored.

This dependency creates an enormous vulnerability. Whether we are speaking of individuals, businesses, governments, or any other entity, all are vulnerable to interruption. Interruptions can come from computer failure, software mistakes and glitches, prank hacking, malicious worms and viruses, and a host of other hostile attacks. As we connect more and more devices, appliances, vehicles, machinery, infrastructure, financial systems, and organizations to the internet, we are taking our dependencies and vulnerabilities to extreme levels.

There are no perfect security protocols and systems for the software in our devices and in the networks that maintain the internet. And there is no way to entirely limit user blunders (say, clicking on a poison phishing email). As I described in the chapter on technology, the internet itself is at risk of being hacked. And equally serious, the nation's electrical grid is also vulnerable. We know all this, yet we continue to connect as much as possible to the web. In fact, it is the stated goal of the Silicon Valley tech companies to digitize and automate as much as possible and to connect as much as possible to the internet; the explicit purpose behind the Internet of Things is to connect every extant thing to the web.

Could we halt this process? Could we stop connecting items to the internet? In an effort to reduce our digital dependencies and vulnerabilities, could we have a discussion about the wisdom of hyperconnectivity and the Internet of Things?

The answer to all of those questions is no. The U.S. may be a democracy, but the private sector is not. The free market and the private, technology sector will design and invent whatever they want. The American citizenry has not yet—in 50 years—had any say in the development of computer and internet technology, and we will not have any.

Over the long history of inventions, technology, and societies, that is always the way it has been. Scientists, engineers, inventors, tinkerers, and entrepreneurs invent things and produce them, and then society reacts. People invented agriculture, metallurgy, guns, steam engines, gas engines, atomic bombs, nuclear energy, telephones, automobiles, airplanes, plastic, and thousands of other notable items, and didn't ask anybody's permission to do so. Individuals and companies manufacture these products and spread them, and only then do societies face the intended and unintended results and consequences of these inventions.

The story of the development of computers and the internet has been no different. They were invented, developed, and distributed by the market and the private sector, and only now are we starting to see enormous unintended consequences. What is different—in the story of computers and the web—from all previous technologies is the speed, scale, scope, and reach of the advance of this technology. Unlike any previous technology ever invented, that combination of dynamics is causing unprecedented disruption and damage in populations across the globe.

But even if we wanted to—and there isn't much desire to—we couldn't reduce, block, or halt the ongoing march of computerization, digitization, and connectivity that is sweeping over everyone and everything across the world. There are no mechanisms available to do that now. We will continue—driven by capitalism, profit, advertising, politics, and the dominant culture—to pursue the Internet of Things and to connect as much as possible to the web. We will, therefore, continue to multiply our computer dependencies, enlarge and add to our vulnerabilities, and expand the damages being done by computer technology and Webworld.

* * * *

Another consequence of the development of computers has been the growth of new and larger systems of automation. I have outlined examples of the types and magnitude of the automation and robotization that have already occurred, and discussed the automation yet to come. There has already been tremendous job loss—millions of eliminated jobs both here and abroad—caused by computerization and automation, and the world stands to lose tens of millions of jobs in the next twenty years.

It is important to note that—perhaps surprisingly—the elimination of jobs due to automation is not an unintended consequence; it is an intended consequence. And I'm not talking about the long-held desire and practice of businessmen to reduce their labor costs whenever possible. That's a dynamic of capitalism that has always existed, and we are relatively used to fluctuations in the employment rates within typical, normal ranges. No, what I am referring to here is something new. Silicon Valley and the tech companies, as I described in the chapters on technology and Webworld, hold a vision of a utopian future where humans have been removed from the labor market of the economy, and all work is performed by machines, computers, robots, and artificial intelligence. That is the path that Silicon Valley corporations are on, and they don't need anybody's permission to pursue their goals.

Occasionally, if asked how all the unemployed workers of the U.S. will make a living, the tech sector leaders will say that each citizen of the country could receive a guaranteed annual minimum income. Even some academicians and politicians are now discussing this idea. This, according to the Silicon Valley utopia-story, would permit citizens to survive financially while freeing them up for "rewarding creative work" of their own interest. But the annual stipend that is being proposed by a number of thinkers varies widely—anywhere from $3,000 to $25,000 per year. For the vast majority of individuals and families, that income would be woefully inadequate to live on. And at the same time, remember, we will have eliminated—with automation—the possibility of everyone working real jobs to supplement this income. Furthermore, the federal and states' budgets couldn't begin to support even those modest levels of income subsidies, even if we drop our welfare programs, as minimum income proponents propose. The total cost to give payments to all citizens—whether unemployed, employed, or some combination of those—would be staggering (at any level higher than a paltry $13,000 or $14,000 a year, the total outlay would be greater than the entire federal budget of roughly $4.5 trillion). Additionally, because these people would no longer pay all taxes (how could they?) to the government, its annual revenue would decline precipitously. Lastly, unemployed citizens, now much poorer, would not be able to prop up the economy with their present levels of consumer purchasing. So, for many reasons, the proposals for a guaranteed annual minimum income are completely unrealistic. Mathematically, at any level of payments that would be meaningful, they are a non-starter. They are a fantasy and a dishonest diversion while the private tech sector continues to pursue and implement full automation.

What is sort of astounding about the topic of providing guaranteed incomes is the omission of nearly any debate about the sea change of eliminating jobs by the millions. Nowhere in the utopia-story do the Silicon Valley engineers encourage us to ask questions about what they have in mind for society. They don't want us to question their vision. Are we already so blinded, coopted, and accepting of technology and Webworld that we cannot muster even a scintilla of skepticism or resistance? Is a fully automated society what we want? Do we want to eliminate every job that we can? Do we derive meaning from our work? What would we lose if we replace humans with machines in every position from the simplest blue-collar job to the most involved white-collar job? And from a purely technical standpoint, how safe (from malware or other interruptions) would such a hyper-connected and machine-guided world be?

The Silicon Valley vision is a nightmare. It's a goal created unilaterally by emotionally underdeveloped minds and it reflects a one-dimensional idea of human purpose and meaning. It elevates untempered logic, pure mathematics, efficiency, and the beauty of what technically can be accomplished with artificial intelligence, over all other considerations.

Could we stop this march toward full automation if we wanted to? The answer is no. There is no consensus to do that, and there are no mechanisms to halt it anyway. Congress isn't going to vote to prohibit automation. It isn't going to change the tax code to prohibit deductions for the development and procurement of robotic systems, or to change the labor laws to meaningfully strengthen worker representation and interests. The private sector is not going to voluntarily halt the development of artificial intelligence. And citizens have no clue about the capacities of the computers and machine-learning systems that are coming. Many people still cling to the vague idea that sufficient numbers of new jobs will be stimulated and created by the digital revolution, but they don't know that smart computers—not humans—will repair and maintain most of this future automation. Time itself is a factor too, and the advance of automation, robotization, and artificial intelligence is not waiting for society to discuss the wisdom of the present and coming technologies.

So tens of millions of jobs will be eliminated. We'll find out then that the math of guaranteed minimum incomes doesn't remotely work, and we'll find out then that an unemployed citizenry can't pay the taxes that make government work and can't purchase enough stuff to satisfy the constant consumer demand that our capitalist economy requires. In fact, one consequence of automating another 20 or 30 or 40 million jobs may be a permanent recession or the crash of the economy itself. And maybe we'll also find out that an algorithm-software-virtual-reality-world isn't as safe and beneficial and nifty as the computer engineers promised.

* * * *

In addition to the problem of computer technology fueling job loss, the rapid advance of artificial intelligence will soon transform our society and the experience of our lives in other ways. The best way to understand what artificial intelligence is—and why it will never stop expanding—is to think of it not as a discrete product or machine, but as a continuum along the progress-line of the development of software. It is very advanced software—built upon the foundation of earlier software—that has even more capabilities, including the capacity to machine-learn. Artificial intelligence is comprised of algorithms (instructions to the computer) that are advanced enough to analyze reams of data and identify patterns, correlations, various interrelationships, and brand new facts. The artificially intelligent machine may then act on what it identifies, making choices, decisions, giving instructions, and operating other machinery. Some degree of A.I. is today involved with the machine technologies of speech recognition and machine-speaking, virtual reality sites and experiences, online video games, facial recognition, autonomous vehicles, automated manufacturing, medical diagnoses, robotics, and innumerable other applications.

In the near future, there will be no escape from constant interactions with AI. It will be the omnipresent filter, organizer, manager, and data recorder through which we experience or operate in every occupation, entertainment, school, location, or communication. Using it, or being used by it, will not be optional. Every store, online shopping site, restaurant, business, corporation, bank, delivery service, government agency, website, chat room, social media platform, search engine, email provider, media newsfeed, smartphone app, GPS device, health monitor, exercise wristband, lawnmower, golf club, tennis racket, coffee pot, appliance, automobile, parking meter, and object will be connected and AI-capable and will maintain a digital record—data—of our interactions with it. This data will be shared universally and in all directions among the Webworld platforms, the Internet of Things, and the businesses and corporations we use.

In, say, five to fifteen years, fed by so much data, AI will be so powerful, so adept, and so capable of machine-learning that it will dominate the administration, management, and presentation of nearly every aspect of work, play, life, and even sex. In the chapter on Webworld, I mentioned the relationship-busting dynamics today of online porn. Well, that's nothing compared to what's coming. Soon, many people will choose to have sex with sexbots, AI "robots" that are life-sized, anatomically correct copies of humans (actual, specific humans too, such as movie stars, if you wish) and that can be programmed to do whatever their users want. Millions of people will come to prefer having sex with these bots rather than with imperfect humans. Among many other consequences, this will have the effect of diminishing society's collective emotional intelligence and its capacity for empathy, with further negative consequences stemming from these shortfalls.

Much else that we do, though it will be done mostly via screens or smartglasses or other intermediary device, will feel equally tailored to our personal desires and identities. Computers, data collection, the internet, and AI-powered online content will become the mediators of everything. Data will be weaponized to present us with material on computer screens that gives us the illusion of choice. But in reality we will have less control over everything, and we will have less choice over everything. We will be being manipulated constantly by Webworld and AI. But by then, as we can see already today, we either won't care or we'll actively like the whole operation. Also, by then, we may no longer be sharp enough to discern the extent to which our lives are mediated.

How much AI do we want? Do we really want algorithms presenting the world—whatever part of the world we are interacting with at a given moment—to us in a manner that they (the algorithms) think all the data in their processors indicate? Do we want to work and play and live in such a data-driven tyranny? Do we want to be presented constantly only with menus of distilled and restricted choices?

Well, at this point, it doesn't matter what we want because artificial intelligence has already progressed to a level where machine learning is irresistibly advanced. The biggest American tech companies—Google, Amazon, Apple, Microsoft, IBM, and Facebook—are committed to enlarging and employing AI wherever possible. Even if we had the will (we don't) to question the nature and wisdom of these technological advances, we simply have no mechanisms adequate to do so. In America we have no history, tradition, or sentiment to block or restrain technological innovation while it is yet happening.

Some people have suggested international advisory boards or governmental commissions to examine the issues around artificial intelligence and to formulate guidelines and principles for good practice. That idea sounds reasonable, but the speed alone of AI development and proliferation makes it an ineffective response. We will be living in a thoroughly AI-managed world long before any commission could develop and enforce specific rules and regulations. Today, we are yearly—headlong—weaving the world with shocking amounts of automation, connectivity, data dependence, AI dependence, and other networked computerization. This enormous investment in digital infrastructure is quickly replacing previous control systems and simply cannot be reversed or unwound.

And as I have described, in the western nations the tech companies are driven by two motives. They hold a vision of the future in which humans play a marginal role in the production and management operations of the economy; and they are driven to make money. Silicon Valley thinks that humans—whether working, playing, or shopping—are inefficient and need help being efficient. In that view, automation and artificial intelligence are bringing superior and welcome interventions and mediations, and organizing every aspect of life better than people can. Secondly, the data that facilitates all this mediating technology is simultaneously weaponized to get us to use the technology, use the internet, buy more stuff, be entertained, stay online longer, and thus feed more data into the tech companies, which then build even stronger and smarter AI. It is a circular process. We are already roped into it, and it will only become more and more imprisoning. The tech companies operate under a financial model that gives them every incentive to continue to increase our dependence on digital technology. As artificial intelligence advances in sophistication, it simply makes it easier for the tech companies to make more money, and lots of money.

There is another reason that America is not going to slow its transformation into an AI-driven society and economy. Today we are in a competition with China to see which country will be dominant in any number of ways. China, whose economy is largely directed by the country's authoritarian government, is pushing to develop its AI capabilities in as many areas as possible. Artificial intelligence is used throughout its economy, military, social life, and surveillance apparatus. Three big tech companies—Alibaba, Tencent, and Baidu—work closely within the Chinese government's policies and toward its goals as they continually advance AI. The government has no ambivalence about computerization; it sees pervasively deployed AI as the key to monitoring and controlling its citizenry, and it sees advanced AI as critical to creating robotic weaponry of all types and to creating software weapons capable of hacking into and bringing down American computer systems, infrastructure, the internet, and the electrical grid.

Ironically (there are many ironies in this entire story), because China is a communist country, its stable, unchanging government is capable of long-term planning, and following long-term policies. There is no doubt that it will continue to build the perfect surveillance society. With its unparalleled AI systems watching literally every action of every citizen, and with a system of rewards and punishments, it will continue to create a docile, obedient citizenry. In China, every citizen receives a social credit score which is a continuously running and continually updated measure of their conformity and value to society. Here in the U.S., without central planning or monitoring by the government, we are nonetheless creating the same docile, obedient citizenry. Here it is mostly the private sector that produces the behavior that the power elite want. In America we don't need overt authoritarianism to control the population; here, the incentives, pleasures, seductions, and advertising of the market system and Webworld produce a compliant, conformist, ignorant, and mostly trapped citizenry. Many of us exist solely to buy things or live online. What China—with AI, data, and surveillance—accomplishes on behalf of government control, the U.S.—with Webworld, data, and mass consumption—accomplishes on behalf of corporate and wealth control.

So, in both countries, the continued development and spread of artificial intelligence is absolutely critical to the dominant economic forces, the dominant culture, and the dominant powers—be they capitalists or communists. And to top it all off, the infinite potential of AI in military applications guarantees that the two nations (among others) will continue their digital competition. We are in an arms race with China; the next generation of "smart" weaponry and remote delivery systems will rely heavily on advanced software and robotics. The U.S. political-military-technological consortium will lobby hard for AI weapons programs to keep up with Chinese advances.

Is there an analogy here to nuclear weapons and that arms race? Might we control AI with international treaties? No. After the U.S. and the Soviet Union realized the danger and futility of the nuclear competition, they created truces and treaties to restrain and control nuclear proliferation. But that was possible only because few nations were involved, and because developing nuclear technologies was a mission able to be undertaken only by nations—and even then it took large amounts of resources, money, machinery, and scientific know-how. Developing artificial intelligence is different. Many nations, many companies, and many non-state actors have access to it. And they are not controllable. In America, as I've described, private sector companies are developing AI, putting its software on the web, and promoting its use. It is too employed and too widespread already, and too integral to capitalism's wealth to rein in now.

In short, pervasive and profound levels of artificial intelligence will come to dominate the experience of life. In China and authoritarian nations, that will mean citizen compliance with the government's wishes. In the United States and democratic nations, that will mean citizen conformity to and compliance with the social, economic, occupational, leisure, and organizational norms that corporations and the powers of the private sector put in place. In the U.S., none of this will be the result of a conspiracy, and only a bit of it will stem from bad intentions. Things will just come together this way as a result of all of the circumstances that I have been outlining in this book. We won't be in China, but we'll be in a tyranny nonetheless. (Ironically, those Americans who most obsess over "freedom," and who are commensurately vigilant about the least government intervention or planning lest they lose some of their precious personal "freedom," probably won't even be able to identify the tyranny that the private sector has created.)

WEBWORLD

The first thing to remember when we think about the internet and the possibilities and likelihood that we can and will reform it is that it is a "world." I call it "Webworld," and with a capital W, because increasingly, and for more and more people, the web is becoming a place, a destination, a home for them. Many people today aren't from Massachusetts, or Boston, or Cleveland, or Dallas, or the United States; they are from Webworld. Their lives take little identification or energy from anything other than what they do or see online.

In the chapter on Webworld, I described the myriad problems besetting the internet. We know how to fix some of them, but others have no remedy. Regardless, we will not meaningfully reform the web.

The operation and dynamics of Webworld are wrapped up in politics, capitalism, technology, media, and human nature, and that reality makes the problems afflicting Webworld tenacious, complicated, and impossible to solve without simultaneously addressing the dynamics and power embodied in those other related forces. And all of this is reciprocal: unwinding the problems in almost any of the forces discussed in this book would require simultaneously addressing the qualities and operation of the internet and the other forces.

One of the biggest factors of life for the internet platforms—that they rely on advertisers for their income and profit—creates a major obstacle to reforming the web. First, it places the advertisers ahead of the users— you and me—in terms of who the platforms must satisfy, and in terms of who the internet is good for. Second, because advertisers naturally want as many people as possible to see their ads, and will pay the internet accordingly, the platform companies have every incentive to increase user engagement on their sites, apps, products, and services. They want us to spend as much time online as we can, and they want us to click, like, share, post, and send messages as much as we can. The larger the audience the platforms can record, and the more user engagement the platforms can demonstrate, then the larger the prices they can charge the advertisers.

This creates the problems that I described in the chapter on Webworld. While online, we see thousands of advertisements, and we are conditioned in many unhelpful ways by that exposure. We buy deeper into an unthoughtful capitalism, a damaging materialism, and a superficial set of values. We also—so swamped by 24/7 advertising—stop recognizing it for what it is—obnoxious, intrusive propaganda.

Our incessant time online also reinforces the cognitive and emotional silos we live in, the opinions we hold, and our divisions from other citizens. It makes us more vulnerable to the destructive misinformation that overflows the web.

The platforms' need for clicks and eyeballs drives them to highlight the nastiest, most sensational and outrageous, most controversial, and most emotional content they can find. Human nature being what it is, we find it hard to look away.

All attempts to reform the web—to make it predominantly a force for good—will run up against the platforms' financial need for clickbait. The platforms will continue to resist any significant reduction in their content.

A special category of content that has been spectacularly damaging is that of fake news, fake stories, and conspiracy theories. Whether we are referring to American alt-right content, white nationalism, Russian hacking and trolling, or the political confusion sown by Macedonian teenagers, false narratives and tales are wreaking havoc on many American minds. Closely related to fake news are the extremists who use the web to gather into groups to promote deranged interpretations of the world, and to foment actual violence. ISIS, neo-Nazis, anti-Islamists, anti-government fanatics, and right-wing nutcases place non-stop content on the web.

Even with this content, the internet companies have performed miserably. First, they are reluctant and unhappy to remove anything. At heart, they still maintain the libertarian ethos that first animated the worldwide web's inventors. Those designers envisioned the internet as an open, decentralized, accessible-to-all framework that would be used in an egalitarian and beneficial way—without the need for an internet administrator or internet "police." Today, we know the blind spots held within that vision. When the open web meets (or encourages) the worst of human nature, really horrible content is put online. The web platforms have finally recognized this problem, but they are still struggling to internalize its implications. They are still struggling to craft responses to it. Although they do remove the most obvious and undisputed filth and violence that is put on the platforms—material such as child pornography, ISIS beheadings, and explicit incitements to violence—they are often slow and imperfect in identifying the material.

Second, they are reluctant to be viewed as censors; they just don't want that role. However, in the face of increasing pressure from government and citizens, the social media companies and web platforms are now working harder to identify and eliminate the most false and the most destructive messaging and information from the web. This task is invariably controversial; even when removing the vilest and most uncivil content of right-wing political extremists, for example, the platforms are attacked by conservatives (and President Trump) who accuse the tech companies of bias. When Facebook banned Alex Jones, Louis Farrakhan, and Milo Yiannopoulos from its online products, conservatives claimed that it was removing legitimate political commentary that it just didn't favor. This reaction bodes ill for possible legislation to support the platforms in online content removal efforts; Republican congressmen will continue to oppose any aggressive policing of Webworld. The removal of disinformation, deliberately divisive political content, fake news, knowingly false advertising (political or otherwise), or even material that attempts to interfere with elections will be left solely in the hands of the private internet companies.

Third, it isn't always easy to discern what content crosses the line from odd minority or fringe viewpoint into unacceptable poison. Since 2016 or so, the tech companies have done a pretty good job of screening out overt terrorist text and video—such as that used by ISIS—and eliminating the worst child pornography and perversions on the web. Most of this worst-cases-content can be caught by artificial intelligence and algorithms. What still evades the AI filters is the more nuanced text content that mimics legitimate political and scientific discourse. This is a huge problem, and large volumes of destructive messaging makes its way onto the web. The web platforms employ tens of thousands of human reviewers in an effort to accurately identify malicious content, but reams of it overwhelm these moderators.

The real and insurmountable problem of reviewing web content is one of magnitude. There is, every day, just too much material placed onto the internet to ever effectively screen and control it. That's true now, and it'll be true forever; in fact, as more people connect to the web, and as the dynamics of the web and the other large forces in society continue to work against us, the problem will only grow worse. This will be true in spades in the U.S., but it will also be true in other developed nations across the world. (China and Russia can control their closed internets, but those countries strictly police expression in their populations.)

We can barely grasp the magnitude of internet use. Four billion people are already connected, linking, blogging, emailing, messaging, and sharing. Google handles approximately 10 billion search queries every day. Facebook, used by 2 billion people, receives tens of billions of posts every day. WhatsApp is used by 1.5 billion people. Twitter manages 500 million tweets a day. YouTube loads 500 hours of video every minute. On TikTok alone, 1 billion videos are viewed daily. This quantity of material is staggering. And it doesn't even include the articles, comments, photos, and videos—billions of them—on websites, blogs, apps, and the dark web across the globe.

Although most major platforms, media outlets, and websites have reviewers, filters, moderators, and site administrators, monitoring all of that content is impossible. Take a look at Facebook's operation to get a feel for the difficulties involved. As of July, 2019, Facebook had 15,000 content moderators and 15,000 security reviewers located around the world in about twenty facilities. Between them, they work in about 100 different languages and—ideally—would be conversant in at least that many cultures. Each moderator is expected to review 300 to 400 posts, photos, or other items per day, and the work is grueling. Both the pace of the work and the poisonous quality of the material being reviewed are relentless. In photos and video, suicides, slashings, gruesome accidents, child molestation, torture, gore, animal abuse, domestic violence, sexual horror, and other visual nightmares abound. In text form, bullying, abuse, lies, hate, cruelty, accusations, conspiracy-mongering, and threats are common.

Facebook moderators rarely last longer than one year on the job; they often leave after six months or so. Almost all of them become either seriously unsettled by the content they review, or actually traumatized. Many of them start to doubt much about the world; they lose their grounding and they're not sure they can trust their judgement about things. They develop severe anxiety and suffer panic attacks. The subcontractors (to Facebook) who hire them know that the daily diet of horrors that they will read or watch will so disturb them that an on-site therapist or counselor is in attendance daily at every location. The fate of these content moderators is telling; if proof is needed, they are proof that watching or reading the worst material that humans can create is destructive to the mental health of anyone and everyone. And short of actually damaging the reviewers' mental health, just the fact that they lose their bearings—become disoriented—regarding what's "normal" or "right" is an indication of the power of the effects that the web is delivering, and not just to professional moderators. Overall, the human Facebook moderators review about 10 million items a week. This is an impressive number, but remember, the company sees tens of billions of posts per week. Huge amounts of absolutely terrible materials go online every day.

At the current time, the internet platforms in the U.S. have no legal liability for content displayed on their sites and products. Present regulations in the "Communications Decency Act" give them immunity. But even if we change the law—make the tech companies liable for dangerous content that they host—they still wouldn't be able to control all of the material on their portions of the web. Although some platforms and products—such as some of those owned by Facebook and Google—have improved their monitoring and removal of pornography and ISIS videos, content review remains an extremely difficult job and a highly imperfect one. Even with new legal requirements to excise destructive online material, there would still be too many postings to screen, and technically, the problem of discerning fake or malicious content from legitimate content would still exist. And there would still be plenty of pirate sites and less-than-conscientious service hosts that would fall between the enforcement cracks. Europe does have stricter regulations on hate speech than the U.S., and is currently considering tougher rules to control disinformation and fake news, but that combination still won't eliminate the problem of destructive forces on the web. Languages and culture are too complicated, and they contain too much nuance, for either humans or AI to catch all the garbage that is daily posted on the internet. Furthermore, the national tradition in America is strongly in favor of unfettered free speech; that makes it unlikely that we'll ever impose substantial speech or content monitoring on web expression. The most that the American Congress will try to require of the web platforms is a greater degree of privacy for the data we give to the tech companies. That won't solve the problem of malicious content. And ultimately, with the wide Internet of Things and pervasive connectivity yielding voluminous and nonstop data, privacy and the protection of it will be an illusion too.

In the chapter on Webworld, I described some of the hacking and malicious posting carried out by Russian intelligence agencies in 2015, 2016, and continuing today. Russian cyber operations against the U.S. and other countries illustrate all of the difficulties we face in policing the web. The Russians exploit every natural vulnerability in Webworld, human nature, and the dynamics of society. They pose as Americans, create false accounts, purchase advertising, write fake-news articles, foment division between groups, employ fear tactics, and utilize both bots and humans to do all this. Furthermore, they spread their efforts across many sites, platforms, and apps, and do it in sufficient magnitudes to have an effect. And just as they have done and are continuing to do in America, they are utilizing the same tactics in Europe. The Russians today continue to seed the internet maliciously in England (especially regarding Brexit), France, Hungary, Austria, Ukraine, and many other countries. Their goal is to promote confusion, distrust, polarization, and anger within the democratic countries of the world. Because many Europeans already feel those emotions—as in America—the Russian efforts at digital agitation fall on fertile ground. And as I've discussed, fighting back against these cyber initiatives is extremely difficult, and to a significant degree, impossible.

Again, the magnitude of the task is shocking. Utilizing artificial intelligence and human filtering, hundreds of millions of items of unacceptable material are removed from the internet every day. But this is a hopeless, futile exercise. Much nasty content, once removed, simply gets reposted under a new title, name, or account, or in a different location or on a different platform. Or the content itself can be edited or manipulated somewhat in order to look like a new, first-time post. After the mass shooting in Christchurch, New Zealand in March 2019, the video of the act (which had been live-streamed) repeatedly appeared online in slightly altered versions, in order to defeat efforts to expunge it from the web.

And of course, while moderators are fighting any given batch of unredeeming content, new horrible or destructive postings are continuing to pile up, relentlessly 24/7, overwhelming the systems we use to review and remove poisonous material. The bad actors on the web also use artificial intelligence, bots, algorithms, and encryption too, to try to be more clever than the content reviewers. The destructive content, and the AI that posts it, are moving targets; they are evolving just as the AI of the platforms is constantly improving. (Facebook alone, for example, removes something like 2 billion deceptive, malicious accounts every year. Facebook's AI does this, but the AI of the "black hats" makes adjustments and returns 2 billion new fake accounts to the web.) Each side—good and bad—is trying to outwit the other. The nefarious users of the web are smart and resourceful and motivated, and they change their content, tactics, appearances, targets, and approaches all the time. They have the advantages of the elements of surprise and lawlessness. Taking all the factors into account, meaningfully reducing the dangerous and destructive content on the web is a losing battle, and there is no answer for it, whether employing human reviewers or artificial intelligence.

I've mentioned how vast quantities of data feed the advance of artificial intelligence. It is also the massive collection of data gathered from all our Webworld interactions that permits better and better microtargeting of each one of us literally at the individual level—for the purposes of manipulating us and conditioning us. The platforms share this data with commercial advertisers, thereby permitting them to persuade us to buy their merchandise. Increasingly, the data collected and the profiles of us that it creates—which describe us more intimately and more fully all the time, physically, behaviorally, mentally, socially, and demographically—will also be used by a widening array of businesses and service providers who will tailor their terms according to the details and qualities of our profiled identity. Nonstop data collection also enables us to be targeted politically and socially in numerous ways. When bad actors like Russia or any authoritarian or populist political side want to influence gullible web users or angry voters, they can use data and user profiles to select the citizens most likely to be receptive to their messages. Similarly, the comprehensive information on each one of us that is constantly accumulating in many places can be used by the internet platforms to keep us isolated in opinion bubbles and narrowing worldviews. As I've described, this has a large range of negative effects.

As a consequence of data collection, microtargeting, and the echo-chamber tribal bubble we each inhabit, Webworld encourages emotional responses and reinforces our political immaturity. It divides society into warring camps, destroys the ideas of nuance and complexity and compromise, makes us less competent as citizens, and undermines democracy.

Could we end data collection and microtargeting? Could we thus put a stop to both the commercial exploitation and the political compartmentalization that they enable?

There is no chance of that happening. The internet frameworks and the way they operate are now so far advanced—and so interwoven with capitalism and politics—that there is no unwinding them. We have no chance of stopping advertising, and no chance of meaningfully reining in the collection of data. With the exception of a relatively small percentage of the population, we aren't going to be willing to pay for all of the services now provided for free by the internet platforms.

There are no reasons to think that data collection will slow. On the contrary, it will increase. The continuing financial imperatives behind the internet platforms and the burgeoning Internet of Things—where literally everything is connected and online—and our enthusiastic use of all of it will generate ever-increasing amounts of data. Citizens, through the political process, don't have the knowledge, power, will, consensus, or choice to shut down data collection.

Webworld affects all users, but it has a special power over children and young people, as I outlined in the chapter on Webworld. Currently, there are almost no reforms on the horizon that would meaningfully address this problem. To the contrary, in our elementary, middle, and high schools, we are pushing computers, coding, and the digital world onto the kids. With the exception of, ironically, some Silicon Valley schools, where tech-savvy parents insist on web-free teaching to protect their children from being internet-conditioned, we are integrating STEM (mostly computer technology and engineering) education into the curricula, and encouraging the students toward careers in computer science. In primary schools, if not before, we equip children with laptops, and parents give them tablets and smartphones at early ages. Adult generations—the ones old enough to straddle the pre-digital and Webworld eras—can sometimes discern the differences that the internet has wrought. Even so, those generations have proven impotent at preventing the damages that have resulted. Younger generations today—those who don't know any time that wasn't digital—do not and will not even recognize the differences and damages created by Webworld. They may be technically, digitally, more proficient with software and social media, but they are, and will be, so conditioned by Webworld that there will be no likelihood that they'll institute the necessary reforms. We have left young people completely vulnerable to the web platform companies. Very few teens or young adults under the age of 30 or so will admit to that, but that is because their epistemology knows only a world mediated by computers, social media, and online-everything. Naturally, they deny that they have been sucked in. Who among us wants to admit that we have lost our agency? What if we can't even identify the agency we've lost? So, regarding the dynamics of Webworld, young people are not the hope of the future.

Really, against both youth and adults, Webworld has perpetrated one of the greatest heists of all time. It is the perfect crime, for which we have no answer. Webworld has stolen our attention and mindfulness and agency, while substantially deemphasizing its methods and motivations. Webworld conditions us so smoothly, seamlessly, gradually, pleasurably, competently, invisibly, and conveniently that we willingly surrender to it. The genius of the heist is partly this: we think it's a robbery in plain sight, and we think it's benign, so we are disarmed and not skeptical. Living in Webworld, we think we are exercising free will and making free choices, but in reality our playing field is circumscribed by a screen, a headset, maybe some VR goggles, and a given set of algorithms. Our situation reminds me of the story of the fish who cannot understand that they swim in water (the writer David Foster Wallace told this story during a commencement talk he gave at Kenyon College in 2005).

Should we bring anti-trust actions against the biggest tech companies; and break them up as well? Should Google, Facebook, and Amazon each be divided into multiple smaller companies? Although there is certainly more talk in political circles of these possibilities, there is far from a consensus about whether those sorts of actions would be wise. And with the power and influence of Silicon Valley—the industry's lobbyists and big donations to congressmen both affecting the likelihood and substance of any major reform legislation—it'll be a long time before the tech companies are constrained in any significant way. Furthermore, not many congressmen or citizens have a sophisticated grasp of the myriad intricacies of Webworld, and not many are convinced that—overall—the internet is a disaster. Therefore, the chances of effective, timely regulation are extremely low.

Over the past few years, for antitrust violations, European regulators have fined Google many billions of dollars. The U.S. Department of Justice is currently investigating the company too for antitrust actions. The U.S. Federal Trade Commission has fined Facebook for mishandling users' private data and is investigating whether the company has engaged in anticompetitive practices. Good steps all, but too little too late to checkmate the damages already wrought by and embedded in Webworld.

There is another set of circumstances that would render moot most regulation of the web and, indeed, even break-up of the internet platform companies. That is because the worst effects of Webworld can't be fixed with regulation. The destruction of critical thinking, the erosion of the idea of expertise, the diminishment of attention span and patience, the degradation of values, the distortion of perspective, and the promotion of outrage, self-centeredness, and a host of other damaging emotional states that are the consequences of repeated and extended time online won't go away with smaller tech platforms or various anti-trust measures. The problems and damages that Webworld causes are products of the fundamental ways it operates; the dynamics of Webworld and what that online world is doing to us are baked into the internet's entire ecology and human nature's interaction with it. No regulations can have an answer for that; no regulations can repeal or remake human nature. No regulations will have an answer for internet content that daily, relentlessly, chips away at kindness, comity, cooperation, reflection, compromise, order, society, and people themselves. In combination with all of the other forces and circumstances that I have described, Webworld is besieging us. In the developed world, we and our societies are—and are becoming more—absurd, dysfunctional, unhealthy, traumatized, and unsustainable. There are many reasons for this, but Webworld is the force that is ensuring that we will remain on that path.

POLITICS

As I described in the chapter on politics, we are today in a terrible place with regard to that subject. Our political dysfunction mirrors our societal dysfunction and our individual, personal distress. The American citizenry is angry, polarized, ill-informed, and alienated. We are divided into many different groups, and each one thinks that it alone knows the truth, the story, the way things are. Each group listens to its own web-siloed-news, talks only with itself, and feels that other groups are ignorant, unpatriotic, prejudiced, elite, or any of many other negative descriptions.

Woven into that societal tapestry, many people struggle financially and emotionally with life today. The forces of capitalism, Webworld, and technology are buffeting everyone, and they distort our democracy simultaneously. We are in a time when all of the forces described in this book, and politics, and the condition of the citizenry, blend into a sort of low-grade assault of overlapping challenges to order, stability, and predictability. Every force and every aspect of society and human nature contribute to the story of where we are. Every aspect of this tapestry of forces and circumstances is both cause and effect of our condition today.

We certainly know of some reforms that could be instituted to improve our democracy. Foremost among them would be reducing the role of money in the political arena. That would be critical. In the chapter on politics, I outlined the enormous presence of money in the political process, and the numerous ways that it is deployed. Through political action committees, "educational" organizations, corporate donations, personal donations, advertisements, and other vehicles, money is distributed freely, anonymously, and in great sums to buy access and influence and to affect elections and legislation.

We already know how to limit or prohibit money in the political system; and we know how to require transparency and accountability in the funding and spending on behalf of candidates and campaigns. We used to have much stricter regulations in those areas. But we've been steadily repealing those rules, and today political money can essentially do what it wants. There is no reason to think that we'll successfully address this problem. No meaningful action will occur. Although Democratic politicians are somewhat inclined toward campaign finance reform, they have an inadequate and timid sense of the magnitude and scope of the restrictions that are needed. Consequently, their proposals will not go far enough. In any case, Republican officeholders will steadfastly oppose any and all attempts at finance reform, and many citizens will join that opposition. Foolishly, many ordinary citizens have been persuaded by the conservative and Republican argument that money is the equivalent of free speech, and therefore should be largely unregulated. This is a bizarre argument that simply ignores the damages created by political money, and it simply ignores the reality that government is today effectively owned by corporate money and influence. Of course, the Supreme Court—a majority of whom also believe that money is speech, and that corporations have "personhood" rights—is the ultimate obstacle to removing money from politics. Even if Democrats in the future are able to legislate finance reform, the court will strike down any truly formidable restrictions.

In light of the conservative majority on the Supreme Court, some reformers have advocated for a constitutional amendment to address money in politics. For example, an amendment could strip personhood rights from corporations and also stipulate that money is not identical to free speech, thereby allowing donations to be regulated. But there is zero chance (now or anytime relevant) of two-thirds of the Senate and House supporting such a proposal. And two-thirds of the state legislatures are not going to propose it either. Not to mention then getting ratification from three-quarters of the state legislatures.

Similarly, we will be unable to restrict the roles of lobbyists, corporations, and special interests, and the corruption of the revolving door between public service and jobs in the private, corporate sector. Here, there is less difference between Democratic and Republican officeholders; once they retire from office, congressmen and Senators from both parties happily take jobs with lobbying firms, corporations, and trade groups. They use their influence with former colleagues and are able to gain easy access to congress on behalf of the companies that they represent. The activities of lobbyists should be strictly reduced, and there should be a lifetime (not one- or two-year) firewall between public service and later employment at the companies that ex-politicians join. No ex-officeholder should be permitted to lobby for corporations he once regulated or legislated about. There is no chance that meaningful reforms of this type will be enacted.

Another area of politics that requires changing is the practice of gerrymandering. Like lobbying, both parties engage in it, so it should be a reform that could be instituted. Eliminating gerrymandering would help to promote representation in Congress that more accurately reflects the politics of the citizenry. Because state legislatures have mostly been unable to rein in the practice of gerrymandering, and because so few states have established independent redistricting commissions, reformers have repeatedly appealed to the Supreme Court to rule against gerrymandering and to establish some legal guidelines to prevent it in the future. The court has refused to do so, and in a ruling in June 2019, basically declared that it has no interest in adjudicating this issue. The court, in a 5—4 decision, ruled that it has no authority to judge what it identifies as strictly "political" issues. The ruling was ominous; the legislative manipulation of districts will continue.

Of course, in a further irony, even had the Supreme Court struck down gerrymandering, politics have become so dysfunctional that honest electoral maps would not make a meaningful difference in restoring our overall political health.

We also need to do what we can to reduce voter suppression. With time, this may or may not be possible, but in the end it will not contribute significantly to ending the crisis in our democracy.

In assessing the likelihood of any limits being placed on either campaign finance or professional lobbying, or of reducing the frequency of gerrymandering and voter suppression, we can count on the objections of—in addition to Republican politicians—the media ecology of Fox News, conservative talk radio, and Webworld to promote disinformation, emotion, and resistance regarding these specific issues. While the producers and audience for that particular media content are predominantly Republican, there are other areas of needed reform that will challenge both Republicans and Democrats. Redesigning capitalism, for example, into something truly sustainable will be an enormous challenge for both groups.

Really, if politics were to be made healthy once again, it would require a dismantling of the vehicles that are used to promote the poison and disinformation and false characterizations that so many citizens are brainwashed with. A critical mass of citizens really is seriously ill-informed about the important forces warping society, and when assessing our prospects for the future, we must weigh the likelihood of our taking steps to become informed and knowledgeable. Sabotaged, in a sense, by those who want us ignorant, we are highly unlikely to do the new reading, viewing, or listening that would be necessary.

To make politics—and by extension, society—healthy would require the citizenry of the United States to understand the lies in the narrative—foisted on them for 40 years—that deceive them into accepting the shapes of capitalism, technology, Webworld, and politics today. Yet I truly despair when I consider the likelihood of that sort of education occurring. Nearly all of the media outlets that most citizens use are just not set up to facilitate that type of adult education in any meaningful or unavoidable way. That said, there are plenty of great, informative articles in plenty of media (print, TV, or web). But people and media producers are only human, and we all easily and frequently select entertainment, sensation, drama, conflict, and distraction over the work of being informed citizens. There's blame and irresponsibility enough to be shared by both citizens and media.

What citizens need most are honest explanations of their world and what is happening. Such explanations are long, complex, and maybe demanding. While serious magazines and newspapers and books offer this material, it doesn't get read by enough people. How do we get them to read it? Most people instead are watching TV or listening to talk radio or looking at the internet or interacting with social media. How do we get those media platforms to be serious and not silly, to focus on important truths and not distractions? How do we get the media platforms—especially conservative talk radio and the entire agglomeration that is Webworld—to present content that would, if widely understood, undermine themselves? And how would we get citizens to pay attention to it?

How do we counter the narrative, adhered to by so many ordinary people here in the U.S. and across the world, that hammers government in general, disparages public servants, views taxes as confiscation of "my hard-earned money," thinks a conspiring intellectual elite or a "deep state" controls the nation's agenda, and is convinced that undeserving minorities, welfare recipients, migrants, and other "takers" are getting ahead of them?

Of all the stories that have been told and sold to the Republican half of the American electorate—and to workers around the world—the absolutely most damaging one has been the idea that the "free market" and the private sector are working on behalf of the average working man and serving him well economically. This narrative has lifted the "entrepreneur" and job "makers" into mythic status and at the same time painted the public sector as something that just gets in the way of wealth production. The truth is that this story has served as cover while the top ranks of the private and corporate world have looted revenue, income, and resources from the rest of us. Along the way, building for the past 40 years or so, the damages to conditions in America and societies across the globe have been piling up.

Citizens in the U.S. and the world are right to feel the economic insecurity, the inroads of automation, the onlining of everything, the con of the gig economy, and the volatility of it all. They are right to feel angry, powerless, distrustful, and alienated. They are right to see the wave of refugees to Europe and the Central American migrants to the U.S. and feel nervous. Among other dynamics, these population displacements are a sign that societies—somewhere—are breaking down. That these migrants can be used as scapegoats is just another indication that average citizens don't know who or what is to blame and aren't prepared to unite in solidarity against the very forces that create a world where migration is the only option for destitute and victimized people. In a world of unprecedented wealth, resources, and capabilities—enough for all people to share—we still have civil war, gang warfare, corrupt governments, horrible and unfair allocation of income, and the repression or exploitation of powerless poor people. It is a sick sight to see the poorest, least empowered citizens of the U.S. and Europe thinking that the poorest, least empowered refugees from the south are the enemy.

It is a lot to ask of citizens that they become informed about their world, their government, their economy, and how it all works together. But if they want to keep their democracies, there is no alternative to that. Political power, runaway capitalism, and technological unilateralism are untouchable if citizens remain ignorant and easily manipulated. Becoming clear about the major forces in society—from money in politics to the current formulation of capitalism to the poison on the web to the lies in the anti-government narrative—is the necessary prerequisite for citizens to become wise and helpful to their own best interests.

This is a job for both Democrats and Republicans, but I do think ordinary Republican citizens have a heavier burden in this regard; they are at a greater disadvantage than Democrats. On the right, in contrast with the left, there is more promotion of fear, anger, resentment, and sense of grievance. There is more explicit reference to political opposites as not just wrong (which liberals label the right as just as frequently) but also unpatriotic or un-American or socialist or even communist. On the right, the triad of Fox News, conservative talk radio, and the internet really combine together powerfully to promote a picture of American society—and then politics—that is distorted in very hostile and aggressive ways. Fox News and talk radio—which reach millions of listeners—don't educate their audiences about what is behind the runaway capitalism that has redistributed wealth upward and is busy automating jobs as fast as it can. Those news outlets won't discuss executive compensation or the notion of fairness in the tax code. Instead, they are blaming liberals and some vague, intellectual elite for globalization and bad trade deals. And they continually disparage the idea of expertise and the facts of science.

The left too has its siloed media, and that does its part as well to divide citizens from each other. But Republican citizens and politicians have hooked their loyalties to President Trump and his lies and unfitness and unpreparedness for office. This further distances the Republican Party from reality and damages the thinking of Republican citizens. Trump incorrectly denies the crisis of climate change and continues the promotion of the simple-minded anti-taxes, anti-government narrative. He attacks the institution of the press, behaves like an internet troll, and actively, deliberately, divides the electorate. His demeanor and his policies are corrosive to our country and, most critically, they are bad for the ordinary citizens who voted for him.

A good example of the dishonesty of President Trump and the politicians of the Republican Party today can be seen in Trump's references to "draining the swamp." In an understandably appealing line to eager voters, he as a candidate said that he would "drain the swamp." There is indeed a swamp to drain in politics, but neither he nor Republican politicians will tell citizens honestly what the swamp is and who made it. This is ironic because Trump's supporters—many of whom are not doing well financially—might be impressed by honest information and straight talk about the economy, deregulation, and the tax code, and how those items have been designed to serve wealthy and powerful interests rather than the working class. Indeed, Trump's voters praised him for "telling it like it is." They just didn't know that he was telling them, really, nothing. Or, if he told them something, it was heavy on emotional, irrelevant, or deceptive content.

Had Trump been honest or knowledgeable, he could have described the swamp, and his supporters would have learned something real. The swamp actually is the collection of players and their relationships that for 40 years has created the character and shape of the politics and forces that I have been describing. Populated by a cadre—whose composition can shift slowly over time—of officeholders, congressional staffers, regulatory agencies, lobbyists, lawyers, bankers, businessmen, and other movers and shakers, these individuals are power brokers who usually represent specific and often narrow interests. They usually are not safeguarding the wide public interest but instead are often following agendas that are motivated by greed and the desire for power, money, government contracts, market share, absence of regulation, or other advantages or rewards. Oftentimes, it is political donations, revolving-door jobs, or the trading of votes or favors that are the coin of the swamp.

The power of swamplike political behavior waxes and wanes, but it is winning when the political system is producing results and politics that are damaging to the broad public interest. The swamp is winning when the citizenry knows—as it does today—that it is not being well represented by its government. Over the past 40 years, both Democrats and Republicans have at times been guilty of representing narrow interests; both parties certainly are responsible for the substantial deregulation of the financial sector of the economy, the sector that precipitated the disastrous Wall Street meltdown (the parties differ markedly in their support for new oversight however).

But Trump and his Republican enablers in Congress won't explain any of this. They would have us believe that the swamp consists exclusively of Democrats, liberal judges, intellectuals, academics, and lifelong government bureaucrats. Trump, during his campaign, repeatedly led citizens astray, accusing Clinton ("lock her up"), immigrants ("build that wall"), and unpatriotic Democrats ("make America great again") of being part of the swamp, of being responsible for globalization, job loss, and the economic insecurity of so many Americans. And all of those distortions and half-truths were echoed 24/7 by Fox News, conservative talk radio, and the right-wing silos of Webworld.

Ironically, before becoming President, Trump was a bona fide member of the true swamp, pushing his real estate ventures and casinos by working the banks, zoning boards, press, politicians, and gatekeepers for such endeavors. During his campaign, he bragged about his reciprocal back-scratching relationships with politicians and how he used them and they used him. This "straight talk" thrilled Trump's supporters and they may have thought he'd do something big about cracking down on these practices. But he has done nothing about them, and he has no intention of doing anything. In fact, irony on top of irony, he supports the role of political contributions and he has appointed judges and Supreme Court justices who believe political donations are equivalent to free speech and therefore cannot be constrained. Similarly, as I've mentioned, he supports corporate personhood and full deregulation of pretty much everything. Those policy positions are just gifts and invitations to the swamp.

On this topic—the swamp and the corruption of government—Trump, Republican congressmen, and right-wing media outlets are furthering some of the most damaged and damaging aspects of the practice of politics today. They are facilitating the continued corruption of government. And they are misleading and miseducating American citizens while doing it. President Trump is not going to drain the swamp; he is adding to the already-corrupted realities that are degrading both democracy and capitalism.

As a candidate, Trump tapped into the legitimate rage of many screwed Americans; as a president, he has managed to distract them and con them while actually doing very little of substance for them.

Given the circumstance around us—a divided and confused citizenry, a powerful Webworld, a sociopathic capitalism, and a continuously weakening press—I don't think that we'll meaningfully repair our politics. A significant portion of our citizenry is sufficiently mistrustful, traumatized, poisoned, or victimized, or so captured by Webworld that they are incapable of responding beneficially to any reform initiatives. And the politicians and Congress, while showing some signs of desire for change, will not be able to go far enough without the support of and push from the people.

We have advanced to a point already where Webworld has neutered or enfeebled many people's minds. That damage cannot be repaired as long as the internet exists. Politics, in the United States and across the world, will not cease to be effectively dysfunctional as long as the internet exists.

Whether President Trump is reelected in 2020 or not will not alter the basic problems in either the electorate or the political system. These problems—embedded in the forces I have been describing—will remain even if a liberal Democrat were to win the presidency. If anything, the problems are bigger, deeper, and more institutionalized than when Obama was President.

* * * *

Given the condition of politics today, let's consider the current presidential race and the potential impacts of its progression and outcome.

First, during the primary season, what forums exist for a candidate—any candidate—to tell the story of America and the world today, the story of where we are now, how we got here, and where we are headed? That's a long story, an unfamiliar story, but the one that needs to be told. In all its details—especially with regard to the need to restrain or redesign capitalism, technology, and Webworld—it would be an unwelcome story. How could a candidate begin to describe honestly what forces and actors have for 40 years manipulated citizens? How could he or she inform voters, unite them, and rally them to see that only solidarity with their fellow ordinary citizens—regardless of party, religion, race, or education—would have a prayer of meeting the most significant global challenges we face? How could a candidate get all citizens—Republican and Democratic, white and black—to see that the largest forces threatening us trump the many other important concerns we hold and that divide us? The American electorate repeatedly allows itself to be split apart by disagreements over abortion, gun control, gay or transgender measures, slavery reparations, the death penalty, sentencing issues, immigration, health care, and other subjects.

The presidential primary debates are only partially helpful in this regard. On the Democratic side, there are too many candidates and too little speaking time for much of any story to be told or any startling education to occur. And though each candidate has good and constructive things to say, the wide range of focuses among them—from women's issues to race injustices to veterans' treatment—indicates that there is still an insufficient grasp of what truly is threatening society as a whole. A number of the candidates do talk about some of the forces I describe; there is significant discussion of runaway capitalism, income inequality, tax fairness, climate change, and the need to examine the size and performance of the biggest internet companies. But let's see how much agreement there is on these issues—and the urgency of addressing them—among the candidates.

It will matter which Democratic candidate receives the nomination. Most of them are not adequately explaining the relationships that link the major forces—for example, the seismic role of the web in dividing and damaging the public—nor are they describing fully the magnitude of the problems and thus the startling nature of the solutions that are required. This is understandable, and it reflects the capacities of human nature to hear bad news and the abilities of human nature to deliver that bad news. When a candidate is trying to win office, the reality is that there are limits to what he or she can explain or propose, and still expect to get elected. Is the American electorate prepared to receive, for example, the analysis of capitalism, technology, Webworld, and the environment that I present in this book? How would we react to the presidential candidate who tells us that nearly everything about the ways we live has to change? Are the upper classes especially—both Democrats and Republicans—prepared to live far more modestly than they do now? How many voters—Republican or Democratic—will accept that a civilization-ending set of developments is bearing down on us?

On the Republican side, President Trump will not—for a variety of reasons—speak honestly or competently about the major forces that are determining the path of society. This is too bad, because many of the people who voted for him did so precisely because those forces are damaging their lives. If there are Republican debates, it is unclear what subjects will be discussed.

Once the Democratic presidential nominee is selected, and he or she is in televised debates with President Trump, there is certainly more potential for meaningful discussion to occur. Whether it does occur will depend upon the two candidates, the moderators, the debate questions, and the formats. It may depend on the courage of the Democratic nominee to tell the story of where we are today and where we're headed. One thing is sure: the differences between the candidates will be large.

If Trump is reelected there really is nothing I can add to what I have already written in this book about society's sure demise in the face of the forces that are unraveling it and the ecosphere. Trump simply won't address these forces with any meaningful policies. The Democrats are extremely unlikely to win the Senate in any case, so Congress too would be a bystander to our dissolution.

If a Democrat were to be elected in 2020, it wouldn't alter my belief that we are headed for the abyss. A Democrat in the White House would change many things—from the tone of presidential rhetoric to the beliefs of judicial nominees to the actual policies proposed by the new administration—but he or she would not fundamentally alter the powers and relationships and forces that have propelled us to this place-of-crises today. Remember, Donald Trump did not create our crises; they are products of 40 years of developments.

Any Democratic President—whether centrist or progressive—would have to contend with all of the realities that shape our society today. For the reasons and circumstances I've outlined, our citizens and our politicians are not going to implement the solutions we need in the time span necessary to be meaningful.

MEDIA

The ongoing dismemberment of the press is an existential threat to democracy. A critical counterweight to political dishonesty and manipulation, its continuing reduction in size and effectiveness bodes ill for the future. It should not continue to distort or sensationalize itself to compete with clickbait. But we have passed the point where it can be saved. The internet and Webworld, and the destructive voices on the right, are subduing the serious and responsible press. Even if the legacy media's financial model could be restored (it can't), the internet has assured that there aren't enough minds left that would read it.

If the internet platforms decided to behave like newspapers, things would not be so desperate. They could—if they chose to—assume responsibility and accountability for the content on their platforms. That would require them to read, review, edit, cull, and include or reject the writings, photos, videos, advertising, and memes that could appear on their platforms. The tech companies have no intention of assuming those responsibilities; they now consistently remove content only in certain categories that are indisputably malicious, violent, or inciteful. Furthermore, as I described earlier, the sheer magnitude of the material posted on the web 24/7 overwhelms the capacity of any platform company to screen it. We invented the internet, and now it is beyond controlling.

Another reform that the platforms could make—but won't—would be to give all users the same news and content in our news-feeds, search results, advertisements, and other programs. Especially with news-feeds, the tech companies could fill them with the most significant, most important news of the world. Again, this is what traditional newspapers did. The editors made a judgement regarding what informed citizens should know, and that's what made the papers. Same with search results; the platforms could stop tailoring then to our personal opinions and start filling them with uncanted, objective truth. But beyond occasional adjustments— Facebook recently tweaked its news-feed—the platforms won't abandon a formula that so thoroughly hooks the user. Ironically, it isn't even clear that the users want these reforms. We like being the center of our own media service. We like receiving news and advertisements when both flatter us with what we are interested in. And it is now popular, especially on the political right, to point out that newspapers never were really unbiased anyway—as if that simple critique explains the whole story and makes today's websites into paragons of "real" news.

Some critics have suggested reinstating the Fairness Doctrine (repealed in 1987) with a version that would be updated to apply to the contemporary media landscape. That would mean that its provisions requiring media to highlight and explain divergent points of view would apply to radio, television, print, and the internet platforms. Ideally, a modern Fairness Doctrine could stimulate media to expose citizens to political ideas that they otherwise would never see or hear. But this new regulation is extremely unlikely to be implemented. The web platform companies and the political right would fight it effectively. Silicon Valley certainly doesn't want to rewrite its algorithms to take us out of our silos; and because talk radio is hugely influential and overwhelmingly conservative, Republican legislators will not be eager to rein it in. In addition, the Big Money of the many established forces across our economy—the ones that have been doing well for 40 years—will be brought to bear in Congress to assure the defeat of this reform.

It is also possible that instituting a Fairness Doctrine at this point would have no effect anyway. We may have reached a condition where citizens are so entrenched in their own respective narratives that no amount of new (to them) information will penetrate and shake their worldviews. For at least 20 or 30 years, powerful dynamics have worked very hard—deliberately—to make citizens dumber, sillier, and less responsible generally, and now they may simply be beyond reaching when we need them the most.

We could also reinstitute some stricter version of the Telecommunications Act. Rather than allowing huge media corporations to own cross-media companies—in TV, radio, newspapers, movies, and the web—we could restrict them to one type of platform and smaller markets. This would diminish their size and power and the synergies they now exploit with mixed-media campaigns. As I mentioned though in discussing possible reforms to Webworld and the tech companies, Silicon Valley is well represented by lobbyists in Washington, D.C. And it is far from clear whether either the general public or politicians support significant fragmentation of the current shape of the largest media conglomerates.

Some version of the death of traditional media reporting and the rise of the internet is now afflicting nearly every nation on earth. Webworld is nearly universal, it is constantly growing, and it is feeding anger, emotion, simple-mindedness, propaganda, and extremism across the world. Webworld will make impossible the solving of our biggest and most important media problems.

EDUCATION

With the loss of sober and honest media—a slow, steady reduction in the number of professional-grade newspapers and journalists—we are losing a major vehicle of adult education and thus one of the principal methods of preparing to address our problems. Without a competent press, and a citizenry that is reading it to be informed, we cannot hope to solve our problems. Instead, in Webworld, which is replacing the press, many of us—a critical mass of us—are becoming sillier and less knowledgeable about the world. We are also becoming more rigid about what we think we know. We have long believed narratives that no longer reflect realities. They really never did, but now their contradictions and falseness have become too obvious against the backdrop of real circumstances and what people are experiencing in their own lives. But the internet, because of its financial structure, is committed to adhering to and reinforcing those narratives. As large corporations that depend for their survival upon advertising, materialism, and consumerism, the internet platforms cannot point out the fundamental contradictions of capitalism and they cannot educate us about the dangers of data collection and the very artificial intelligence that they are developing and utilizing to manipulate us.

Understanding the problems and forces that I describe in this book—even being able to consider the thesis of this book—takes a mind open to looking at familiar realities in new and different ways. It takes habits of mind—the habits that a good education gives us—that Webworld is destroying. The dynamics of Webworld, in fact, are actually uneducating us; they are making us stupider, more impulsive, less able to think critically, and less able to change our minds. As long as Webworld exists, we will be unable to educate the citizenry sufficiently. We will not be able to create a population informed enough that they are willing to challenge and change the forces that are right now deciding the present and future.

This is such a disappointing judgement on the web, when we think about its potential. Ideally, as its founders had in mind, the internet should be an extraordinary educational tool and vehicle. With infinite information, videos, and photos, the internet contains so much material—easily accessed—for the genuinely curious person. One can read, view, and travel on the web; one can learn many things. And indeed, some users do. But as I described in the chapter on human nature, society cannot advance beyond the limits of the mental health and emotional maturity of the population interacting as a whole. And the web retards that health and maturity. So, while plenty of smart, conscientious citizens use the internet to learn and grow, nobody is immune to its effects. The best of us are still siloed and buffeted by Webworld, and it affects our perspectives and responses. The worst of us—those who have the most difficulties—can be really limited and damaged by the internet. We are all diminished by Web-world, and it reduces the scope and capabilities of our possible responses to the problems of society.

If education alone were going to be our savior, it would already be effective and powerful in ways that it clearly isn't. If we're adults in the U.S., we've all gone to school—at least through high school—and there are plenty of awesome books and academic articles that we could continue to learn from. But most of us don't pursue continuing education in any broad way. It is important to remember that any effort at educating people—especially adults—doesn't occur in neutral, perfect circumstances. Life doesn't stop while we learn new things. In today's world, with so many competing messages, so much chaff, and so much political cant, it isn't easy to learn what's what. And the content of the education that I am suggesting is necessary presents a particular challenge to the adult student. It is material that will contradict much that he has been told about the world. If he believes the new material—if he learns the story—it will unsettle him, cause him anxiety, and pose large and difficult questions to him about the ways of our society. What he learns will implicitly demand change. We know how difficult change is for people. Adult students will struggle, in many ways. And while our student considers new information, there will be plenty of voices telling him that it is flawed or wrong. And as I referred to in the chapters on education and human nature, our epistemology too can be a profound obstacle to overcome; at the very least, it is a collection of emotions, observations, data, and settled beliefs that we must negotiate as we are exposed to potential new learning.

Some observers, recognizing that today's adults are not going to meaningfully address the contemporary forces defining society, place their hopes in young people. They think that, with the right education and without a long epistemology to overcome, young students can learn accurately where the world stands. I don't think this is the case.

First, they don't have a new, substantially different epistemology—at least in any way that would lead them to question technology and Web-world. We adults, who have designed both their world and their school curricula, have surrounded them from birth with gadgets, devices, computers, and screens. We have given them tablets, smartphones, apps, social media, video games, 24/7 brand advertising, and hyperconsumerism. That is all they have known; why would they question the validity of the very existence of all of those things?

Furthermore, we have given students a "STEM" education, with the emphasis placed on computer science! What bigger message and endorsement of the digital culture could we have given them? We teach them on laptops, teach them to code, and teach them to be software writers; and then we expect that they'll conclude that the internet and Webworld are doing more harm than good?

Second, with regard to the current realities in politics and capitalism that are distorting our economy and creating alienation and polarization in our citizenry, some observers believe that young people could lead a new effort at better and more engaged citizenship. This is equally fantasy-thinking. Do you see the adults across the nation designing a new civics curriculum for all the schools in all the states? Do you think Americans today could remotely agree on a new course of studies intended to produce unusually enlightened, discerning, wise high school graduates?

Young people, especially as they transition into their high school years and beyond, are subject to the same influencers, conditioning, pressures, and need to earn money as their parents. There'll be no magic, enlightened generation just determined to save the world. There's no magic, period. That's key, by the way; to produce students with a new attitude, they would have to be consciously designed, primed, and groomed by specific curricula, messages, values, socialization, and adult modeling. We adults have not done that—we've done the opposite in fact—and we're not going to. We continually underestimate the power, subtlety, stealth, tenacity, and process of development of epistemology. Mostly, especially in young people, epistemology is a product, not something we choose or have thorough control over. Children largely don't choose their families, parents, place of birth and residence, experiences, and cultural milieu. By the time we are old enough to consciously exert more control over our learning and experiences, we have to a great degree been formed and influenced. Many people, of any age, even with will and exposure to new education, cannot fully rise above or grow beyond their long (or short) epistemology.

Young people have the same human nature as the rest of us, with flaws, weaknesses, and other imperfections. Today, young people are nearly as polarized and alienated as adults, and they have the poorest voter turnout of all age groups. Finally, because they were born and raised in

Webworld times, and are enamored of technology and social media, they are unable to measure and gauge fully what has already been lost regarding so much about our habits of mind, the nature of work, the media, and the sane rhythms of life. The young will not rescue us because they will not be able to see that the dynamics of the internet—an ecology that has never not been in their lives—will prevent society from being able to address the forces propelling it.

HUMAN NATURE

Human nature is a force, and it is also a thing that the other forces act on. I have described how Webworld and politics and the condition of the world today are impacting our human nature, and in many cases they are preying on it. Webworld, especially, takes advantage of its vulnerabilities.

There is absolutely no possibility of changing human nature (at least not without genetic modification). So the consequences of being human in this world of forces cannot be avoided. In the face of all the technology, conflict, capitalism, politics, and other realities in this complex and turbulent world, we will always respond like the emotional animals we are, not like some perfectly rational creatures.

There is a limit, then, to how much logic and wisdom we can deploy, and we should be realistic about this. Human nature is not perfectable, and society much less so. Sometimes, at the individual level, one can come close to a high degree of wisdom and awareness. But at the level of American society today—a collection of 330 million diverse individuals executing an infinite array of endeavors—the complexities and compromises and institutions and factors that are required or in play simply make impossible anything approaching a sane, stable, and sustainable community.

Human nature has always existed, and every society has had to find the ways to harness, channel, or restrain it. What is different today is the existence of the internet. Webworld is designed to victimize us, through our human nature. As it is doing that, it is killing our restraint, responsibility, humility, self-awareness, and tolerance for ambiguity and uncertainty. It is blinding us to the damage—in so many areas—that we are doing. It masks the lies, contradictions, distortions, chaos, insanities, and unsustainabilities of our culture. Standing inside that culture, and hailing more and more from Webworld, we cannot see that.

Every society that has existed before us has had to cope with and manage human nature. Most eventually failed. We, however, have invented machinery that makes it impossible to control our nature. We are, therefore, overwhelming ourselves. We aren't going to change human nature, or reform Webworld in timely and meaningful ways, so we are not going to solve the problems that threaten us.

We have invented a technology that is lethal to human nature. Once before, we did something similar—we invented nuclear weapons, lethal to life itself. After Hiroshima and Nagasaki, we realized that we had on our hands a technology that couldn't be used. So it is possible to invent clever devices that produce results that are either too uncontrollable or too destructive. We haven't used nuclear weapons again, and we hope never to. Webworld is such a device. Acting toxically on human nature, it produces results that are uncontrollable and ultimately lethal to society.

It is tempting to think that we could reform the web, make it safe for humans. But that idea makes two mistakes. First, it imagines that we could ever change the web sufficiently to render it mostly harmless, on balance. That, as I described earlier, cannot be achieved technically, and it won't be done meaningfully in our current political and financial culture. Second, the idea ignores the entire point of recognizing that human nature is a force and that it contains—in many people—the energies to take advantage of others. We can improve the web, but hackers, trolls, terrorists, and con men would still exist. Because of the scale and dynamics of Webworld, and the existence of human nature, we have created an unsolvable problem.

THE ENVIRONMENT

I have described the dire conditions of our natural world. They have been caused by political, economic, technological, and cultural systems and arrangements that have been based on ideas which have no relationship to the fact that we live on a planet with finite resources.

As the concepts, values, and literal, tangible expression of the Western idea of "progress" advance steadily across the world, our environmental problems only worsen. The materialism, consumerism, and standard of living that our version of capitalism promotes require a use of resources and a despoiling of the natural world that are not sustainable. We are depleting or damaging our soil, fresh water, forests, oceans, minerals, atmosphere, and habitats.

A total, certain ecological catastrophe awaits in this century. Nature and nature's systems have already begun to unravel in many parts of the world, but because the deterioration is as yet seemingly sporadic and dispersed, and because we in the United States don't see much of it, we remain uninformed and unimpressed.

To arrest the damage that we are doing to the ecosphere would require steps that are huge, shocking, wrenching, and unthinkable to most Americans. They are measures that would change everything, touch everything, and transform life as we currently live it. Implementing these measures would be expensive and jarring and inconvenient. Nobody, including environmentalists, would like them. Some observers have said that transforming our societies into green, sustainable ones can be done smoothly, without horrible disruption, and for manageable sums. That's just not true; it's a fantasy, and it completely ignores the scope and scale of the transformation that is needed, and the speed at which meaningful change must occur. Although we know what reforms are necessary to stop damaging our world, there is no chance that we are going to implement the changes in any meaningful or timely way. I am not referring to any changes that we as individual citizens may or could make, such as buying a hybrid car, recycling diligently, watering our lawns less, planting a tree, living in the city, or just living more modestly in general. The changes I am referring to are big reforms in the structures of our capitalism, the market, industry, politics, and transportation. And they are changes that have to be implemented in nations across the globe.

There is some recognition, primarily among Democrats, of the size of the energy transformation that is needed to slow and halt carbon dioxide emissions. The "Green New Deal," for example, the proposed legislation often discussed by the Democratic candidates for president, sets as its goal the complete elimination of the use of fossil fuels. That's a frank acknowledgement of one very large source of the climate crisis, but nowhere in the legislation—which also proposes more and better jobs, health care, housing, education, public transit, and infrastructure—does it hint at the transformations also necessary in capitalism and the consumption society. Instead, it contains an upbeat implication that we could simply, productively, redirect our resources and energies and build a smarter, more energy-efficient, industrial society; it'll be costly, yes, but we'll end up prosperous and comfortable, like we are now. In fact, it views the needed greening of society as a good opportunity to create new jobs and new technologies that will save our society and preserve our economy at the same time. The Green New Deal is a good document—a start—but it is a telling indication that we don't yet recognize what a sustainable world will require.

* * * *

The primary reform needed is to halt all burning of fossil fuels— wood, coal, gas, and oil—across the entire globe, and do it immediately. Just think about that. Think about the global and domestic fossil fuel network and infrastructure: oil and gas fields, drilling rigs, refineries, tanker ships, storage tanks, distribution lines, power plants, and gas stations. Now think about the users: billions of buildings, factories, houses, vehicles, ships, airplanes, tools, and motors. Think about the coal mines and forestry lumber infrastructure. Nearly every bit of the entire existing fossil fuel apparatus around the world would have to be shut down and replaced by solar, wind, hydroelectric, and other renewable energy technologies.

Just imagine the scale of that task even if every person on the planet were in favor of doing it. The scope, scale, cost, logistics, waste, and disruption would be staggering. And the manufacturing and placement of new energy infrastructure across the globe would require, ironically, the use of phenomenal amounts of land, water, resources, and fossil fuel energy.

Now think about trying to accomplish that goal in our current, real world, with all of the disagreement, resistance, economics, and politics that have so far prevented us from achieving meaningful progress. The task moves from just staggering to impossible. Today, despite at least twenty years of high-profile efforts to raise a mass consciousness and a movement to transition toward renewable energies, the fossil-fuel industries are still enjoying full-throttle prosperity and use. They are still thoroughly interwoven into the fabric and financial dynamics of our capitalist system and the health and operation of the global economy. They are an integral part of stock markets and in the portfolios of a large and diverse group of investment funds. We haven't remotely begun to figure out how to abandon an enormous sector of the economy and account financially for the "stranded assets" of the fossil-fuel infrastructure. Remember, this change must occur immediately.

It is true that we have made some progress in developing renewable energy technology and use. In various nations of the world, including the U.S. and China, impressive installations of wind turbines and solar photovoltaics have been built in the past twenty years. But the deployment of green technologies has moved approximately at the speed of normal market and political conditions only, without the urgency and policies that are truly needed. The current rate of deployment is woefully insufficient.

Politically today, the fossil-fuel industries are still supremely powerful, with lobbyists, trade regulators, Senators, and congressmen often supporting their interests. With the role of money, lobbying, and revolving-door jobs still relatively unfettered, enormous resistance exists to block and retard progress toward green energy. The institutional advantages of the fossil-fuel sector will not quickly weaken.

Furthermore, our capitalism does not reflect a society ready or able to forego fossil fuels and the economic society they make possible. Are we going to eliminate consumerism and materialism? Do citizens in the developed world—even so-called "green" ones—really understand what standard of living is ecologically possible for 2 billion, 4 billion, 10 billion earthlings? Are we Americans ready to accept that a sustainable life must provide shelter, heat, clothing, food, water, medical care, and safety, but little else in terms of material goods and consumption? Or are we intent on holding onto the incredible luxuries and conveniences that we have become used to?

Are we going to redesign capitalism so that it can continue to exist without an ecosphere-destroying consumerism? Consumer purchasing—goaded by advertising—fuels approximately 70 percent of the gross domestic product and millions of jobs. Would our economy collapse if that percentage is dramatically reduced? And if we somehow create a new and more modest capitalism, can we provide enough jobs for workers in the United States—and the world?

Would we be willing to ban most advertising? For in the current design of capitalism, ads play a huge role in conditioning us to think in all the ways that support consumption, materialism, and capitalism itself. We are taught to want things, want more things, want new things, want newer things, and aspire to status, fashion, and superiority. We are persuaded by ads that we need luxuries, toys, more devices, and more entertainment. We are conditioned to believe that buying things will make us happier, prettier, more desirable to others, and more fulfilled.

And could human nature itself become reconciled with a static, steady-state world? We are striving, constructive beings, full of creative energies and never-resting minds. We are insatiable in every way, and we chafe at restraints. We build things. The human spirit is a bounding power and it cannot be restrained by force, necessity, or reason. It is simultaneously our strength and our weakness. The nature of human nature is, in fact, one of the reasons that capitalism has mostly beat out any system of pure social-ism; capitalism (for better and worse) allows for the full expression of individual autonomy, initiative, inventiveness, and athletic or intellectual potential. It is very hard to imagine modern man returning to and main-taining a subsistence society.

One of the features of Webworld demonstrates how difficult it would be to transform our society. Computers and the internet, as I described, came out of an idealistic, academic, Californian culture that had the right values and intentions. The earliest Silicon Valley computer nerds wanted an online network to connect all the bright and curious minds of the scientific community, a community that would share openness, honesty, transparency, positive and beneficial ideas, research, and learn enthusiasti-cally from each other. And it is fair to say that, especially in the 1960s and '70s, this community was more environmentally conscious and more able to critique the flaws in capitalism than the population as a whole.

Yet even that more progressive scientific community was unable to hold off the development of the web into an overwhelmingly commer-cial enterprise—one that is sustained almost exclusively by advertising. The nerds who invented the internet were unprepared for the forces of both human nature and for-profit capitalism; they didn't anticipate the malevolence that today inundates Webworld, nor the imperatives of an all-encompassing capitalism. Most telling, even today, when Google, Face-book, Amazon, Apple, Microsoft, and IBM—all staffed predominantly by progressive types—all recognize the terrible problems and contradictions in a Webworld propelled by advertising and consumerism, they cannot bring themselves to meaningfully restrain or reform their business models and practices. The high-tech corporate community is as trapped by the current design and rewards of capitalism as the fossil-fuel industry is. We are all trapped by the treadmill of capitalism. That is why a radical and rapid transformation of society and the economy would be so difficult.

If we aren't going to halt the use of fossil fuels, and are going to continue increasing the amount of carbon dioxide in the oceans and atmosphere, perhaps there are formidable new technologies that can somehow save us? A number have been proposed, but none of them offers reason for hope. None of them comes remotely close to reducing or solving the realities of our CO_2 problem. There is no technological magic bullet waiting to be employed.

Under the label of "geoengineering" solutions, carbon sequestration is often talked about. Sequestration is the idea of capturing the carbon dioxide already in the atmosphere, or as it is being produced by a power plant, and holding it in a reservoir that is leak-proof. Most often suggested as a container have been the caverns and voids somewhere below the surface grade of the landscape. The CO_2 would have to be injected with pressure into relatively deep (maybe a mile or two down) voids. This approach has many major problems: the voids required to accommodate the enormous volume of CO_2 involved would have to be huge; they would have to be leak-proof, so that the gas could not leak back out into the atmosphere; and they would have to hold the CO_2 forever. The sequestration and injection process itself would consume large amounts of energy, and produce its own large quantities of CO_2 emissions. At the scale that would be required, it would be costly, unreliable, and bizarre. It is never going to happen.

Another specious geoengineering idea is to dump large amounts of iron filings into the oceans to stimulate the growth of plankton, which absorbs CO_2 during photosynthesis. Some portion of the vegetation would be eaten by fish and other sea life while another portion would eventually sink to the seabed and sequester the carbon for a good long time. But a "fertilization" intervention such as this, on the scale needed to make a difference, is risky and unwise. We have no idea what the consequences would be; we don't know which sea life would eat the plankton, what unforeseen qualities—perhaps toxic—the algae could have, and most serious of all, we don't understand what possible consequences might ripple across the larger ecosystem.

In the same risk category as ocean fertilization is seeding the atmosphere with sulfur particles or gases. Some scientists propose releasing fine particles of sulfur dioxide or other synthetic chemicals into the stratosphere at an altitude of twelve miles or so. The idea is to block some portion of sunlight from reaching earth, thus tempering the rise of global warming. We would have to do this every year. Of course, the consequences of doing this are completely unknown; it would certainly reduce solar heat gain at the earth's surface but it would also alter the winds, ocean currents, rainfall, and circulatory patterns and distribution of climate characteristics across the globe. It would produce different results in different parts of the world, perhaps reducing monsoon intensity in one location and increasing it elsewhere. Its consequences could also damage the ozone layer or other critical atmospheric-geophysical relationships. We could destabilize longstanding ecological balances that we are not even aware of. We would be deliberately producing acid rain.

Injecting enormous quantities of man-made chemicals into the atmosphere, seas, or earth would be a dangerous and desperate act. The consequences would be unpredictable and not able to be controlled or recalled. What is thoroughly frightening is this: because we are not going to meaningfully address global warming with CO_2 reduction measures, we will eventually, almost assuredly, take these extraordinary geoengineering steps as we witness both the biosphere and civilization collapsing. We will feel there is no longer anything to lose. And if some sense of caution restrains most of the nations of the world from gambling with geoengineering, there will certainly be some countries that unilaterally execute these measures. And lastly, because there are so many private citizens with personal fortunes of literally billions of dollars, some of them will no doubt finance private-sector efforts at climate modification. There will be no way to stop them.

There are other bizarre interventions that are being discussed. Some groups have considered installing big mirrors in the deserts, or producing reflective pavement, or spraying everything white, all to reflect more sunlight. There is nothing wrong with improvements such as white roofs (architects specify them now on many flat roofs), but to think seriously about huge mirrors to control the earth's temperature is just lunacy.

Another gimmick that—unlike geoengineering—is already in use is the con game called "carbon offsets." A company or utility or land developer who is either producing CO_2 emissions or cutting down natural forests can pay for the planting or preservation of a new forest preserve in some other location. The CO_2 absorbed by the new trees is supposed to match (and offset) the quantity of CO_2 emitted by the utility, or match the oxygen production lost by developing previously green lands. This is a bogus set of procedures for practical reasons; it requires constant, permanent monitoring and enforcement, and the new forests in remote locations must be maintained forever, even as they too come under the inevitable pressures for land development. There are many other types of offset projects as well, all of which are even harder to verify and monitor. The entire concept of allowing CO_2 pollution to continue while we compensate for it elsewhere has been proven to be unmanageable and unrealistic in the real world.

Similarly, the idea of putting a tax on carbon emissions is an idea whose time has passed. First proposed at least 20 years ago, but defeated politically over and over again, it had offered a way to use the market system to encourage a managed transition from fossil fuels to greener energy. By taxing CO_2 pollution, we could have created healthy financial incentives—almost like a subsidy—to assist in the adoption of solar and wind energy. Fossil fuel energy would slowly have become more expensive while renewable energy would gradually become less expensive. The normal dynamics of competition and choice would then have worked their magic—we had presumed—to create a happy result. But now we are out of time. We don't have 10 or 20 years to make a market transition; and the atmosphere is already too saturated with CO_2 to continue polluting it—no matter how much the fossil fuel industries are willing to pay for that practice.

Never mind curtailing CO_2 production, we cannot even halt or control our relentless destruction of forests, marshes, prairies, and other natural landscapes. Every day, land development around the world burns or bulldozes thousands of acres of previously untouched wildlands. Even the Amazon rainforest remains under assault and shrinks in area every year. The soils and vegetation and natural water aquifers of the ecosphere—the things that keep our planet cleansed and healthy—are disappearing. As man and his industries, buildings, roads, and farming spread like an uncontrollable plague across the natural world, we are simply eviscerating it.

Some observers have advocated nuclear power as a substitute for fossil-fuel energy. Leaving aside the unresolved nuclear waste disposal issues, this path is unavailable. Nuclear plants are incredibly complex and take years to plan and build; and as solar photovoltaic and wind turbine power have come down in price, nuclear power has become prohibitively expensive. We would need thousands of plants built immediately (and this ignores wide citizen opposition), and even then, nuclear power serves predominantly electrical demand and cannot satisfy all of the applications powered by oil and gas. It is way too late in our ecological crisis for new nuclear power plants to be able to play any meaningful role.

* * * *

We are not going to halt the damage that we are doing to every aspect of the ecosphere. We are not going to redesign our capitalism, consumerism, standard of living, or insatiable aspirations. We are not going to remove the money from politics, nor shut down the internet and Webworld. We aren't going to redesign human nature. All of those forces will prevent us from addressing global warming.

Currently, very few people anywhere—including most environmentalists in the U.S.—have any idea of what life would be like for everyone if we were to live in an ecologically sustainable way. We simply don't grasp how big the gap is now between the way we live, and the way we'd have to live. It is a gulf.

So, meanwhile, because "progress" is marching on, and because societies—however unevenly—are getting richer, we will continue in the immediate decades to use more fossil-fuel energy, produce more carbon dioxide, and foul more and more of the natural world. And as the human population continues to climb toward at least 9.5 billion, we will every year clear more forests, pave more land, destroy more habitats and natural resources, and make certain the environmental calamities that await us within this century.

HUMAN POPULATION

I have reviewed the facts of human population today. Standing now at 7.8 billion people, we will reach approximately 9.5 or 10 billion around 2050. After that, the global population total may go up or down, no one knows.

Why is today different from any other time? There are many differences, but an obvious one is the number of people on the planet. In 1800, as the Industrial Revolution was gathering force, there were only 1 billion earthlings.

Our industries, our endeavors, and our indefatigable creativity have given an increasing proportion of people better standards of living and better lives than ever before in history. But this wonderful result—a testament to the cooperation and work ethic of people everywhere—is, ironically, severely damaging the biosphere. The ecosphere cannot remain in balance while we use it and overload it in the manner that we do.

Our human population is one of the forces that is combining with the other forces described in this book. Within the next 10 or 20 years, there is nothing we are going to do to change the globe's rising population; after that, any of a number of horrible scenarios may unfold. So, as a factor today, contributing to the crises that we are in, the overall population is immutable. It is too late to change that. Whatever else we do or don't do regarding the other forces wracking society, the human population will not stand still. Between now and 2050, we will add another 2 billion people to the planet, each one needing to fed, clothed, housed, educated, and employed. Their resource consumption and footprint on the land will just pile onto the staggering loads that we are already imposing within the ecosphere.

TRANSPORTATION

I have described the state of our traffic and mass transit today. Public transit in America has been long neglected, and today it is a shadow of what it should be given the populations and densities of our cities and suburbs. Consequently, automobile traffic is a significant and negative force in the daily lives of many people; it has damaging psychological and physiological effects. Additionally, because large, global corporations are primarily in control of the technological development of the car, it is becoming highly computerized and partially automated. Steadily, the experience of being in an automobile is being imbued with the guiding philosophies of Silicon Valley. Being in a car is increasingly like being in Webworld; we are encouraged to be connected, online, entertained, detached from our actual surroundings and the passing landscape, navigate by app, and generally recreate the digital silo that we inhabit when not in a car. More and more, the modern car carries us in a private filter bubble, one that conditions us into not looking out the windows, and not caring about the condition of the physical landscape.

The change that is needed—both in the U.S. and across the globe—is a massive initiative to build public transportation systems. To halt suburban sprawl and wasteful land use, preserve energy and the natural environment, reduce traffic and debilitating commutes, avoid the digital vulnerabilities of connected vehicles, and generally resist the data collection and Webworlding of every aspect of life, we need more subways, trolleys, trains, and buses.

That, however, is not going to happen. The public constituency for it is simply too small and too weak while the forces promoting the car—political, technological, economic—are huge, global, and powerful. Those forces are intent on selling hundreds of millions of cars, SUVs, and pickups in China, India, and the rest of the world. Eventually, cars may become partly or mostly self-driving, but that will not alleviate growing traffic. It will simply increase data collection.

MISCELLANEOUS FORCES

In the preceding chapter I briefly outlined a number of forces that are important to many people, but which do not rise to the level of directing American society. Those forces are: immigration and refugee migrations; terrorism; black-white relations; health care; student loan debt; gene editing; war and nuclear war; and religion. They do not have a grip on society as a whole in the manner of, say, capitalism and technology and the major forces. In many cases, they are a product of or a part of or are woven through the larger forces. They are subjects that need attention and reform or responses of many types, but at this moment today they do not have the influence over our lives that the major forces do (as I acknowledged in the preceding chapter, however, they are literally life-or-death issues for many people). If we were to somehow eliminate all of these second-tier issues, the story that I am telling in this book—the status of where we are today and where we're headed—would not change.

It is worth noting, however, that 10, 15, 20, and more years from now, some of the secondary forces could develop into primary threats. As we fail to address the growing crises in America and the world, and as all sorts of conditions and circumstances therefore deteriorate, factors such as terrorism, war, and refugee migrations will increase in power. Around the world, as people start to starve, or die of heat and drought, and their communities shatter in the face of environmental degradation, they will seek safety by migrating. And without question, accompanying those population dislocations will be violence, terrorism, and killing.

CHAPTER 13

SUMMARY

Today, we are in a really bad place. This is true across the globe, whether you live in America, China, Norway, Italy, Pakistan, or Chad. The barely restrained forces of capitalism, technology, and Webworld are sweeping across the world and warping or damaging the cultures, habits, media, politics, religions, natural environments, and human nature of diverse peoples everywhere.

There are differences, of course, in how these forces are playing out in different nations. Some countries are struggling more than others. But the citizens of almost every nation see or feel the changes being wrought by these forces, and many people—a critical mass—are angry, alienated, confused, sickened, or disempowered by them.

I have identified ten major forces—capitalism, technology, Webworld, politics, media, education, human nature, the environment, human population, and transportation—that are combining today in ways that have come to dominate the world. Together, as a juggernaut of factors, they are defining and deciding the path of the world; the interplay of their dynamics is defining what is possible, and what is not possible.

The interplay of these forces—many of them do not have discernible boundaries between them—is the story of our world today. If you do not understand them, and their development over the past 45 or 50 years, you do not understand the world.

With the exception of Webworld, none of these forces is new. Yet—without question—the present time is vastly different and vastly more threatening than at any other time in human history. The danger that we face is nothing less than the unraveling of civilization across the planet.

Today, the forces I describe in this book have become extreme. Their dynamics or expression or condition have become either toxic or are being exploited—with destructive results.

To review ever so briefly, capitalism has become rapacious and out of control. It has a magnitude, scale, reach, and power never before seen. It is insufficiently regulated and its worst practitioners—who are many—have become greedy and without ethics, honor, or restraint. They have ripped up the social contract. Capitalism today is at war with the biosphere and every culture around the world that has not yet fully aligned itself with materialism and consumerism. Finally, in an unprecedented development, and with unprecedented power and effectiveness, capitalism utilizes and exploits technology, Webworld, politics, and human nature to prevail with and spread its agenda and values. We do not have a political system that will challenge contemporary capitalism and remake it into a version that works for all people and classes, and we do not have a citizenry sufficiently educated about what needs to be done. And those two unfortunate realities will not change meaningfully enough or quickly enough to avert any of a number of disasters.

With the invention of computers and the internet, and the continuing advance of artificial intelligence, technology stepped into a whole new world and created problems for society that have no parallel in history. With computers, connectivity and the digitization of all objects, and the inevitable imperfections of software and human nature, technology has made—and is continuing to make—our infrastructure and world more and more fragile and vulnerable. We continue to increase our dependencies on digital networks and we continue therefore to build our vulnerabilities. Unilaterally, Silicon Valley is imposing on us its vision of utopia. Additionally, automation is eliminating jobs, and no ordinary citizens anywhere have requested that. With bots and artificial intelligence, automation and the replacement of human workers will continue into true crisis levels. There are no politics or mechanisms equal to the task of stopping those private-sector developments. As A.I. and machine learning take advantage of all of the data everywhere that will circulate through networked devices, we will come to live in a digital tyranny. We may remain technically "free," but our choices will be determined by social, economic, and organizational norms that we didn't choose.

Technology, of course, makes Webworld possible. In the history of mankind, we have never seen anything with the power, reach, and synergies of Webworld. Its overwhelming impact on societies everywhere is negative. Taking advantage of the natural weaknesses and vulnerabilities in human nature, it works with capitalism, politics, education, and the media to replace beneficial values and practices with poisonous and destructive ones. It is undermining democracy, society, cooperation, brotherhood, tolerance, patience, thoughtfulness, reason, and emotional intelligence. Webworld is instrumental in promoting consumerism and all sorts of chaff; we have become a shockingly silly and distracted people, incapable of discerning and focusing on the story of the crises around us. It has put us in silos—divided us—and made it impossible to imagine the lives of other people, and it thereby erodes empathy for and trust in the others. Human nature is just no match for the power, speed, relentlessness, vituperation, seductions, tools, and algorithms of Webworld. As long as it exists, we will not rise to meet the existential threats we face, nor will we survive as a civilization. Whether we ultimately succumb—sometime this century—because of ecological collapse, civil war, disease, famine, or technological vulnerabilities, the foundational reason will be the very existence of Webworld. For today it fuels, lubricates, and empowers all the other forces creating, directing, and diminishing the paths that we are on.

Politics today in the United States and nearly everywhere are becoming increasingly dysfunctional. In many nations, large proportions of citizens are angry, alienated, emotional, and ill-informed. They may have legitimate grievances—having been victimized for forty years or so by the forces I describe—but they don't truly know the story of contemporary society. They have often bought into narratives that are misleading and that have been sold to them by politicians, corporations, and interests that are manipulating them. In the U.S. especially, national politics and Congress are co-opted by moneyed interests, and no longer work for the health and welfare of the citizens and country as a whole. With no way to remove money from politics, and no way to counter the poison and distortions promoted by Fox News, right-wing talk-radio extremism, and Webworld, there is no avenue to repairing our political dysfunction. The election of Donald Trump to the presidency was an expression of that dysfunction, not its cause; it was evidence of the desperation of many good, ordinary citizens who have been screwed for forty years. If a Democrat is elected president in 2020, we will still remain a desperately divided nation without the tools to bring us back together. Even under a Democratic president, the forces I've described will remain empowered and effective because in significant ways they aren't Democratic or Republican forces.

The media no longer offers hope that sober and professional journalism could educate the adult population about the story of our time. The responsible press is steadily shrinking in size, financial health, power, and influence. Large traditional newspapers—pre-internet—at least often in their news sections (as opposed to their editorials and op-eds) aspired to write for a diverse audience and attempted to present events that we should care about. Yes, they did this job imperfectly and sometimes with plenty of biases and support for unwise courses of action. But today, the web is a much worse and far more reckless vehicle than newspapers were. It and its dynamics are killing professional journalism and killing the possibility of common understanding about anything.

Web media are dividing us and embittering us. This is happening in the U.S. and all over the world as social media and targeted internet news-feeds narrow our perspectives, reinforce our fears, and corrode the very foundations of society and comity. And although there are Webworld extremists on both the left and the right, and close-minded choirs on each side, there is far more damage being done by internet media on the right. In the U.S., when ordinary citizens on the right are being taught that the press is the enemy of the people, we have a measure of how neutered reason and citizenship have become.

Similarly, education itself is no longer available as a path to enlightenment. With the continuing diminishment of serious journalism, and the ever-expanding influence of Webworld, the human population is losing its competencies and capacities. We are prey for web media, for propaganda, and for hucksters. Webworld is methodically unraveling us and literally de-educating us.

All of the extraordinary effectiveness of Webworld is made possible by human nature. We are remarkable beings, with the potential to be brilliant and generous, or small, stupid, and destructive. For 15,000 years or so, we have shown both capabilities, with societies and civilizations rising, falling, and rising anew over the epochs. We have made mistakes, invented unpredictable technologies, and even suffered through grievous environmental catastrophes. But today, with the invention of the internet and the development of Webworld, we have created a sort of digital phenomenon-machine that we cannot cope with. Webworld is nearly diabolical; we cannot catch up to it. It is not static; it is a moving, morphing target. Next to it, our human nature is a child-like, helpless, predictable constant. Humans throughout history have often taken advantage of our nature and our emotions. But this is the first time in human history that those who would manipulate us are equipped with a force like Webworld; they have a weapon comprised of infinite amounts of data, essentially infinite amounts of computer power, the ability to model and analyze nearly infinite behavioral modification incentives, and the willing (or unwilling) collaboration of four billion online (and growing) mostly clueless humans.

Of all the threats we face, the ongoing destabilization of the biosphere is probably the ultimate one. There are other catastrophes that could occur first—such as a mammoth long-term failure of the worldwide web or of the national electric grid—which would be deadly, but in the absence of those it will be environmental chaos that spells the end of civilization as we know it. That will occur this century. There are simply too many significant obstacles woven through all the aspects of our culture and economy—locally and globally—for us to be able to respond quickly and effectively to the ecological crises around us. We just can't redesign every single thing—capitalism, economics, the market, consumerism, politics, the energy infrastructure, standards of living, and our own attitudes and understandings—in any relevant time span, if ever.

* * * *

This is the story of our time. It's a story about a host of forces that worked reasonably well for many people (not everyone) for a long time, but now have grown out of control, dysfunctional, destructive, or outmatched. They now—in a variety of ways—threaten the continued existence of our societies.

This is not an easy story to understand, and it's even harder to accept it and the conclusion that we cannot fix it. It's very hard for people to believe that this time—this period in history—is different. We've often figured our way through terrible adversity—the Civil War, the Depression, World

War II, the civil rights struggle—and citizens may think that we'll do it again. After all, they think, we survived the dislocations of the Industrial Revolution, the consequences of the automobile, and other shocks to the norm.

But today, the forces are working together in ways that foreclose effective intervention. They have unprecedented power and they interact with unprecedented velocity. And they are working on a planet that for the first time ever has eight billion people on it, and in a biosphere that has never been in worse shape. The atmosphere contains considerably more carbon dioxide today than at any point in human habitation of the planet. The CO_2 levels are still growing globally and we will not stop them.

Perhaps the easiest way to grasp the futility and delusion of hope is to think about the internet. Because of its dynamics, we will remain unable to address our problems as long as it and social media exist. But what chance is there of turning off the web, eliminating connectivity, shunning social media, and halting the advance of artificial intelligence and data collection? There is zero chance.

There is a nice phrase, "Be the change you wish to see." But it's misleading and counter-productive. In 2019, the scope and magnitude of the problems we have cannot be addressed or solved at the individual level. Our problems are massive and structural; they are cultural, technological, institutional, and organizational. They require societal movement.

If we understand that our problems have evolved somewhat organically up and through our economy, industry, society, and culture, we can feel some equanimity about the spot we're in. The more we understand about the forces in society and how they came to look like they look today, the less angry we'll be with our fellow ordinary Americans—whatever our political differences. For if there's blame to be apportioned, it is mostly not to be put on average working people.

Your average (meaning not the corporate and political leaders) citizen grew up in an American culture that helped to form and shape his epistemology; it taught him the rules and it conditioned his norms, values, and expectations. Politically, he may have been Republican or Democratic, but he didn't have much to do with establishing the policies, leadership, and tone of either party. Regarding our material lives, lifestyles, and levels of consumption, we varied considerably by class and race, but large swaths of us also matched each other. And those differences and similarities among the population didn't necessarily correspond to political leanings. Regarding our attitudes toward technology and globalization, we mostly followed the same evolution. Whether we were Republican or Democratic, the negative consequences of automation and globalization unfolded over the decades and accumulated against us all (other than the top 5 or 10 percent of income earners) fairly equally. In that way, overall, through the past forty years of developments, ordinary citizens have pretty much all just been as American as one another. We all got taken advantage of.

Average Americans certainly vary in the personal details of epistemology though, and we should bear this uppermost in mind when we wonder how things have gone wrong. Each one of us grew out of a specific context and has lived a specific life of experiences; we grew up in a particular location, in a particular community, with a family, a religion (or not), an education, relationships, successes and failures, trauma, and experiences. We have also been shaped by radio, television, Webworld, and advertisements. We are all products of a culture. Most of the time, most of us behave in the ways we have learned and gotten used to over a long period of time. Our varying epistemologies don't absolve us from agency or responsibility or the civic duty to be informed but they sure help to explain both our similar and dissimilar behavior as ordinary Americans. And if we could understand that reality better, and grasp its significance, we could feel more solidarity with our fellow citizens, and be less easily manipulated into dividing from them.

If there is a group of Americans (and other nationalities) that deserves significant blame for the crises upon us, it would be the political leaders, corporate leaders, and well-educated citizens in positions of power or authority who understood what was happening to the earth and to ordinary citizens but nonetheless did nothing to halt the damage. In many cases, in fact, they plowed ahead with greed, irresponsibility, and unaccountability, compounding the injuries and guaranteeing the crises. For the past forty years, capitalism, technology, globalization, finance, and politics increasingly blended into an interconnected mosaic of forces that overwhelmingly benefited the powerful and the wealthy and actually victimized everyone else. Some of this evolution unfolded inadvertently, or by default, but the majority of it occurred by design. It was a result of tax policies, deregulation, legislation, Supreme Court rulings, corporate behavior, lobbying, and other political activities or neglect. And much of it was advanced by outright fraud and deception.

Who are the powerful people who designed those many components and details of the forces and the system that produced the outcomes we see today? Do they share a political party or some philosophy, education, university, or agreement? Was it all a conspiracy?

There is much talk today of a boogeyman called "the elite," especially from conservative commentators or Republican politicians trying to make populist appeals. They brand intellectuals, academics, or liberals—especially "East coast liberals"—as elite. They promote the idea that all of the difficulties that ordinary citizens are having are caused by an elite—all from the Democratic Party—that is pushing its own narrow and practically un-American agenda onto an unwilling country.

But that is inaccurate, dishonest, and misleading. It is a story told to manipulate ordinary people, perhaps especially Republican voters. The truth is that the actual elites in this country are the powerful or wealthy (or both) individuals who design and move the levers and institutions of the government, economy, market, corporations, and banks, both nationally and globally. They are Democrats and Republicans, conservative and liberal, and white, black, ethnic, well-educated, and not formally educated. They are not a conspiracy; they don't need to be. And that is because they all share some major understandings and one overarching goal. They understand how nations, economies, politics, and power work; they understand how to accumulate power and—if they desire—also wealth. And they share a common need to reinforce and perpetuate the system that they have mastered and in which they are successful. They have little need to discuss these dynamics with each other for it is all understood.

For forty years there has indeed been a sort of silent class warfare. But it hasn't been liberals against conservatives, or intellectuals versus the working man, or even Democrats versus Republicans. It certainly hasn't been the poor attacking the rich. No, the real class war has been the power elite—the people doing really well—waging war against all of the rest of us. They have both helped foster the forces I describe and have taken advantage of their dynamics.

After 1965 or so, and in the decades hence, if there had ever been a chance for ordinary Americans to fight back against the power elite and the dominant forces shaping society, it would have required a solidarity among citizens, a solidarity that crossed party lines, educational levels, religious beliefs, and other important differences. The solidarity would have had to span blue- and white-collar workers and even black and white people. It would have had to unite rural and urban residents, and middle-class and poor people.

But forming such a union of purpose is a difficult task. The bottom 90 percent or so of income earners is a hugely diverse group. An agreement—explicit or implicit—among them to safeguard their economic interests would have had to be given priority over the many other issues that could have divided them (and did). Important to many ordinary Americans are abortion rights, gun rights, business freedoms, patriotism, military service, affirmative action, gay marriage, religious tradition, social mores, and scores of other issues. These can be difficult and emotional subjects, and in individual lives they can at moments become paramount concerns. So, for hundreds of millions of Americans to keep them relegated to a sort of secondary tier of interest—subservient to a coalition of compromise necessary to maintaining citizen solidarity—was and is just impossible.

Now add to the natural arduousness of uniting diverse ordinary citizens another whole element of force trying its hardest to divide them. Over the decades there have been plenty of voices who inveighed against compromise with "the other side," and who fed division, distraction, fear, incitement, misdirection, and misinformation to citizens. Achieving solidarity among ordinary citizens would have required them to understand the story of their lives, the story of America, and the story of the evolution of the forces described in this book. That would have been a hard job under any circumstances.

But as I described in the chapters on politics and capitalism, the victimization of American workers and voters unfolded slowly and incrementally without announcements from the power elite. It wasn't easy to see clearly what was going on and for how long it would go on. Furthermore, to increase the obscurity of events, conservative talk radio, conventional economic market theory, and many Republican (and some Democratic) officeholders fed the false narrative that all was well with capitalism and the meritocracy. In a nutshell, that everyone from rich to poor was getting what their work was worth, and that everything from college admissions to job hunting to market competition was conducted on a fair and level playing field. That government regulations and taxes were just ways to take your money and control and freedom. And that government itself was a barely legitimate enterprise that unfortunately we must have—at least to wage war, pave the streets, and provide law enforcement.

It must be said here that while the power elite contains both Democrats and Republicans, and while both have profited mightily, there are some real and important differences between many of them. While Democratic politicians and Democratic industrialists have benefited from the arrangements of capitalism, technology, and politics, some of them have nonetheless tried to reform the system. Plenty of powerful or wealthy Democrats have tried to reduce the level of money in politics, add tempering regulations to the growing winner-takes-all consequences of capitalism, sponsored labor retraining for displaced workers, and supported legislation to tax or reduce carbon emissions. The Democrats haven't been perfect, but generally speaking they have been readier than the Republican Party to address the root causes of the powerful forces rending society today. This is a significant and genuine difference between the two parties.

We have not a chance however of significant or timely reform. We are a supremely divided nation. Ordinary Republican citizens are still being deceived and manipulated by their leaders, and Democratic citizens and politicians are unsure how to proceed—whether to pursue compromise or seek partisan victory.

And the internet and social media—Webworld—just ensure that citizens will remain substantially ignorant, distracted, unreflective, and divided. Webworld was a total and inadvertent gift to the power elite; they could not have dreamed of such a drug for promoting frenzy and impotence and emotional incompetence among the citizenry. If ever the American people had had a chance to create solidarity among our ranks, it was before the spread of the world-wide web. Today, effectively neutered in a thousand ways by Webworld, we have lost.

So, for many real reasons, most of us are not in a good or happy way. We are angry, resentful, confused, sick at heart, traumatized, worried, fearful, or in a state of conscious coping. And many citizens in countries all over the world are in similar emotional states. While many countries have their own specific problems, they also face the same global forces of capitalism, technology, Webworld, political dysfunction, media transformation, and environmental deterioration that we do. And just as in the U.S., the forces undermine the health, sanity, cooperation, and resilience of the people of other nations. The limits to the possibilities of education and the vulnerabilities and weaknesses in human nature are universal and apply to every society on this earth.

People are uninformed and they are nervous and scared; they do not know what the future will bring. But they observe the realities around them and can see the changes, breakdowns, and deterioration of order or longstanding patterns around them. Especially in the developed world, they see or sense irresponsibility or unaccountability in their political, corporate, and institutional leaders; immigration and refugee migrations around the world remind them that much is in flux, and may continue to be in flux.

In the United States, President Trump was elected by a worried and unsettled electorate. Although we can't take our fascinated eyes off him at present—for a 73-year-old man, he is so vain, bizarre, and undeveloped—the true fact is he's just a temporary sideshow, a Twitter troll elected by people who felt they had no good alternative and little else to lose. Whether he is reelected or a Democrat is elected in 2020, the real forces in our society and world will still be in full play and control. The citizenry will still be dysfunctional and divided. The internet and Webworld will still make impossible the reforms that need to be made. And human nature and human emotion will only become ever bigger factors as all sorts of chaos and deterioration come closer.

* * * *

Despite a growing awareness of the looming environmental crises, and despite all the talk of the importance of our responses between now and 2030, we will fail miserably—in the U.S. and elsewhere—to redesign the world. The next ten years will be the last decade in the U.S. when citizens will live as though we can live this way forever. After 2030 or so, too many unsettling events and experiences will be occurring and too frequently—for anyone to think or act as though the future is stable or safe, or even there at all.

I used to think that the power elite would respond to this sure future, would have already responded. After all, they have children too, don't they? But I was mistaken. Because the elite have wealth, power, and achievement, I made the error of ascribing to them more wisdom and caring than they actually have. In reality, they may have mastered one or two things, but they are no more well-rounded or forward-looking than any-one else in society. They possess the same multifaceted human nature as us ordinary citizens. In fact, they may be less generous and less responsible than us. Certainly many of them, like the Wall Street financial cowboys or the Silicon Valley utopians I have mentioned, may be so taken with their own agency and visions that they have an outright myopia when it comes to the ability to see beyond their own worlds and relatively narrow areas of expertise.

So I think the power elite will just ride this out. They'll work, live, play, and direct the forces of society largely as they do now—until they can't. In the end, their money, mobility, and resources may perhaps allow them to delay slightly their fates (same as our fates), but probably not by much.

For about 25 years, until a year ago, I had some investments in the stock market. Because financial investing was not a strength or interest of mine, I used a prestigious large bank with personal investment advi-sors who manage individual portfolios. My portfolio of holdings was the typical, unexceptional, broadly diversified collection of stocks and bonds. Over all those years, including through the Wall Street meltdown of 2008, I just observed the ups and downs of the market and the advice and behav-ior of my financial advisor. It slowly dawned on me that he basically never said anything other than "maintain your course with a diversified portfo-lio; don't leave the market." When the stock market went up and down arbitrarily, when big world events happened, when environmental disas-ters or foreign affairs shook the market, he just said, "stay your course." It finally occurred to me that that was all he was ever going to say. I envi-sioned Manhattan submerged and the world-wide internet frozen, and my advisor would call to tell me, "no adjustments are needed."

I laugh at myself now, but I thought having a paid expert watch my retirement account meant that one day I would get a phone call or an email from him and he would say, "Something really bad is going to occur next week, so I'm calling (or writing) to warn you to take your savings out of the stock market now; it will probably fall dramatically and soon." What I finally learned is that no ordinary citizen gets a call like that.

Well, all of the potential disasters awaiting us are like the stock mar-ket. They could occur at any time, and without warning. But we are expecting warnings. We think with all of the powerful and knowledgeable politicians, capitalists, financiers, technologists, internet administrators, and computer scientists, how could we not get warnings? It is true that we are getting some, and in the various fields. But they don't dominate the conversation, and they largely don't change our behavior, the economy's structure, or the big-picture approach to anything. The one exception to the dearth of warnings comes from the ecologists. For any person paying even a modicum of attention, stories about the state of the biosphere now and in the near future are everywhere.

But even many of those warnings pull their punches, speak of hope, possible near-term changes that can be made, and ignore the interconnected house of cards we've created with our highly interdependent and highly fragile computerization, connectivity, and burgeoning Internet of Things. The reality is, if you survey the shocking vulnerabilities across the fields, and you examine the path that the forces have us on, you can see the abyss from here.

* * * *

Here in the United States, through the good luck of being at the right location on the globe with respect to latitude and major atmospheric and ocean currents, we will be among the countries that experience ecological horrors toward the later stages of the global crisis, if the crisis that comes first is ecological. It is possible, but not a sure thing, that we will be able to witness the earliest mass migrations of hundreds of millions of people from Asian and Pacific shoreside and low-lying areas, and also from vulnerable areas in South and Central America. The world is interconnected in innumerable ways today so it is unclear when—as the rest of the world's societies begin to collapse—the U.S. will start to suffer breakdown. Because we are a very large, rich, resource-laden, talented, and almost physically isolated nation, it is possible that we'll fall apart with the last tier of nations.

As societies collapse and waves of refugees migrate across large distances, we will see starvation, disease, and dying. Especially as the populations of the southern hemisphere move toward the north, we will see conflict along national borders. Will the developed countries of Europe, and the United States, attempt to close their borders? Will we shoot refugees as they try to climb our walls?

If the first crisis that occurs is not environmental but instead is technological or political or economic, then all the countries of the world will be thrown into chaos simultaneously. If, for example, the internet fails or is hacked, that will create a cascading series of failures and breakdowns across all sectors of society and the global economy. As heating, cooling, water, food production and distribution, electrical, energy, and transportation systems all come to a halt across the world, civilization will quickly deteriorate. Almost immediately, starvation, freezing, overheating, infections, diseases, and human violence against humans will kill people everywhere. In every country, including the U.S., merely surviving at all will become unlikely. Billions of people will die in relatively short order.

* * * *

If you look, you can see the abyss from here. Recklessness and irresponsibility surround us. Those two qualities characterize our political and corporate leaders, our economic and technological systems, and our approach to the biosphere. Those two qualities are baked into the structure, algorithms, and operation of the internet, connectivity, and Webworld.

We just lost sight of everything. Egged on by a loud and pressing paradigm that made it nearly impossible to keep our wits about us, we chose the wrong gods.

Here in the United States, one day soon, certainly before 2040 or 2050, we will look back at life in 2019 and marvel at what we had. We had warmth, cool, food, water, shelter, order, safety, and a society. Until that time comes when we are forced to experience that perspective, we can instead be grateful that we have those incredible basic fulfillments now. We can feel care, responsibility, gratitude, and generosity of spirit for those things.

Feeling that way might seem small and inadequate in the face of the story of our time, but it isn't. It will be a triumph of the best of yourself over the forces in society that thrive on disempowering your humanity and the idea of brotherhood. It won't save the world, won't change the outcome that's coming, but it'll show you that you understand this story and that you're taking back your responsibility, your command of what's right and sane, and your soul. And with all the ordinary people and natural organisms of the world, you can feel a right and healing solidarity.

BIBLIOGRAPHY

THE BIBLIOGRAPHY THAT FOLLOWS is a partial list of books that provided information and insights as I put together my thoughts for this story. In addition to these, there are literally hundreds of others—read over decades—that have contributed to my understanding of the subjects of this book.

In addition to books, I have relied on years of closely following the news and current events here in the U.S. and across the world. Although I have always read widely across both "conservative" and "liberal" magazines and newspapers, my favored periodicals and newspapers have been the *New York Times, Boston Globe, The Guardian, The New Yorker, The New York Review of Books, Columbia Journalism Review*, and *The Atlantic*.

Finally, in the never-ending task of understanding humans and their behavior and epistemology, nothing beats actually talking with them. Countless conversations with people of every stripe and occupation have been important to this story.

Please note that while the book titles that follow are listed in subject categories, many of them do not really fall neatly within those divisions. Remember, the categories too are not really discrete subjects; there isn't any line between technology and Webworld, for example; or between Webworld and media. Most of these books, in fact, are far broader than any single topic, and they more accurately straddle subjects. Many of the books could be placed into a different heading than where I located them.

CHAPTER 1—CAPITALISM

Barber, Benjamin. *Jihad vs. McWorld*. New York: Times Books, 1995.

Bregman, Rutger. *Utopia for Realists*. Boston: Little, Brown, 2017.

Brown, Lester. *Eco-Economy*. New York: W.W. Norton, 2001.

Cohen, Tyler. *Average Is Over*. New York: Penguin Group, 2013.

Daily, Gretchen. *Nature's Services*. Washington, D.C.: Island Press, 1997.

———, and Katherine Ellison. *The New Economy of Nature*. Washington, D.C.: Island Press, 2002

Daly, Herman, and John Cobb. *For the Common Good*. Boston: Beacon Press, 1989.

———, and Kenneth Townsend. *Valuing the Earth*. Cambridge, MA: MIT Press, 1993.

Davidson, Eric A. *You Can't Eat GNP*. Cambridge, MA: Perseus Publishing, 2000.

Derber, Charles. *Sociopathic Society*. Boulder, CO: Paradigm Publishers, 2013.

Durning, Alan. *How Much Is Enough?* New York: W.W. Norton, 1992.

Ehrenreich, Barbara. *Bait and Switch*. New York: Henry Holt, 2005.

———. *Nickel and Dimed*. New York: Henry Holt, 2001.

Greider, William. *One World, Ready or Not*. New York: Simon & Schuster, 1997.

———. *Who Will Tell the People*. New York: Simon & Schuster, 1992.

Gutta, John. *For A Fair America*. Charleston, SC: self-published, 2014.

Hawken, Paul. *The Ecology of Commerce*. New York: HarperCollins, 1993.

———, et al. *Natural Capitalism*. Boston: Little, Brown, 1999.

Heilbroner, Robert L., and Lester Thurow. *Five Economic Challenges*. Englewood Cliffs, NJ: Prentice-Hall, 1981.

Klein, Naomi. *No Logo*. New York: Picador, 2000.

Korten, David. *When Corporations Rule the World*. Bloomfield, CT: Kumarian Press, 1995.

Krugman, Paul. *End This Depression Now!* New York: W.W. Norton, 2012.

Lewis, Michael. *The Big Short*. New York: W.W. Norton, 2010.

Lynn, Barry. *Cornered*. New York: John Wiley & Sons, 2010.

McDonough, William. *Cradle to Cradle*. New York: North Point Press, 2002.

Monbiot, George. *Out of the Wreckage*. Brooklyn, NY: Verso Books, 2017.

Papanek, Victor. *The Green Imperative*. New York: Thames and Hudson, 1995.

Pearlstein, Steven. *Can American Capitalism Survive?* New York: St. Martin's Press, 2018.

Perkins, John. *Confessions of an Economic Hit Man*. San Francisco: Berrett-Koehler, 2004.

Piven, Francis Fox, and Richard Cloward. *Regulating the Poor*. New York: Random House, 1971.

Quart, Alissa. *Branded*. New York: Perseus, 2003.

Rand, Ayn. *For the New Intellectual*. New York: Random House, 1961.

———. *The Fountainhead*. New York: Bobbs-Merrill, 1943.

Reich, Robert. *Aftershock*. New York: Alfred Knopf, 2010.

———. *Saving Capitalism*. New York: Alfred Knopf, 2015.

Schumacher, E.F. *Small Is Beautiful*. New York: Harper & Row, 1973.

Stiglitz, Joseph. *Freefall*. New York: W.W. Norton, 2010.

———. *Globalization and Its Discontents*. New York: W.W. Norton, 2002.

Thurow, Lester. *The Zero-Sum Society*. New York: Basic Books, 1980.

Wapshott, Nicholas. *Keynes Hayek*. New York: W.W. Norton, 2011.

Wilson, William Julius. *When Work Disappears*. New York: Alfred Knopf, 1996.

Zizek, Slavoj. *Demanding the Impossible*. Malden, MA: Polity Press, 2013.

———. *The Year of Dreaming Dangerously*. Brooklyn, NY: Verso, 2012.

CHAPTER 2—TECHNOLOGY

Bowden, Mark. *Worm*. New York: Grove Press, 2011.

Ford, Martin. *Rise of the Robots*. New York: Basic Books, 2015.

Koppel, Ted. *Lights Out*. New York: Crown Publishing, 2015.

Markoff, John. *Machines of Loving Grace*. New York: HarperCollins, 2015.

McKibben, Bill. *Enough*. New York: Henry Holt, 2003.

Postman, Neil. *Technopoly*. New York: Alfred Knopf, 1992.

Rifkin, Jeremy. *Zero Marginal Cost Society*. New York: Palgrave Macmillan, 2014.

Sale, Kirkpatrick. *Rebels Against the Future*. Reading, MA: Addison-Wesley, 1995.

CHAPTER 3—WEBWORLD

Carr, Nicholas. *The Glass Cage*. New York: W.W. Norton, 2014.

———. *The Shallows*. New York: W.W. Norton, 2010.

Eggers, Dave. *The Circle*. New York: Alfred Knopf, 2013.

Feffer, John. *Splinterlands*. Chicago: Haymarket Books, 2016.

Foer, Franklin. *World Without Mind*. New York: Penguin Press, 2017.

Galloway, Scott. *The Four*. New York: Penguin Random House, 2017.

Gitlin, Todd. *The Twilight of Common Dreams*. New York: Henry Holt, 1995.

Healy, Jane. *Failure to Connect*. New York: Simon & Schuster, 1998.

Hedges, Chris. *Empire of Illusion*. New York: Nation Books, 2009.

Hindman, Matthew. *The Myth of Digital Democracy*. Princeton, NJ: Princeton Univ. Press, 2008.

Huxley, Aldous. *Brave New World*. New York: Harper & Brothers, 1932.

Lagorio-Chafkin, Christine. *We Are the Nerds*. New York: Hachette Books, 2018.

Lynch, Michael. *The Internet of Us*. New York: W.W. Norton, 2016.

McNamee, Roger. *Zucked*. New York: Penguin Press, 2019.

Morozov, Evgeny. *The Net Delusion*. New York: PublicAffairs Books, 2011.

Mukherjee, Ashesh. *The Internet Trap*. Princeton, NJ: Princeton Univ. Press, 2018.

Nichols, Tom. *The Death of Expertise*. New York: Oxford Univ. Press, 2017.

Pariser, Eli. *The Filter Bubble*. New York: Penguin Random House, 2012.

Pegues, Jeff. *Kompromat*. Blue Ridge Summit, PA: Prometheus, 2018.

Stoll, Clifford. *Silicon Snake Oil*. New York: Doubleday, 1995.

Taplin, Jonathan. *Move Fast and Break Things*. New York: Little, Brown, 2017.

Vaidhyanathan, Siva. *Anti-Social Media*. New York: Oxford Univ. Press, 2018.

Watts, Clint. *Messing With the Enemy*. New York: HarperCollins, 2018.

Webb, Amy. *The Big Nine*. New York: PublicAffairs Books, 2019.

Zuboff, Shoshana. *The Age of Surveillance Capitalism*. New York: PublicAffairs Books, 2019.

CHAPTER 4—POLITICS

Annenberg Democracy Project. *A Republic Divided*. New York: Oxford Univ. Press, 2007.

Bellah, Robert, et al. *Habits of the Heart*. Los Angeles: Univ. of California Press, 1985.

Berman, Morris. *Dark Ages America*. New York: W.W. Norton, 2006.

———. *The Twilight of American Culture*. New York: W.W. Norton, 2000.

Brinkley, Alan. *Voices of Protest*. New York: Alfred Knopf, 1982.

Crawford, Alan. *Thunder on the Right*. New York: Pantheon Books, 1980.

Engler, Mark, and Paul Engler. *This Is An Uprising*. New York: PublicAffairs, 2016.

Fisher, Roger, and William Ury. *Getting to Yes*. Boston: Houghton Mifflin, 1981.

Frank, Thomas. *What's the Matter with Kansas?* New York: Henry Holt, 2004.

Gitlin, Todd. *The Sixties*. New York: Bantam Books, 1987.

Hacker, Jacob, and Paul Pierson. *Winner-Take-All Politics*. New York: Simon & Schuster, 2010.

Havel, Vaclav. *Disturbing the Peace*. New York: Alfred Knopf, 1990.

———. *Open Letters*. New York: Alfred Knopf, 1991.

Heilbroner, Robert L. *An Inquiry into the Human Prospect*. New York: W.W. Norton, 1974.

Hemmer, Nicole. *Messengers of the Right*. Philadelphia: Univ. of Pennsylvania Press, 2016.

Hochschild, Arlie. *Strangers in Their Own Land*. New York: The New Press, 2016.

Judt, Tony. *Ill Fares the Land*. New York: Penguin Press, 2010.

———. *When the Facts Change*. New York: Penguin Random House, 2015.

Kaplan, Robert D. *An Empire Wilderness*. New York: Random House, 1998.

———. *The Coming Anarchy*. New York: Random House, 2000.

Kuttner, Robert. *Revolt of the Haves*. New York: Simon & Schuster, 1980.

Lakoff, George. *Don't Think of an Elephant!* White River Junction, VT: Chelsea Green, 2004.

Lapham, Lewis. *Waiting for the Barbarians*. New York: Verso, 1997.

Lepore, Jill. *The Whites of Their Eyes*. Princeton, NJ: Princeton Univ. Press, 2010.

Levitsky, Steven, and Daniel Ziblatt. *How Democracies Die*. New York: Penguin Random House, 2018.

Lilla, Mark. *The Once and Future Liberal*. New York: HarperCollins, 2017.

MacMillan, Margaret. *Paris 1919*. New York: Random House, 2001.

Mann, Thomas, and Norman Ornstein. *It's Even Worse Than It Looks*. New York: Basic Books, 2012.

Mayer, Jane. *Dark Money*. New York: Doubleday, 2016.

Miller, James. *Democracy Is in the Streets*. New York: Simon & Schuster, 1987.

Mills, C. Wright. *The Power Elite*. New York: Oxford Univ. Press, 1956.

Neustadt, Richard, and Ernest May. *Thinking In Time*. New York: Macmillan, 1986.

Sandel, Michael. *Justice*. New York: Farrar, Straus and Giroux, 2009.

Shutkin, William. *The Land That Could Be*. Cambridge, MA: MIT Press, 2000.

Valby, Karen. *Welcome to Utopia*. Austin, TX: Univ. of Texas Press, 2010.

Walesa, Lech. *A Way of Hope*. New York: Henry Holt, 1987.

Wills, Garry. *A Necessary Evil*. New York: Simon & Schuster, 1999.

Zantovsky, Michael. *Havel a Life*. New York: Grove Atlantic, 2014.

CHAPTER 5—MEDIA

Fallows, James. *Breaking the News*. New York: Pantheon Books, 1996.

Hamill, Pete. *News Is a Verb*. New York: Random House, 1998.

McChesney, Robert. *Rich Media, Poor Democracy*. Champaign, IL: Univ. of Illinois Press, 1999.

Postman, Neil. *Amusing Ourselves to Death*. New York: Viking Penguin, 1985.

———. *Conscientious Objections*. New York: Alfred Knopf, 1988.

Rosen, Jay. *What Are Journalists For?* New Haven, CT: Yale Univ. Press, 1999.

Terkel, Studs. *Talking to Myself*. New York: Pantheon Books, 1973.

Trow, George W. S. *Within the Context of No Context*. Boston: Little, Brown, 1981.

CHAPTER 6—EDUCATION

Friedenberg, Edgar. *Coming of Age in America*. New York: Random House, 1963.

Gardner, Howard. *The Disciplined Mind*. New York: Simon & Schuster, 1999.

Glasser, William. *Choice Theory in the Classroom*. New York: HarperCollins, 1986.

———. *The Quality School*. New York: HarperCollins, 1990.

Goodman, Paul. *Growing Up Absurd*. New York: Random House, 1956.

Kozol, Jonathan. *Savage Inequalities*. New York: Crown Publishers, 1991.

Meier, Deborah. *The Power of Their Ideas*. Boston: Beacon Press, 1995.

Postman, Neil. *The End of Education*. New York: Alfred Knopf, 1995.

Sizer, Theodore R. *Horace's Hope*. New York: Houghton Mifflin, 1996.

———, and Nancy Sizer. *The Students Are Watching*. Boston: Beacon Press, 1999.

Steel, Ronald. *Walter Lippmann and the American Century*. Boston: Little, Brown, 1980.

Tough, Paul. *Whatever It Takes*. New York: Houghton Mifflin Harcourt, 2008.

Vance, J.D. *Hillbilly Elegy*. New York: HarperCollins, 2016.

Westbrook, Robert. *John Dewey and American Democracy*. Ithaca, NY: Cornell Univ. Press, 1991.

Westover, Tara. *Educated*. New York: Random House, 2018.

CHAPTER 7—HUMAN NATURE

Anouilh, Jean. *Becket*. New York: Coward-McCann, 1960.

Alston, William. *Religious Belief and Philosophical Thought*. New York: Harcourt, Brace & World, 1963.

Bloom, Allan. *The Republic of Plato*. New York: Perseus Books, 1968.

Bolt, Robert. *A Man for All Seasons*. New York: Random House, 1960.

Buruma, Ian. *Murder in Amsterdam*. New York: Penguin Press, 2006.

Cahalan, Susannah. *Brain on Fire*. New York: Simon & Schuster, 2012.

Chase, Alston. *A Mind for Murder*. New York: W.W. Norton, 2003.

Didion, Joan. *The Year of Magical Thinking*. New York: Alfred Knopf, 2005.

Forrest, David. *Slots*. Harrison, NY: Delphinium Books, 2012.

Frankl, Viktor E. *Man's Search for Meaning*. Boston: Beacon Press, 2006 (originally published in German in 1946).

Gardner, Howard. *Changing Minds*. Boston: Harvard Business School Press, 2004.

Goleman, Daniel. *Emotional Intelligence*. New York: Random House, 1995.

Goodman, Robert. *The Luck Business*. New York: Simon & Schuster, 1995.

Gyatso, Tensin (Dalai Lama). *Ethics for the New Millennium*. New York: Penguin Putnam, 1999.

Herman, Judith. *Trauma and Recovery*. New York: Basic Books, 1992.

Hofstadter, Richard. *Anti-Intellectualism in American Life*. New York: Random House, 1962.

King, David. *The Ha-Ha*. New York: Little, Brown, 2005.

Lazarus, Richard, and Bernice Lazarus. *Passion and Reason*. New York: Oxford Univ. Press, 1994.

Lenski, Gerhard. *Human Societies*. New York: McGraw-Hill, 1970.

Lessing, Doris. *Prisons We Choose to Live Inside*. New York: Harper & Row, 1987.

Levine, Bruce. *Surviving America's Depression Epidemic*. White River Junction, VT: Chelsea Green, 2007.

Lightman, Alan. *The Diagnosis*. New York: Pantheon Books, 2000.

Lilla, Mark. *The Reckless Mind*. New York: New York Review of Books, 2001.

Maas, Peter. *Marie: A True Story*. New York: Random House, 1983.

Milburn, Michael, and Sheree Conrad. *Raised to Rage*. Cambridge, MA: MIT Press, 2016.

Mishra, Pankaj. *Age of Anger*. New York: Farrar, Strauss and Giroux, 2017.

Moisi, Dominique. *The Geopolitics of Emotion*. New York: Doubleday, 2009.

Myss, Caroline. *Anatomy of the Spirit*. New York: Harmony Books, 1996.

Niebuhr, Reinhold. *Moral Man and Immoral Society*. New York: Charles Scribner's Sons, 1932.

———. *The Nature and Destiny of Man*. New York: Charles Scribner's Sons, 1941.

Potok, Chaim. *My Name Is Asher Lev*. New York: Alfred Knopf, 1972.

Schull, Natasha Dow. *Addiction By Design*. Princeton, NJ: Princeton Univ. Press, 2012.

Schwartz, Richard. *Internal Family Systems Therapy*. New York: Guilford Press, 1995.

Shay, Jonathan. *Achilles in Vietnam*. New York: Simon & Schuster, 1994.

———. *Odysseus in America*. New York: Simon & Schuster, 2002.

Shepard, Paul. *Nature and Madness*. San Francisco: Sierra Club Books, 1982.

Solzhenitsyn, Aleksandr. *The First Circle*. New York: Harper & Row, 1968.

Strauss, Darin. *Half A Life*. New York: Random House, 2010.

Toews, Miriam. *Swing Low*. New York: HarperCollins, 2000.

Viscott, David. *Emotional Resilience*. New York: Harmony Books, 1996.

Wallace, David Foster. *This Is Water*. New York: Little, Brown, 2009.

Wilson, Edward O. *The Meaning of Human Existence*. New York: W.W. Norton, 2014.

CHAPTER 8—THE ENVIRONMENT

Allaby, Michael. *Basics of Environmental Science*. New York: Routledge, 1996.

Bergoglio, Jorge Mario (Pope Francis). *Encyclical on Climate Change & Inequality*. Brooklyn, NY: Melville House, 2015.

Berry, Wendell. *What Are People For?* New York: Farrar, Strauss and Giroux, 1990.

Beston, Henry. *The Outermost House*. New York: Holt, Rinehart and Winston, 1928.

Commoner, Barry. *The Closing Circle*. New York: Alfred Knopf, 1971.

Diamond, Jared. *Collapse*. New York: Viking Penguin, 2005.

Eiseley, Loren. *The Firmament of Time*. New York: Atheneum, 1971.

———. *The Immense Journey*. New York: Random House, 1957.

Gelbspan, Ross. *Boiling Point*. New York: Basic Books, 2004.

———. *The Heat Is On*. Reading, MA: Addison-Wesley, 1997.

Ghosh, Amitav. *The Great Derangement*. Chicago: Univ. of Chicago Press, 2016.

Gore, Al. *Earth in the Balance*. New York: Houghton Mifflin, 1992.

Hecht, Susanna, and Alexander Cockburn. *The Fate of the Forest*. New York: HarperCollins, 1990.

Heinrich, Bernd. *The Trees in My Forest*. New York: HarperCollins, 1997.

Hertsgaard, Mark. *Earth Odyssey*. New York: Broadway Books, 1998.

Houghton, John. *Global Warming*. Cambridge, UK: Cambridge University Press, 1997.

Kormondy, Edward. *Concepts of Ecology*. Englewood Cliffs, NJ: Prentice-Hall, 1969.

McAlester, A. Lee. *The Earth*. Englewood Cliffs, NJ: Prentice-Hall, 1973.

McCarthy, Cormac. *The Road*. New York: Alfred Knopf, 2006.

McHarg, Ian. *Design with Nature*. Philadelphia: Natural history Press, 1969.

McKibben, Bill. *Eaarth*. New York: Henry Holt, 2010.

———. *The End of Nature*. New York: Random House, 1989.

———. *Hope, Human and Wild*. New York: Little, Brown, 1995.

Oreskes, Naomi, and Erik Conway. *The Collapse of Western Civilization*. New York: Columbia Univ. Press, 2014.

Orr, David W. *Dangerous Years*. New Haven, CT: Yale University Press, 2016.

———. *Down to the Wire*. New York: Oxford Univ. Press, 2009.

———. *Earth in Mind*. Washington, D.C.: Island Press, 1994.

———. *Ecological Literacy*. Albany, NY: State University of New York Press, 1992.

Spirn, Anne. *The Granite Garden*. New York: Basic Books, 1984.

Tokar, Brian. *Earth for Sale*. Cambridge, MA: South End Press, 1997.

Weisman, Alan. *Gaviotas*. White River Junction, VT: Chelsea Green, 1998.

———. *The World Without Us*. New York: St. Martin's Press, 2007.

Wilson, Edward O. *The Diversity of Life*. Cambridge, MA: Harvard Univ. Press, 1992.

———. *The Future of Life*. New York: Alfred Knopf, 2002.

CHAPTER 10—TRANSPORTATION

Caro, Robert A. *The Power Broker*. New York: Alfred Knopf, 1974.

Cullen, Gordon. *Townscape*. New York: Van Nostrand Reinhold, 1961.

Duany, Andres, Elizabeth Plater-Zyberk, and Jeff Speck. *Suburban Nation*. New York: North Point Press, 2000.

Fischler, Stanley I. *Moving Millions*. New York: Harper & Row, 1979.

Flink, James. *The Automobile Age*. Cambridge, MA: MIT Press, 1988.

Gans, Herbert J. *The Levittowners*. London: Allen Lane The Penguin Press, 1967.

———. *The Urban Villagers*. New York: Macmillan Publishing, 1962.

Garreau, Joel. *Edge City*. New York: Doubleday, 1991.

Goddard, Stephen. *Getting There*. New York: HarperCollins, 1994.

Jacobs, Jane. *The Death and Life of Great American Cities*. New York: Random House, 1961.

Kay, Jane Holtz. *Asphalt Nation*. New York: Crown Publishers, 1997.

Keller, Suzanne. *The Urban Neighborhood*. New York: Random House, 1968.

Kunstler, James. *The Geography of Nowhere*. New York: Simon & Schuster, 1993.

———. *Home from Nowhere*. New York: Simon & Schuster, 1996.

Lynch, Kevin. *The Image of the City*. Cambridge, MA: MIT Press, 1960.

Moe, Richard, and Carter Wilkie. *Changing Places*. New York: Henry Holt, 1997.

Whitt, J. Allen. *Urban Elites and Mass Transportation*. Princeton, NJ: Princeton Univ. Press, 1982.

Yago, Glenn. *The Decline of Transit*. Cambridge, UK: Cambridge University Press, 1984.

CHAPTER 11—MISCELLANEOUS FORCES

Black-White Relations

Alexander, Michelle. *The New Jim Crow*. New York: The New Press, 2010.

Baldwin, James. *The Fire Next Time*. New York: Dial Press, 1963.

Branch, Taylor. *Parting the Waters*. New York: Simon & Schuster, 1988.

———. *Pillar of Fire*. New York: Simon & Schuster, 1998.

————. *At Canaan's Edge*. New York: Simon & Schuster, 2006.

Cleaver, Eldridge. *Soul on Ice*. New York: McGraw-Hill, 1968.

Coates, Ta-Nehisi. *Between the World and Me*. New York: Spiegel & Grau, 2015.

DuBois, W.E.B. *The Souls of Black Folk*. Chicago: A.C. McClurg & Co., 1903.

Ellison, Ralph. *Invisible Man*. New York: Random House, 1947.

Garvey, Amy Jacques. *Garvey and Garveyism*. New York: Macmillan, 1963.

Griffin, John Howard. *Black Like Me*. Boston: Houghton Mifflin Harcourt, 1961.

Malcolm X. *The Autobiography of Malcolm X*. New York: Grove Press, 1965.

McCall, Nathan. *Makes Me Wanna Holler*. New York: Random House, 1994.

West, Cornel. *Race Matters*. Boston: Beacon Press, 1993.

Wideman, John Edgar. *Brothers and Keepers*. New York: Holt, Rinehart and Winston, 1984.

Wright, Richard. *Black Boy*. New York: Harper & Brothers, 1945.

Printed in the USA
CPSIA information can be obtained
at www.ICGtesting.com
LVHW042105180224
772178LV00003B/428